iPad

10th Edition

by **Bob LeVitus**
Houston Chronicle "Dr. Mac" columnist

Edward C. Baig
USA Today Personal Tech columnist

Bryan Chaffin
The Mac Observer Editor-in-Chief

for
dummies®
A Wiley Brand

iPad® For Dummies®, 10th Edition

Published by: **John Wiley & Sons, Inc.,** 111 River Street, Hoboken, NJ 07030-5774, www.wiley.com

Copyright © 2018 by John Wiley & Sons, Inc., Hoboken, New Jersey

Published simultaneously in Canada

For general information on our other products and services, please contact our Customer Care Department within the U.S. at 877-762-2974, outside the U.S. at 317-572-3993, or fax 317-572-4002. For technical support, please visit https://hub.wiley.com/community/support/dummies.

Wiley publishes in a variety of print and electronic formats and by print-on-demand. Some material included with standard print versions of this book may not be included in e-books or in print-on-demand. If this book refers to media such as a CD or DVD that is not included in the version you purchased, you may download this material at http://booksupport.wiley.com. For more information about Wiley products, visit www.wiley.com.

Library of Congress Control Number: 2017958917

ISBN 978-1-11-941712-5 (pbk); ISBN 978-1-119-41710-1 (ebk); ISBN 978-1-119-41714-9 (ebk)

Manufactured in the United States of America

10 9 8 7 6 5 4 3 2 1

Contents at a Glance

Table of Contents

Introduction

s Yogi Berra would say, "It was déjà vu all over again": front-page treatment, top billing on network TV and cable, and diehards lining up for days to ensure landing a highly lusted-after product from Apple. The products generating the most buzz lately are the iPad Pro models and their accessories, the Apple Pencil and Smart Keyboard. Every iPad is a magical device and the iPad Pro lineup might be the most magical yet.

We hope you bought this book to find out how to get the most magic out of your iPad, regardless of its model. Our goal is to deliver the information you need in a light and breezy fashion. We expect you to have fun using your iPad and we hope you have fun spending time with us.

About This Book

We need to get one thing out of the way right from the get-go. We think you're pretty darn smart for buying a *For Dummies* book. That says to us that you have the confidence and intelligence to know what you don't know. The *For Dummies* franchise is built around the core notion that everyone feels insecure about certain topics when tackling them for the first time, especially when those topics have to do with technology.

As with most Apple products, iPads are beautifully designed and intuitive to use. And though our editors may not want us to reveal this dirty little secret (especially on the first page, for goodness' sake), the truth is you'll get pretty far just by exploring the iPad's many functions and features on your own, without the help of this (or any other) book.

Okay, now that we've spilled the beans, we'll tell you why you shouldn't run back to the bookstore and request a refund. This book is chock-full of useful tips, advice, and other nuggets that should make your iPad experience all the more pleasurable. We'll even go so far as to say that you won't find some of these nuggets anywhere else. So keep this book nearby and consult it often.

Foolish Assumptions

Although we know what happens when one makes assumptions, we've made a few anyway. First, we assume that you, gentle reader, know nothing about using an iPad or iOS — beyond knowing what an iPad is, that you want to use iOS, that you want to understand your iPad and its operating system without digesting an incomprehensible technical manual, and that you made the right choice by selecting this particular book.

And so, we do our best to explain each new concept in full and loving detail. Perhaps that's foolish, but . . . oh, well.

One last thing: We also assume that you can read. If you can't, please ignore this paragraph.

Icons Used in This Book

Little round pictures (or *icons*) appear in the left margins throughout this book. Consider these icons as miniature road signs, telling you something extra about the topic at hand or hammering a point home. Here's what the five icons used in this book look like and mean.

These juicy morsels, shortcuts, and recommendations might make the task at hand faster or easier.

This icon emphasizes the stuff we think you ought to retain. You may even jot down a note to yourself on the iPad.

Put on your propeller beanie hat and insert your pocket protector; this text includes the truly geeky stuff. You can safely ignore this material, but if it weren't interesting or informative, we wouldn't have bothered to write it.

You wouldn't intentionally run a stop sign, would you? In the same fashion, ignoring warnings may be hazardous to your iPad and (by extension) your wallet. There, you now know how these warning icons work, for you have just received your very first warning!

We put a New icon next to anything that's new or improved in iOS 11.

We wrote a bunch of things that just didn't fit in the print version of this book. Rather than leave them on the cutting room floor, we've posted the most useful bits online in a cheat sheet for your enjoyment and edification.

To find them, go to www.dummies.com, and then type *iPad For Dummies cheat sheet*. And here's what you'll find: info on using the iPad's buttons and icons, tips for mastering multitouch, and where to find additional help if your iPad is acting contrary.

Where to Go from Here

Why, go straight to Chapter 1, of course (without passing Go).

In all seriousness, we wrote this book for you, so please let us know what you think. If we screwed up, confused you, left out something, or — heaven forbid — made you angry, drop us a note. And if we hit you with one pun too many, it helps to know that as well. Because writers are people too (believe it or not), we also encourage positive feedback if you think it's warranted. So kindly send email to Ed at Baigdummies@gmail.com and to Bob at iPadLeVitus@boblevitus.com. We do our best to respond to reasonably polite email in a timely fashion. Most of all, we want to thank you for buying our book. Please enjoy it along with your new iPad.

Note: At the time we wrote this book, all the information it contained was accurate for all Wi-Fi and Wi-Fi + 3G and 4G iPads with the exception of the first- through third-generation iPads, which can't run iOS 11 and are not covered. The book is also based on version 11 of the iOS (operating system) and version 12.7 of iTunes. Apple is likely to introduce new iPad models and new versions of iOS and iTunes between book editions, so if the hardware or user interface on your new iPad or the version of iTunes on your computer looks a little different, be sure to check out what Apple has to say at www.apple.com/ipad. You'll no doubt find updates on the company's latest releases.

1

Getting to Know Your iPad

Get basic training for getting along with your iPad.

Enjoy a gentle introduction to your iPad.

Take a peek at your iPad hardware and software and explore the way it works.

Discover the joys of synchronization over USB or Wi-Fi and find out how to get your data — contacts, appointments, movies, songs, podcasts, books, and so on — from a computer (or iCloud) onto your iPad, quickly and painlessly.

Chapter **1**

Unveiling the iPad

Congratulations! You've selected one of the most incredible handheld devices we've ever seen. Of course, the iPad is a combination of a killer audio and video player, an e-book reader, a powerful Internet communications device, a superb handheld gaming device, a still and video camera, and a platform for over 2.2 million apps at the time this was written — and probably a lot more by the time you read this.

REMEMBER

Apple has produced 14 iPad models so far: The original iPad (2010), the iPad 2 (2011), the iPad third generation (Spring 2012), the iPad fourth generation (Fall 2012), the iPad mini (Fall 2012), the iPad Air and the iPad mini 2 (Fall 2013), the iPad Air 2 and iPad mini 3 (Fall 2014), the 12.9-inch iPad Pro and iPad mini 4 (Fall 2015); the 9.7-inch iPad Pro (Spring 2016), the 9.7-inch iPad (Spring 2017), and the 10.5-inch iPad Pro (Summer 2017).

Note that we're *not* covering the four original full-sized iPads — the ones that don't have Air, mini, or Pro as their surname. The reason is not that we didn't want to cover them; the current version of the operating system (iOS 11) doesn't run on them.

If you're the owner of one of those models, you can still find a lot of handy information here, but some things might look or work differently. You might want to rummage around for a previous edition of this book.

Moving right along, in this chapter, we offer a gentle introduction to all the pieces that make up your iPad, plus overviews of its revolutionary hardware and software features.

Exploring the iPad's Big Picture

The iPad has many best-of-class features, but perhaps its most notable feature is that there's no physical keyboard or stylus in the box. Instead, every iPad includes a super-high-resolution touchscreen that you operate using a pointing device you're already intimately familiar with: It's called your finger. (Apple did, however, introduce its first optional stylus and keyboard — the $149 Apple Pencil and $169 Smart Keyboard, both of which work with only iPad Pro models.)

Every iPad ever built has a beautiful screen, and since the third-generation they've sported Apple's exclusive high-definition Retina display, which is easily the most beautiful screen we've ever seen on a tablet.

Other things we love include the iPad's plethora of built-in sensors. It has an *accelerometer* to detect when you rotate the device from portrait to landscape mode — and instantly adjust what's on the display accordingly.

TIP

The screen rotates — that is, unless the screen orientation lock is engaged. We tell you more about this feature shortly.

A light sensor adjusts the display's brightness in response to the current ambient lighting conditions. Then there's a three-axis gyro sensor that works with the accelerometer and built-in compass. And most models — the iPad Air 2, iPad mini 4, 9.7-inch iPad, and all iPad Pro models — also include Apple's Touch ID sensor, which lets you unlock your iPad with your fingerprint.

Last, but definitely not least, all iPads since the third generation include Siri, a voice-controlled personal assistant happy to do almost anything you ask (as long as your iPad is running iOS 6 or later).

In the following sections, we're not just marveling about the wonderful screen and sensors. Now it's time to take a brief look at the rest of the iPad's features, broken down by product category.

The iPad as a media player

We agree with the late Steve Jobs on this one: The iPad is magical — and without a doubt the best iPod (that is, media player) Apple has ever produced. You can enjoy all your existing media — music, audiobooks, audio and video podcasts, iTunes U courses, music videos, television shows, and movies — on the gorgeous color display found on every iPad ever made (even the oldest iPads have gorgeous color displays).

Here's the bottom line: If you can get the media file — be it video, audio, or whatever — into iTunes on your Mac or PC, you can synchronize it and watch or listen to it on your iPad. And, of course, you can always buy or rent content on your iPad in the iTunes Store.

Chapter 3 is all about syncing (transferring media from your computer to your iPad), but for now, just know that some video content may need to be converted to an iPad-compatible format, with the proper resolution, frame rate, bit rate, and file format to play on your iPad. If you try to sync an incompatible video file, iTunes alerts you that an issue exists.

If you get an error message about an incompatible video file, select the file in iTunes and choose File ⇨ Create New Version. When the conversion is finished, sync again. Chapter 8 covers video and video compatibility in more detail.

The iPad as an Internet communications device

But wait — there's more! Not only is the iPad a stellar media player, but it's also a full-featured Internet communications device with — we're about to drop some industry jargon on you — an email client that's compatible with most POP and IMAP mail services, with support for Microsoft Exchange ActiveSync. (For more on this topic, see Chapter 5.) Also onboard is a world-class web browser (Safari) that makes web surfing fun and easy on the eyes, unlike what's on many mobile devices. Chapter 4 explains how to surf the web using Safari.

Another cool Internet feature is Maps, a killer mapping app that's improved in iOS 11. By using GPS (3G or 4G models) or triangulation (Wi-Fi only models), the iPad can determine your location, let you view maps and satellite imagery, and obtain driving directions and traffic information regardless of where you happen to be. (See Chapter 6 for the scoop on Maps.) You can also find businesses (such as gas stations, pizza restaurants, hospitals, and Apple Stores) with just a few taps.

And in iOS 11, you can even use Maps to get directions for public transportation in many US cities (and China), with more cities in both countries coming soon.

New in iOS 11 are indoor maps of large spaces such as malls, airports, and transportation hubs. That's the good news. The bad news is that indoor maps are few and far between so far; only a handful appear, even in big cities.

Maps is useful over Wi-Fi but more useful and more accurate on cellular iPads with 3G or 4G.

We dare say that the Internet experience on an iPad is far superior to the Internet experience on any other handheld device.

The iPad as an e-book reader

Download the free iBooks app if you don't already have it, or any of the excellent (and free) third-party e-book readers such as the Kindle and Nook apps, and you'll discover a new way of finding and reading books. The iBooks Store and News app (covered in Chapter 10) are chock-full of good reading at prices that are lower than what you'd pay for a printed copy. Better still, when you read an e-book, you're helping the environment and saving trees. Furthermore, some (if not many) titles include audio, video, or graphical content not available in the printed editions. Plus, a great number of good books are free. And best of all, you can carry your entire library in one hand. If you've never read a book on your iPad, give it a try. We think you'll like (or love) it.

The iPad as a multimedia powerhouse

The Retina display on all iPads since the third generation makes the experience even more extraordinary. Add an adapter cable or Apple TV, and your iPad turns into a superb device for watching video on an HDTV (or even a non-HD TV), with support for output resolutions up to 1080p.

TIP

You won't need the (admittedly less expensive) adapter cable if you choose an Apple TV (from $69), which is a marvelous little device that, among other things, lets you stream audio and video from your iPad to your HDTV wirelessly.

And iPads include a pair of cameras and the FaceTime video-chatting app, taking the iPad's multimedia acumen to new heights. Chapter 8 gets you started with FaceTime.

The iPad as a platform for third-party apps

At the time of this writing, more than 2.2 million apps were available in the App Store, with over 180 billion downloads to date in categories such as games, business, education, entertainment, healthcare and fitness, music, photography, productivity, travel, and sports. The cool thing is that most of them, even ones designed for the iPhone or iPod touch, also run flawlessly on the iPad.

Of those 2 million+ apps, well over half are designed specifically for the iPad's larger screen, with more arriving daily.

Chapter 11 helps you fill your iPad with all the cool apps your heart desires. We share our favorite free and for-pay apps in Chapters 18 and 19, respectively.

What do you need to use an iPad?

To *use* your iPad, only a few simple things are required. Here's a list of everything you need:

>> An iPad

>> An Apple ID (assuming that you want to acquire content such as apps, videos, music, iBooks, and podcasts, which you almost certainly do)

>> Internet access — broadband wireless Internet access is recommended

Several years ago, we said you *needed* a computer with iTunes to sync your iPad. That's no longer true; these days you can activate, set up, update, back up, and restore an iPad wirelessly without ever introducing it to a computer.

Although you don't technically *need* a computer, it's nice to have a symbiotic relationship between your iPad and your Mac or PC because some common tasks are faster and easier when you use iTunes on a computer with a larger display and real keyboard than on your iPad.

If you do decide to introduce your iPad to your computer (and we think you should), you need one of the following for syncing (which we discuss at length in Chapter 3):

>> A Mac with a USB 2.0 or 3.0 port, Mac OS X version 10.8.5 or later, and iTunes 12.7 or later

>> A PC with a USB 2.0 or 3.0 port, Windows 7 or later, and iTunes 12.7 or later

iTunes is a free download, available at www.itunes.com/download.

Touring the iPad Exterior

The iPad is a harmonious combination of hardware and software. In the following sections, we take a brief look at the hardware — what's on the outside.

On the top

On the top of your iPad, you find the headphone jack, microphone, and the sleep/wake button, as shown in Figure 1-1. Note that iPad Pro models also have two of their four speakers on the top:

REMEMBER

>> **Sleep/wake button:** This button is used to put your iPad's screen to sleep or to wake it up. It's also how you turn your iPad on or off. To put it to sleep or wake it up, just press the button. To turn it on or off, press and hold down the button for a few seconds.

   Your iPad's battery will run down faster when your iPad is awake, so we suggest that you make a habit of putting it to sleep when you're not using it.

   When your iPad is sleeping, nothing happens if you touch its screen. To wake it up, merely press the button again or press the Home button on the front of the device (as described in a moment).

   If you use an Apple Smart Cover or Smart Case (or any of the third-party cases that use the Smart Cover mechanism), you can just open the cover to wake your iPad and close the cover to put it to sleep.

   In Chapter 15, you can find out how to make your iPad go to sleep automatically after a period of inactivity.

   If you have an iPad Pro model, two of the four speakers are on the top of the device.

>> **Headphone jack:** This jack lets you plug in a headset. You can use the Apple headsets or headphones that came with your iPhone or iPod. Or you can use pretty much any headphones or headset that plugs into a 3.5-mm stereo headphone jack.

   Throughout this book, we use the words headphones, earphones, and headset interchangeably. Strictly speaking, a headset includes a microphone so that you can talk (or record) as well as listen; headphones or earphones are for listening only. Either type works with your iPad, as do most wireless Bluetooth headsets and newer headsets with Lightning connectors (for iPhone 7, 7 Plus, 8, 8 Plus, and X).

>> **Microphone:** The tiny dot in the middle of the top is actually a pretty good microphone. (*Hint:* You'll sound better if you use a headset — any headset.)

FIGURE 1-1:
The top
of the iPad.

Headphone jack

Stereo speakers (Pro models only)

Sleep/wake button

On the bottom

On the bottom of your iPad are the speakers (two of the four speakers on iPad Pro models) and Lightning connector, as shown in Figure 1-2:

>> **Speakers:** The speakers plays audio — music or video soundtracks — if no headset is plugged in.

>> **Lightning connector:** This connector has three purposes:

- *Recharge your iPad's battery:* Simply connect one end of the included cable to the iPad's Lightning port and the other end to a USB port.

- *Synchronize your iPad:* Connect one end of the same cable to the Lightning connector and the other end to a USB port on your Mac or PC.

- *Connect your iPad to cameras or televisions using adapters:* Such connectors include the camera connection kit or other adapter cables. Make sure to use an adapter that works with the Lightning connector.

REMEMBER

If you connect the USB cable to USB ports on your keyboard, USB hub, display, or other external device, or even the USB ports on an older Mac or PC, you may be able to sync, but more than likely you can't charge the battery. For the most part, only your computer's built-in USB ports (and only recent-vintage computers at that) have enough juice to recharge the battery. If you use an external USB port on a hub, you'll probably see a *Not Charging* message next to the battery icon at the top of the screen (unless the hub has its own AC power source).

FIGURE 1-2:
The bottom of the iPad.

Speaker   Lightning connector   Speaker

On the sides

On the right side of your iPad are the volume up and volume down buttons, as shown in Figure 1-3. Press the upper button to increase the volume; press the lower button to decreases the volume.

TIP

The Camera app uses the volume up button as an alternative shutter release button to the on-screen shutter release button. Press either one to shoot a picture or start and stop video recording.

On the left side of your iPad, if it's a cellular model, you'll find the SIM card tray.

FIGURE 1-3:
The right side
of the iPad.

Nano-SIM tray
(cellular models only)

Volume up and down buttons

TIP

Apple used to include a SIM card eject tool with iPads and iPhones. If you don't have one lying around, you can straighten a paper clip and use it as a faux SIM card eject tool.

On the front and back

On the front and back of your iPad, you find the following (labeled in Figure 1-4):

>> **Touchscreen:** You find out how to use the iPad's gorgeous high-resolution color touchscreen in Chapter 2. All we have to say at this time is: Try not to drool all over it.

App icon

Front camera

Rear camera

FIGURE 1-4:
The front and
back of the
iPad: a study
in elegant
simplicity.

Touchscreen

Home button

>> **Home button/Touch ID sensor:** No matter what you're doing, you can press the Home button at any time to display the Home screen, as shown in Figure 1-4. The Home button also doubles as a Touch ID sensor on most iPads, so you can use your fingerprint (or a passcode) to unlock your phone and authenticate purchases.

>> **Front (FaceTime) camera:** The front camera is serviceable and delivers decent-enough video for video chats and such, but it's not particularly good for taking still photos. That is, unless your iPad is a Pro model, which offers 7-megapixel front camera photos (versus 1.2 megapixels on all other models).

>> **App icons:** Each of the icons shown on the screen (see Figure 1-4) launches an included iPad app. You read more about these apps later in this chapter and throughout the rest of the book.

>> **Rear camera:** On the backside, just below the sleep/wake button, iPads have a better camera than the one in front. Pro models have 12-megapixel cameras with an f/1.8 aperture; other iPads have 8-megapixel cameras with f/2.4 apertures. All iPads can record HD video at 1080p; Pro models can record video at up to 4K.

Status bar

The status bar, which is at the top of the screen, displays tiny icons that provide a variety of information about the current state of your iPad:

>> **Airplane mode:** Airplane mode should be enabled when you fly. It turns off all wireless features of your iPad — the cellular, 4G, 3G, GPRS (General Packet Radio Service), and EDGE (Enhanced Datarate for GSM Evolution) networks; Wi-Fi; and Bluetooth — so you can enjoy music, video, games, photos, or any app that doesn't require an Internet connection while you're in the air.

Tap the Settings app and then tap the Airplane Mode switch on (so green is displayed). The icon shown in the margin appears on the left side of your status bar whenever airplane mode is enabled.

REMEMBER

Disable airplane mode when the plane is at the gate before takeoff or after landing so you can send or receive email and iMessages.

There's no need to enable airplane mode on flights that offer onboard Wi-Fi unless you have a cellular-equipped iPad. On such flights it's perfectly safe to use your iPad's Wi-Fi while you're in the air (but not until the captain says so).

To use Wi-Fi in flight with a cellular iPad, first enable airplane mode and then reenable Wi-Fi.

»» **Wi-Fi:** If you see the Wi-Fi icon, your iPad is connected to the Internet over a Wi-Fi network. The more semicircular lines that are lit (up to three), the stronger the Wi-Fi signal. If your iPad has only one or two semicircles of Wi-Fi strength, try moving around a bit. If you don't see the Wi-Fi icon on the status bar, Internet access with Wi-Fi is not currently available.

»» **Personal hotspot:** You see this icon when you're sharing your Internet connection with computers or other devices over Wi-Fi. Personal hotspot is available for every iPad except the iPad 2 and may not be available in all areas or from all carriers. Additional fees may apply. Contact your wireless carrier for more information.

»» **Syncing:** This icon appears on the status bar when your iPad is syncing with iTunes on your Mac or PC.

»» **Activity:** This icon tells you that some network or other activity is occurring, such as over-the-air synchronization, the sending or receiving of email, or the loading of a web page. Some third-party apps use this icon to indicate network or other activity.

»» **VPN:** This icon shows that you're currently connected to a virtual private network (VPN).

»» **Lock:** This icon tells you when your iPad is locked. See Chapter 2 for information on locking and unlocking your iPad.

»» **Screen orientation lock:** This icon appears when the screen orientation lock is engaged.

»» **Location Services:** This icon appears when an app (such as Maps; see Chapter 6 for more about the Maps app) is using Location Services (GPS) to establish your physical location (or at least to establish the physical location of your iPad).

»» **Do Not Disturb:** This icon appears whenever Do Not Disturb is enabled, silencing incoming FaceTime calls and alerts. See Chapter 15 for details on Do Not Disturb.

»» **Play:** This icon informs you that a song is currently playing. You find out more about playing songs in Chapter 7.

»» **Bluetooth:** This icon indicates the current state of your iPad's Bluetooth connection. If you see this icon on the status bar, Bluetooth is on, and a device (such as a wireless headset or keyboard) is connected. If the icon is gray, Bluetooth is turned on, but no device is connected. If the icon is white,

Bluetooth is on, and one (or more) devices are connected. If you don't see a Bluetooth icon, Bluetooth is turned off. Chapter 15 goes into more detail about Bluetooth.

>> **Bluetooth Battery:** Displays the battery level of supported Bluetooth devices (while paired). Only certain devices — mostly headsets and speakers — support this feature. If you see this icon in your status bar, it's telling you the approximate battery level of whichever supported device is currently paired with your iPad.

>> **Battery:** This icon shows the level of your battery's charge, and also indicates when you're connected to a power source. It's completely filled when you aren't connected to a power source and your battery is fully charged. It then empties as your battery becomes depleted. You see an on-screen message when the charge drops to 20 percent or below, and another when it reaches 10 percent.

COMPARING WI-FI, 4G, LTE, 3G, GPRS, AND EDGE

Wireless (that is, cellular) carriers may offer one of three data networks relevant to the iPad as of this writing. For now anyway, only the third-generation and later iPads can take advantage of the speediest 4G or LTE networks, which carriers are rolling out as fast as they can. The second-fastest network is called 3G, and there are older, even slower data networks called EDGE and GPRS. Your iPad starts by trying to connect to the fastest network it supports. If it makes a connection, you see the 4G or 3G icon on the status bar. If it can't connect to a 4G or 3G network, it tries to connect to a slower EDGE or GPRS network, and you see EDGE or GPRS icons on the status bar.

Most Wi-Fi networks, however, are faster than even the fastest 4G cellular data network — and much faster than 3G, EDGE, or GPRS. So, because all iPads can connect to a Wi-Fi network if one is available, they do so, even when a 4G, 3G, GPRS, or EDGE network is also available.

Last but not least, if you don't see 3G, 4G, LTE, GPRS, E (for EDGE), or the Wi-Fi icon, you don't currently have Internet access. Chapter 4 offers more details about these different networks.

Discovering the Delectable Home Screen and Dock Icons

The iPad Home screen and dock display 20 icons, with each icon representing a different built-in app or function. Because the rest of the book covers each and every one of these babies in full and loving detail, we merely provide brief descriptions here.

To get to your Home screen, tap the Home button. If your iPad is asleep when you tap, the unlock screen appears. After your iPad is unlocked, you see whichever page was on the screen when it went to sleep. If that happens to have been the Home screen, you're golden. If it wasn't, merely tap the Home button again to summon your iPad's Home screen.

In the following sections, we tell you briefly about the icons preloaded on your iPad's first Home screen page, as well as the icons you find on the dock that are always accessible from each Home screen.

Home is where the screen is

If you haven't rearranged your icons, you see the following apps on the first Home screen, starting at the top left:

>> **FaceTime:** Use this app to participate in FaceTime video chats, as you discover in Chapter 8.

>> **Calendar:** No matter what calendar program you prefer on your Mac or PC (as long as it's iCal, Calendar, Microsoft Entourage, or Microsoft Outlook or online calendars such as Google or iCloud), you can synchronize events and alerts between your computer and your iPad. Create an event on one device, and the event is automatically synchronized with the other device the next time the two devices are connected. Neat stuff.

>> **Photos:** This app is the iPad's terrific photo manager, which just keeps getting better. It lets you view pictures from a camera or SD card (using the optional camera connection kit), screen shots of your iPad screen, photos synced from your computer, saved from an email or web page, or saved from one of the myriad third-party apps that let you save your handiwork in the Photos app. You can zoom in or out, create slideshows, email photos to friends, crop, do a bit of image editing, and much more. And it's where you'll find the Camera Roll album with photos and videos you've taken with your iPad. To get started, see Chapter 9.

» **Camera:** You use this app to shoot pictures or videos with your iPad's front- or rear-facing camera. You find out more in Chapters 8 (videos) and 9 (camera).

» **Contacts:** This handy little app contains information about the people you know. Like the Calendar app, it synchronizes with the Contacts app on your Mac or PC (as long as you keep your contacts in Address Book, Contacts, Microsoft Entourage, or Microsoft Outlook), and you can synchronize contacts between your computer and your iPad. If you create a contact on one device, the contact is automatically synchronized with the other device the next time your devices are connected. Chapter 12 explains how to start using the Calendar and Contacts apps.

» **Clock:** The Clock app includes alarm clocks, timers, and more. You hear more about this nifty app in Chapter 13.

» **Maps:** This app is among our favorites. View street maps or satellite imagery of locations around the globe, or ask for directions, traffic conditions, or even the location of a nearby pizza joint. You can find your way around the Maps app with the tips you find in Chapter 6.

» **Home:** This app lets you control smart appliances that conform to Apple's HomeKit standard.

» **Notes:** This program enables you to type notes while you're out and about. You can send the notes to yourself or to anyone else through email, or you can just save them on your iPad until you need them. For help as you start using Notes, flip to Chapter 13.

» **Reminders:** This app may be the only to-do list you ever need. It integrates with iCal, Calendar, Outlook, and iCloud, so to-do items and reminders sync automatically with your other devices, both mobile and desktop. You'll hear much more about this great app, but you have to wait until Chapter 13.

» **News:** This app is where you'll find news culled from magazines, newspapers, and websites. You read more about News in Chapter 10.

» **iTunes Store:** Tap this puppy to purchase music, movies, TV shows, audiobooks, and more. You find more info about iTunes (and the Music app) in Chapter 7.

» **App Store:** This icon enables you to connect to and search the iTunes App Store for iPad apps that you can purchase or download for free over a Wi-Fi or cellular data network connection. Chapter 11 is your guide to buying and using apps from the App Store.

» **iBooks:** You use iBooks to read books, which you can buy in the iTunes Store.

» **Settings:** Tap this icon to change settings for your iPad and its apps. With so many settings in the Settings app, you'll be happy to hear that Chapter 15 is dedicated exclusively to Settings.

Now, swipe from right to left across the first Home screen to make the second Home screen appear. Its icons include the following:

>> **Tips:** This app offers tips from Apple on doing more with your iPad. And here's a tip about Tips: Apple pushes new tips to the app every week, so if you haven't looked at the app lately, consider doing so to see what's new.

>> **Podcasts:** Use the Podcasts app to (d'oh!) listen to your favorite podcasts, which you download and subscribe to (let's all say it together this time) in the iTunes Store.

>> **Photo Booth:** This one is a lot like those old-time photo booths, but you don't have to feed it money. You discover details about Photo Booth in Chapter 9.

>> **Find Friends:** See the locations of friends and family who opt in.

>> **Find iPhone:** If your iPad (or iPhone or iPod touch) goes missing, use this app to determine its last known location.

>> **TV:** This handy app is the repository for your movies, TV shows, and music videos. You add videos via iTunes on your Mac or PC or by purchasing them from the iTunes Store with the iTunes app on your iPad. Check out Chapter 8 to find out more.

Sittin' on the dock of the iPad

At the bottom of the iPad screen are the final five icons, sitting on the left side of a special shelflike area called the *dock*.

NEW

New in iOS 11, suggested apps appear on the right side of the dock. These are apps you've used recently or apps that are open on your iPhone or Mac. In Figure 1-4, for example, the three suggested apps (from left to right) are App Store, Settings, and iTunes Store.

REMEMBER

The thing that makes the icons on your dock special is that they're available on every Home screen.

By default, the five icons on the left side of the dividing line in the dock are as follows:

>> **Messages:** This app provides to iPads, iPhones, iPod touches, and Macs a unified messaging service dubbed iMessage. You can exchange unlimited free text or multimedia messages with any other device running iOS 5 or later (the iPad, iPhone, and iPod touch) or Mac OS X Mountain Lion or later. Find out more about iMessage in Chapter 5.

» **Mail:** This app lets you send and receive email with most POP3 and IMAP email systems and, if you work for a company that grants permission, Microsoft Exchange, too. Chapter 5 helps you start emailing everyone you know from your iPad.

» **Safari:** Safari is your web browser. If you're a Mac user, you know that already. If you're a Windows user who hasn't already discovered the wonderful Safari for Windows, think Internet Explorer on steroids. Chapter 4 shows you how to start using Safari on your iPad.

» **Files:** This app (if enabled in Settings ⇨ iCloud ⇨ iCloud Drive) contains all documents you've saved to your iCloud Drive. Apple apps as well as many third-party apps know how to use it.

NEW

» **Music:** Last but not least, this icon unleashes all the power of an iPod right on your iPad so that you can listen to music or podcasts. You discover how the Music app works in Chapter 7.

The dock on all iPads can hold at least six icons; pro models can hold as many as a dozen. Feel free to add icons to or remove icons from the left side of the dock until it feels right to you. To add or remove dock icons, press and hold down on any icon — on your Home screen or in the dock — until all the icons begin to wiggle. Then, drag the icon to the left side of the dock (or wherever you like). When you're satisfied, press the Home button to exit wiggly mode and save your arrangement.

TIP

Two last points:

» Notifications keep getting better and more useful with each new version of iOS. We wanted to mention them even though they don't have an icon of their own. You hear much more about notifications in Chapter 13; to see them now (we know you can't wait), swipe your iPad screen from top to bottom to make them appear. Then swipe from bottom to top to put them away again.

This gesture works anytime — even when your iPad is locked. If it's locked, you'll see your most recent notifications when you swipe down. Then swipe up to see your older notifications.

» We'd be remiss not to mention the even more useful Control Center, with controls for Wi-Fi, Bluetooth, audio playback, and more, all available from any screen in any app. You discover much more about Control Center in Chapter 14, but if you just can't stand the suspense, put your finger at the very bottom of your iPad screen and swipe upward to check out Control Center (and then tap the Home button to put it away).

TIP

Chapter **2**

iPad Basic Training

By now you know that the iPad you hold in your hands is very different from other computers.

You also know that these slate-style machines are rewriting the rule book for mainstream computing. How so? For starters, iPads don't come with a mouse or any other kind of pointing device. They lack traditional computing ports or connectors, such as USB. And they have no physical or built-in keyboard, though Apple will sell you a Smart Keyboard accessory for the iPad Pro models.

iPads even differ from other so-called tablet PCs, some of which feature a pen or stylus and let you write in digital ink. As we point out (pun intended) in Chapter 1, the iPad relies on an input device that you always have with you: your finger. Okay, so the iPad Pros you meet in this book also break that longstanding iPad rule, at least if you spring for the Apple Pencil accessory.

Tablet computers of one form or another have been around since the last century. They just never captured the fancy of Main Street. Apple's very own Newton, an ill-fated 1990s personal digital assistant, was among the machines that barely made a dent in the market.

What's past is past, of course, and technology — not to mention Apple itself — has come a long way since Newton. And suffice it to say that in the future, tablets — led by the iPad brigade, of course — promise to enjoy a much rosier outlook.

If you were caught up in the initial mania surrounding the iPad, you probably plotted for weeks about how to land one. After all, the iPad, like its close cousin the iPhone, rapidly emerged as the hippest computer you could find. (We consider you hip just because you're reading this book.) You had to plot to get subsequent versions as well.

Speaking of the iPhone, if you own one or its close relative, the Apple iPod touch, you already have a gigantic start in figuring out how to master the iPad multitouch method of navigating the interface with your fingers. If you've been using iOS 11 on those devices, you have an even bigger head start. You have our permission to skim the rest of this chapter, but we urge you to stick around anyway because some things on the iPad work in subtly different ways than on the iPhone or iPod touch. If you're a total novice, don't fret. Nothing about multitouch is painful.

Getting Started on Getting Started

We've always said that you needed the following four things to enjoy your new iPad, but starting with iOS 5, you don't *need* a computer (and the connection to iTunes and whatever program you use to store your contacts) to use an iPad. You see, iOS 5 was the first operating system to allow you to activate, set up, and apply iOS updates to an iPad wirelessly, without having to connect it to a computer. All the ensuing versions of iOS continued the tradition. We show you how to get your iPad set up without a computer in the next section, including the new automatic setup that makes things even easier; in Chapter 3, we show you how to set up your iPad with your computer.

Because even though you don't *need* a computer, we think you'll prefer using your iPad with one rather than without.

TIP

In our experience, many tasks — such as iOS software updates — are faster and easier to do using iTunes on a Mac or PC than on the iPad. Having a backup for your data helps, too. Actually, it more than helps. A backup can be a lifesaver.

Now, here are those four things you need to use your iPad:

>> **A computer:** As we point out, you don't really need a computer, though it's helpful to use your iPad with one just the same. The computer can be a Mac running OS X version 10.6.8 or later, or a PC running Windows XP Home or Professional Edition with Service Pack 3 or later.

The iCloud service has higher requirements: Mac OS X Mountain Lion or later, or Windows Vista or later for PCs. Flip to Chapter 3 for details about iCloud.

>> **iTunes software:** More specifically, you need version 10.7 or later of iTunes — emphasis on the *later* because by the time you read this, it will be later. After all, iTunes was up to version 12.7 by the time we were preparing this book.

Apple constantly tweaks iTunes to make it better. You can go to www.itunes. com/download to fetch a copy. Or launch your current version of iTunes and then choose iTunes ⇨ Check for Updates.

The uninitiated might want to know that *iTunes* is the nifty Apple jukebox software that owners of iPods, iPhones, and iPads, not to mention PCs and Macs, use to manage music, videos, apps, and more. iTunes is at the core of the iPad as well, because an iPod is built into the iPad, as part of the Music app. You can use iTunes to synchronize a bunch of stuff from your Mac or PC to and from an iPad, including (but not limited to) photos, movies, TV shows, podcasts, iTunes U lectures, and of course, music.

Syncing is such a vital part of this process that we devote an entire chapter (Chapter 3) to the topic.

>> **An Apple ID account:** Read Chapter 7 for details on how to set up an account. Like most things Apple, the process isn't difficult. You'll want an account to download content from iTunes, the App Store, or to take advantage of iCloud.

>> **Internet access:** Your iPad can connect to the Internet in either of two ways: Wi-Fi or cellular (if you bought an iPad with 3G or 4G capabilities). You can connect your iPad to cyberspace via Wi-Fi in your home, office, school, favorite coffeehouse, bookstore, or numerous other spots.

TECHNICAL STUFF

At press time, 4G (fourth-generation) wireless data connections were available from many carriers in countries too numerous to mention; in the United States, you can choose among AT&T, Sprint, Verizon Wireless, and T-Mobile, with most working on the fastest variety, called *LTE* (Long Term Evolution).

As this book goes to press, data rates (no contract required) are reasonably priced as long as you don't stream or download a lot of movies or watch tons of videos while connected over 3G or 4G. For as little as $5 in some instances, you can purchase a day pass for data instead of opting for a monthly plan.

Figuring out how much data you need beforehand isn't always easy, but it's simple enough to adjust along the way. If you're streaming a lot of music, T-Mobile for one provides a nice benefit: the capability to stream free on most major services, including Spotify and Apple's own Apple Music.

The following are some of the offerings from the major US carriers when we published this book. Keep in mind that all the rate plans cited are subject to change and sometimes tied to shareable family plans that include smartphones. In some instances, you must pay activation or other fees. Promotions are also common:

- AT&T: $15 a month for 250MB, 3GB for $30, and 5GB for $50

- Sprint: $15 a month for 1GB, 3GB for $35, and 6GB for $50

- T-Mobile: $20 a month for 2GB, 10GB for $50, 14GB for $60, and unlimited data for $70

- Verizon: $20 for 2GB, 4GB for $30, 6GB for $40, and 8GB for $50.

A friendly warning pops up on your iPad when you get close to your limit. At that point, you can pay more to add to your data bucket or start from scratch next month. Keep in mind that with 4G, you're likely to consume more data in a hurry. And prices of course are subject to change.

TIP

Whichever carrier you go with, we recommend finding a Wi-Fi network if you want to buy, rent, or watch movies, lest you exhaust your data allotment in a hurry.

iPads with cellular service may include an Apple SIM card that theoretically allows you to bounce from one carrier to another. The process isn't always simple, however, because such SIM cards are sometimes locked down, either by Apple or by the carrier from which you buy the tablet. Moreover, the type of SIM card inside your iPad varies. Some models have nano-SIM cards. Others, including most of the early models dating all the way back to the original iPad, have a micro-SIM. On the other hand, a more recent version — the 9.7-inch iPad Pro Wi-Fi + Cellular model — has both an embedded Apple SIM and a tray for a nano-SIM card.

If you can't get your iPad to work with a chosen wireless carrier, check with that carrier for details.

Turning On and Setting Up the iPad

Unless your iPad is brand-spanking new and fresh out of the box, chances are good that you've already performed the steps that follow. We cover them here because if you choose to use your iPad computer-free, these steps make up the entire setup process.

Apple has taken the time to partially charge your iPad, so you can set it up right away, in one of two ways. We strongly encourage you to use the first method, automatic setup, because it's so easy. However, it does require you to have another iOS 11 device already set up and running with the same Apple ID.

If you don't have another device using iOS 11, never fear! We also show you how to set up your iPad manually. In fact, you can skip straight down to the section called "Manual setup" to get started.

Automatic setup

NEW

Automatic setup, which is new in iOS 11, enables you to transfer your settings and Apple ID–related data from one iOS 11 device to another. As just mentioned, you need another iOS 11 device using the same Apple ID.

1. **Begin the setup process:**

a. *Press and hold down the sleep/wake button on the upper-right edge.* You see the Apple logo, followed by the word *hello* and similar greetings in a bunch of other languages.

b. *When you see a* Press Home to Open *message (in English or another languages), do so.* The language screen appears.

c. *Tap to choose your language, followed by your country or region preferences.* The Quick Start screen appears, along with a blue Set Up Manually button. Resist the urge to tap that one!

2. **Pair the two devices:**

a. *Bring your other iOS 11 device close to your iPad.* And by *close,* we mean a couple of inches away. Make sure this other device is unlocked, and look for the *Set Up New iPad* pop-up notification. The automatic setup magic has begun!

TECHNICAL STUFF

The pairing process uses the camera on one device to view shifting dots on another device. (The dots are a code, like a QR code, generated by your iPad.) This security procedure makes it difficult for someone to hijack this process to steal your Apple ID and other data.

b. *On the second device, tap the gray Continue button.* Your second device displays the instruction Hold Your New iPad Up to the Camera, while the iPad gets a cool screen with a rotating 3D blob of dots. (It will look familiar if you've ever paired an Apple Watch to an iPhone.)

c. *Hold your other iOS 11 device over the iPad you're setting up until the camera is positioned over the blob of dots, as shown in Figure 2-1.* After the camera captures the blob of dots, your other device will say Finish on New iPad, while your iPad asks you to Enter Passcode of Your *Other Device.*

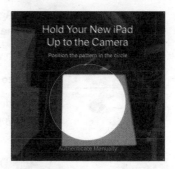

FIGURE 2-1: Maneuvering an iPad to pair with an existing iOS 11 device for automatic setup.

d. Enter on your new iPad the passcode from your second device. This is now the passcode for your iPad, too. (You can change it later, as detailed in Chapter 15.)

   As soon as you enter it successfully, your iPad will automatically display one of two screens: the Touch ID screen (for iPads with Touch ID) or the Apps & Data screen (for iPad Air and iPad mini 2).

3. **If you have an iPad Air or iPad mini 2, the Apps & Data screen will appear, so skip to Step 6.**

   The iPad Air and iPad mini 2 don't support Touch ID.

4. **Set up Touch ID:**

   a. Tap Continue.

   b. Tap the Home button each time you're asked. With each touch, sensors comprehensively map your fingerprint.

   c. When asked, adjust your grip and continue the process until the Complete screen appears.

5. **On the Complete screen, tap Continue.**

   The screen displays *Setting Up Your Apple ID* while your other device and your iPad exchange information, including Contacts, Calendar, and Keychain passwords. Your other device also copies over all your Wi-Fi settings, even passwords, so your iPad automatically joins your normal networks. This process could take a few minutes. When it's finished, the Apps & Data screen appears.

6. **Choose how to set up your iPad by tapping one of the options and following the on-screen prompts.**

   Your four choices are Restore from iCloud Backup, Restore from iTunes Backup, Set Up as New iPad, and Move Data from Android. When the process is complete, the Terms and Conditions screen appears.

7. **Tap Agree to accept the terms and conditions, and then tap Agree again on the pop-up dialog that appears.**

   When you tap Agree the second time, the Location Services screen appears.

8. **Tap to enable or disable Location Services.**

   Location Services are key to making the most out of your iPhone by letting iOS and your apps know where you are. We strongly recommend that you enable this feature.

   When you make your choice, one of two screens appears: the Apple Pay screen (for iPads with Touch ID) or the iPad Analytics screen (for iPad Air and iPad mini 2).

9. **If you have an iPad Air or iPad mini 2, go to Step 12.**

10. **Tap Continue, and then confirm or set up Apple Pay.**

If Apple Pay is set up on your other iOS 11 device, confirm each credit card you've set up. Otherwise, you can now add credit cards one at a time or set up Apple Pay later by tapping the Set Up Later in Settings button. (Learn more about Apple Pay in Chapter 15.)

When you're done, the Siri screen appears.

11. **Tap Continue to Set Up Siri.**

Starting in iOS 11, Siri is activated out of the box, and the Continue button turns on Hey Siri and Press Home for Siri. Otherwise, choose Set Up Later in Settings to turn on or off either method of calling Siri. You can do that by choosing Settings ⇨ Siri & Search when you're done setting up your iPad. For more on using Siri and dictation, see Chapter 14.

When you're done, the iPad Analytics screen appears.

12. **Tap to choose whether or not to share iPad analytics data with Apple.**

iPad analytics data is key to Apple learning more about how you use your iOS devices, including problems and other information. We think the company's privacy policies are best in class, and Apple has committed to anonymizing the data it collects so that it can't be tied to a specific user. Accordingly, we usually tap Share with Apple when setting up our own devices. Once you tap, the App Analytics screen appears.

13. **Decide whether or not to send analytics data to developers.**

In a previous step, you chose whether or not to share analytics data with Apple. Now you're asked if you want to share analytics with developers. If you agree to share with developers, you're not just trusting Apple; you're trusting all those developers, too. When we set up our devices, we often skip this permission.

After you make your choice, the next screen appears. If you have an iPad Pro, the True Tone Display screen appears.

14. **If you don't have an iPad Pro model, the Dock screen will appear, so skip to Step 16.**

15. **Tap Continue to acknowledge your iPad Pro has True Tone Display.**

Embedded sensors on your iPad Pro measure ambient light and adjust your iPad's display to match those conditions. Tap and hold down See without True Tone Display to see what the screen would like without these automatic adjustments. (To turn off the feature, you have to choose Settings ⇨ Display & Brightness later.) We recommend you keep this feature on and not worry about it.

16. **Tap Continue to acknowledge that you know that you can access the dock from anywhere.**

Apple wants to be sure you know about this feature, which is new in iOS 11. Read more about the dock later in this chapter. When you tap Continue, the Switch between Recent Apps screen appears.

17. **Tap Continue to acknowledge that you can switch between recent apps.**

Also new in iOS 11 is the ability to swipe up from the bottom of your screen to get to the app switcher. We talk about that later in this chapter. When you tap Continue, the Welcome to iPad screen appears.

18. **Tap Get Started to use your iPad.**

Congrats! You've completed the automatic setup process.

REMEMBER

If you ever need to restore your iPad to factory condition, follow the same steps, as described in Chapter 16.

Manual setup

If you've already gone through the automatic setup process, you can skip this section. If you want to know how to manually set up your iPad, however, you're in the right place. In the interest of space, we won't repeat details for instructions that are identical to what we explained in the "Automatic setup" section.

1. **Begin the setup process:**

   a. Press and hold down the sleep/wake button on the upper-right edge. You see the Apple logo, followed by the word *hello* and similar greetings in a bunch of other languages.

   b. When you see a Press Home to Open *message (in English or another languages), do so.* The language screen appears.

   c. Tap to choose your language, followed by your country or region preferences. The Quick Start screen appears, along with a blue Set Up Manually button.

2. **Tap the Set Up Manually button.**

3. **Tap to choose an available Wi-Fi network, provide a password (if necessary), and then tap the blue Join button.**

Certain iPad models may allow you to choose a cellular network, if available, and set up or change your Wi-Fi network later. (See Chapter 15 for setting up Wi-Fi in Settings.) After you tap Join, your iPad will automatically advance to the next screen.

4. **If you have an iPad Air or iPad mini 2, you'll see the Passcode screen, so skip to Step 6.**

The iPad Air and iPad mini 2 don't support Touch ID.

5. **Set up Touch ID:**

   a. *Tap Continue.*

   b. *Tap the Home button each time you're asked.* With each touch, sensors comprehensively map your fingerprint.

   c. *When asked, adjust your grip and continue the process until the Complete screen appears.*

6. **Create a passcode.**

Type a 6-digit passcode to unlock your iPad. When the Re-enter Your Passcode screen appears, type your passcode again. The Apps & Data screen appears.

7. **Choose how to set up your iPad by tapping one of the options and following the on-screen prompts.**

Your four choices are Restore from iCloud Backup, Restore from iTunes Backup, Set Up as New iPad, and Move Data from Android. When the process is complete, the Apple ID screen appears.

8. **If you don't have an Apple ID or forgot it:**

   a. *Tap the Don't Have an Apple ID or Forgot It? button.*

   b. *On the next screen, set up a new account or bypass this step until later by tapping Settings ➪ Apple ID.* (See the end of this chapter for an introduction to this service.)

The Terms and Conditions screen appears.

9. **If you have an Apple ID:**

   a. *Enter your Apple ID credentials.*

   b. *If you have activated two-factor authentication (sometimes called 2FA), approve this login on one of your other Apple devices, and then enter a passcode displayed on that device.*

   c. *If you use a different Apple ID for iCloud than you do for iTunes, you can enter both at this stage. Tap the Use Different Apple IDs for iCloud & iTunes? button, and enter your credentials for both.*

When your Apple ID has been set up, the Terms and Conditions screen appears.

10. **Tap Agree to accept the terms and conditions, and then tap Agree again on the pop-up dialog that appears.**

When you tap Agree the second time, the Express Settings screen appears.

11. **Tap Continue to automatically set up Siri, Location Services, and iPad Analytics through the Express Settings screen.**

    With one tap of your finger, Apple now makes it possible to set up all three of those settings at once. We recommend you do so, though you can choose to customize these settings one-by-by one by tapping Customize Settings.

    Siri is activated out of the box. By tapping Continue, you're turning on Hey Siri and Press Home for Siri, which you can turn off later in Settings ⇨ Siri & Search.

    Location Services are key to making the most out of your iPad by letting iOS and your apps know where you are. Data analytics are key to Apple learning more about how you use your iOS devices, including problems and other information. We think the company's privacy policies are best in class, and Apple has committed to anonymizing the data it collects so that it can't be tied to a specific user.

    When Express Settings is finished, one of two screens appears: the Apple Pay screen or the App Analytics screen.

12. **If you have an iPad Air or iPad mini 2, continue with Step 13 in the preceding section, "Automatic setup."**

13. **Tap Continue, and then confirm or set up Apple Pay.**

    If you have Apple Pay already set up with your Apple ID, you'll be asked to confirm each credit card you've set up. Otherwise, you can now add credit cards one at a time or set up Apple Pay later by tapping the Set Up Later in Settings button. (Learn more about Apple Pay in Chapter 15.)

14. **Continue with Step 13 in the preceding section, "Automatic setup."**

REMEMBER

If you ever need to restore your iPad to factory condition, follow the same steps, as described in Chapter 16.

POINTING A FINGER AT TOUCH ID

Apple wants you to give the iPad Air 2, iPad mini 3, iPad mini 4, or every iPad Pro model the finger. But only in a good way. All five devices are equipped with Touch ID, a fingerprint scanner cleverly embedded in the Home button. With a gentle press of any designated finger, you bypass your passcode. (Setting up passcode safeguards is a good idea, and it's something we also touch on in the chapter on Settings, Chapter 15.)

What's more, you can use your own digit (not the numerical kind) to authenticate iTunes and App Store purchases. (Go to Settings ⇨ Touch ID & Passcode and make sure that the iTunes & App Store switch is turned on.) You can also use Touch ID to authorize Apple Pay purchases on the web (but not in bricks-and-mortar retail stores).

Locking the iPad

We can think of several sound reasons for locking your iPad:

>> You won't inadvertently turn it on.

>> You keep prying eyes at bay.

>> You have a persistently inquisitive child.

>> You spare the battery some juice.

Apple makes locking the iPad a cinch.

REMEMBER

You don't need to do anything to lock the iPad; it happens automatically as long as you don't touch the screen for a minute or two. As you find out in Chapter 15, which is all about settings, you can also set the amount of time your iPad must be idle before it automatically locks.

Can't wait? To lock the iPad immediately, press the sleep/wake button.

TIP

If you have an iPad with a Smart Cover (or a third-party equivalent), opening and closing the cover locks and unlocks your iPad, but the Smart Cover has the advantage of awakening your iPad without making you tap the Home button (though you may still have to enter a passcode).

Unlocking the iPad is easy, too. Here's how:

1. **Press the sleep/wake button, or press the Home button on the front of the screen.**

2. **Do one of the following:**

   - *If you have Touch ID, use one of your registered fingers to press the Home button to unlock the iPad and go to your Home screen.*

   - *If you don't have Touch ID or your iPad was just restarted, press Home with another finger and enter your passcode.*

   See Chapter 15 to find out how to password-protect your iPad.

Mastering the Multitouch Interface

The iPad, like the iPhone, dispenses with a physical mouse and keyboard, in favor of a virtual keyboard — a step that seemed revolutionary just a few years ago, but is just-how-it-is today.

In the following sections, you discover how to move around the multitouch interface with ease. Later, we home in on how to make the most of the keyboard.

Training your digits

Rice Krispies have *Snap! Crackle! Pop!* Apple's response for the iPad is *Tap! Flick! Pinch!* Oh yeah, and *Drag!*

Fortunately, tapping, flicking, pinching, and dragging are not challenging gestures, so you can master many of the iPad's features in no time:

>> **Tap:** Tapping is the single most important element of modern multitouch interfaces. Tap to open, tap to play, tap to select, tap to shoot (in games). Sometimes, you *double-tap* (tapping twice in rapid succession), which has the effect of zooming in (or out) of web pages, maps, and emails.

>> **Flick:** A flick of the finger on the screen lets you quickly scroll through lists of songs, emails, and picture thumbnails. Tap the screen to stop scrolling, or merely wait for the scrolling list to stop.

>> **Pinch/spread:** Place two fingers on the screen and spread them apart to zoom in on images, web pages, text, videos, and more. Or pinch your fingers together to make things smaller. Pinching and unpinching are easy to master and quickly become second nature.

>> **Drag:** Here's where you slowly press your finger against the touchscreen without lifting it. You might drag to move around a web page or map that's too large for the iPad's display area.

>> **Drag downward from the top of the screen:** This special gesture displays notifications (which you find out about in Chapter 13). Press your finger at the very top of the screen and drag downward.

>> **Drag downward from any screen without starting at the very top of the screen:** This action summons Search, a discussion for later in this chapter.

>> **Drag from left to right from the first Home screen:** You are summoning the Today screen, where you see the appointments and reminders you have coming up, get app suggestions and News stories, and access Search. The today view is available on the lock screen and the Home screens.

>> **Drag from right to left from the lock screen:** This shortcut action summons the iPad's camera app.

>> **Drag upward from the bottom of the screen:** This time, you're calling up Control Center, a handy repository for music controls, airplane mode (see Chapter 15), Wi-Fi, Bluetooth, do not disturb, mute, volume, orientation lock, timer (Clock app), camera, AirPlay, and brightness controls. Check out Figure 2-2 for one view of Control Center.

>> **Swipe from right edge of the screen:** You can pull in a temporary overlay of another open app, a *slide over* feature we get to later in this chapter. This action requires that you go to Settings ➪ General ➪ Multitasking & Dock and enable the Allow Multiple Apps switch.

>> **Four- or five-finger swipes and pinches:** To quickly multitask or switch among or view running apps (see the later section, "Multitasking"), use four or five fingers to swipe upward. Swipe left or right (only one finger required) to switch between recently used apps. Pinch using four or five fingers to jump to your Home screen. Swipe up (one finger will do the trick) on an app's thumbnail to quit it.

Later in this chapter, you read about a couple of new ways to employ your digits, at least on certain models: slide over and split view.

Navigating beyond the Home screen

FIGURE 2-2:
We think you'll call on Control Center a lot.

The Home screen, which we discuss in Chapter 1, is not the only screen of icons on your tablet. After you start adding apps from the iTunes App Store (which you discover in Chapter 11), you may see a row of two or more tiny dots just above the main apps parked at the bottom of the screen. Those dots denote additional Home screens each containing up to 20 additional icons, not counting the additional icons in your iPad's dock. You can have up to 15 Home screens. You can also have more or fewer icons in your dock, but we can't think of a decent reason why you'd want to ditch any of them. In any case, more on these in a moment.

Here's what you need to know about navigating among the screens:

>> To navigate between screens, flick your finger from right to left or left to right across the middle of the screen, or tap directly on the dots. The number of dots you see represents the current number of screens on your iPad. The all-white dot denotes the screen you're currently viewing. Flicking — or swiping — from right to left from the first Home screen brings up the aforementioned Today screen.

>> Make sure you swipe and not just tap, or you'll probably open one of the apps on the current screen instead of switching screens.

TIP

>> Press the Home button to jump back to the Home screen. Doing so the first time takes you back to whatever Home screen you were on last. Tapping Home a second time takes you to the first Home screen.

>> The dock was radically revamped in iOS 11, as seen in Figure 2-5. You can now put up to 13 apps in it or as few as none. The dock also shows the three most recently opened apps on the right side of the divider line, making for a quick return to an app. You can access the dock from an open app by swiping up from the bottom of your screen.

Select, cut, copy, and paste

Being able to select and then copy and paste from one place on a computer to another has seemingly been a divine right since Moses, and that's the case on the Apple tablet as well. You can copy and paste (and cut) with pizzazz.

On the iPad, you might copy text or a URL from the web and paste it into an email or a note. Or you might copy a bunch of pictures or video into an email.

Suppose you're in the Notes app, jotting down ideas that you'll eventually copy to an email. Here's how you would exploit the copy-and-paste feature:

1. **Press against a word to select it.**

2. **Tap Select All to grab everything.**

You can also tap Select to drag the *grab points* (handles) to select a larger block of text or to contract the text you've already selected, as shown in Figure 2-3. Dragging grab points may take a little practice.

FIGURE 2-3:
Drag the grab handles to select text.

3. **After you select the text, tap Copy. If you want to delete the text block, tap Cut instead.**

4. **Open the Mail program (see Chapter 5) and start composing a message.**

5. **When you decide where to insert the text you just copied, tap the cursor.**

Up pop the Select, Select All, Paste, Quote Level, Insert Photo or Video, and Add Attachment commands, as shown in Figure 2-4. (We get to the last three options in Chapter 5.)

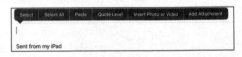

FIGURE 2-4:
Tap Paste and text will appear.

6. **Tap Paste to paste the text into the message.**

TIP

Here's the pizzazz part. If you made a mistake when you were cutting, pasting, or typing, shake the iPad. Doing so undoes the last edit (provided that you tap the Undo Paste or Undo option when it appears and keep the feature enabled in Settings).

You also see these options:

- *Auto-Correct:* If you happen to select a word with a typo, the iPad might underline that word. If you tap the underlined work, the iPad might show you the word it thinks you meant to spell. Tap that suggested word to accept it.

- *Predict:* A predictive word feature reveals up to three word or phrase options in buttons just above the keyboard. If one of these words or phrases is what you had in mind, tap the appropriate button.

- *Replace:* The iPad may show you possible replacement words. For example, replacement words for *test* might be *fest, rest,* or *text.* Tap the word to substitute it for the word you originally typed.

- *Indent Right or Left:* Pretty self-explanatory. With this option, you can indent highlighted text to the right or left.

- *Look Up:* Tap your selected word for a definition, courtesy of the *New Oxford American Dictionary,* the *Oxford Dictionary of English,* an Apple dictionary, or a foreign language dictionary if you've downloaded any dictionaries onto your iPad. But Look Up (which used to be Define) goes well beyond definitions and includes searches that extend to the App Store, Apple Music, Twitter, the web, Wikipedia, and more.

Multitasking

Through *multitasking,* you can run numerous apps in the background simultaneously and easily switch from one app to another. The following examples illustrate what multitasking enables you to do on your iPad:

» A third-party app, such as Slacker Personal Radio, continues to play music while you surf the web, peek at pictures, or check email. Without multitasking, Slacker would shut down the moment you opened another app.

» A navigation app can update your position while you're listening to, say, Pandora Internet radio. From time to time, the navigation app will pipe in with turn-by-turn directions, lowering the volume of the music so that you can hear the instructions.

>> If you're uploading images to a photo website and the process is taking longer than you want, you can switch to another app, confident that the images will continue to upload behind the scenes.

>> Leave voice notes in the Evernote app while checking out a web page.

Multitasking couldn't be easier — and it has improved through the various iOS upgrades. Now your iPad can anticipate your needs. For example, if it detects, over time, that you tend to turn to your social networking apps around the same time every morning, it will make sure the feeds are ready for you.

Here's another example. Double-press the Home button to bring up the app switcher and Control Center. We describe Control Center in depth in Chapter 14, so let's look at the app switcher, as shown in Figure 2-5. You see preview pages with icons just above them for any open apps. Scroll to the left to see more apps. Tap the preview screen for the app you want to switch to; the app remembers where you left off. If you hold the tablet sideways in landscape mode, the previews for your apps appear sideways, too.

App switcher   Control Center

FIGURE 2-5: Scroll to the left to see thé apps you've recently used or are still running.

Dock   Recently opened apps

To remove an app from the multitasking rotation, swipe up the app's preview. Poof — it's gone.

Apple says that multitasking will not overly tax the battery or exhaust system resources. The iPad conserves power and resources by putting apps in a state of suspended animation. And your iPad will schedule updates only during power-efficient times, such as when your device is connected to Wi-Fi.

TIP

You can use the four- or five-finger gesture to swipe upward to reveal your multitasking options.

Now let's take a look at some other tricks that make multitasking even more powerful.

Splitting the screen

All the iPads have larger screens compared to their iOS cousin, the iPhone, especially the 12.9-inch iPad Pro. And you can exploit the extra screen real estate to make multitasking even more productive.

For starters, there's a feature called *slide over.* Launch the first app you want to use and then swipe up from the bottom of the screen to bring out the dock. Drag an app off the dock, and iOS 11 will make a tray on the right side of the screen where you can drop that app. Now it's running side by side with your first app! This split view mode is shown in Figure 2-6. Drag the little gray handle between the two apps to resize them.

Safari   Resizer   Mail

FIGURE 2-6:
iOS 11 split
view in action
with Safari
on the left
and Mail on
the right.

In Safari, you have three ways to open split view when using the iPad in landscape mode. You can long-press a link on a web page and then tap Open in Split View. Or use a two-finger tap on a link to open that link on the other side of the screen. Lastly, drag a tab to the right edge of the screen and release, and a new split view is created.

We bet you can think of all sorts of reasons to run two apps at the same time. Maybe you're composing a message to a friend in the Mail app while scrolling through Safari in the smaller panel to find a place to have lunch. Maybe you're sketching in one app while using a photo in another as a reference point.

Drag down the gray handle at the top of the side app and the iPad switches to pop-over mode. Instead of running side by side, your first app now runs underneath the second one.

When you're done with that secondary app, just slide it away by dragging the gray handle in the middle to the right side of the screen. The slide over feature works with Apple's own apps as well as some third-party apps. Apps that don't support it can still have a second app running on top of them, as described in the preceding tip.

Split view works only on the iPad Air 2, iPad mini 4, iPad Pro, 9.7-inch iPad, and later models.

Picture-in-picture

There's a good possibility that your television at home has a picture-in-picture feature that enables you to watch one channel in the main portion of the TV screen while checking out a second channel in a small window on the screen. You don't really want to miss any of the action in the big game now, do you?

Since iOS 9, your iPad has had the same feature. You're not necessarily watching live TV shows in this smaller window, but you might be. The picture-in-picture feature on the iPad works when you're on a FaceTime video call or watching a video via the Videos app. Both topics are reserved for Chapter 8.

Picture-in-picture couldn't be simpler. While watching a video, press (not tap) the Home button. The video picture shrinks into a small window hanging out in the lower-right corner of the display.

You can pause the video or shut it down by tapping the controls that appear in this diminutive video window. (Tap the window if you don't see the controls.) If you want the video to take over the entire iPad screen, tap the leftmost picture control inside the video window, shown in Figure 2-7.

Meanwhile, if the video window is blocking a portion of the screen that you want to see, you can drag it to another space.

Organizing icons into folders

Finding the single app that you want to use among apps spread out over 15 screens may seem like a daunting task. But Apple felt your pain and added a handy organizational tool: folders. The Folders feature lets you create folder icons, each containing apps that pertain to the name that Apple assigned or you gave to that folder.

To create a folder, follow these steps:

FIGURE 2-7:
Like some TVs, the iPad has a picture-in-picture feature.

1. **Press your finger against an icon until all the icons on the screen wiggle.**

2. **Decide which apps you want to move to a folder and then drag the icon for the first app on top of the second app.**

   The two apps now share living quarters inside a newly created folder. Apple names the folder according to the category of apps inside the folder.

3. **(Optional) Change the folder name by tapping the X on the bar where the folder name appears and typing a new name.**

To launch an app inside a folder, tap that folder's icon and then tap the icon for the app that you want to open.

You have plenty of room for all your apps on the iPad. Indeed, you can put as many as 16 apps inside a folder, stash up to 20 apps or folders per page (not counting up to 5 apps in the dock), and have as many as 15 pages.

When you drag all the apps from a folder, the folder automatically disappears.

Printing

iOS 11's AirPrint feature is Apple's effort to address a glaring shortcoming of older versions of iOS, the ability to print. You can print wirelessly from the iPad to an AirPrint-capable printer, available from all the major printer manufacturers.

AirPrint works with Mail, Photos, Safari, and iBooks (PDF files). You can also print from apps in Apple's iWork software suite, as well as third-party apps with built-in printing.

REMEMBER

An AirPrint printer doesn't need any special software, but it does have to be connected to the same Wi-Fi network as the iPad.

To print, follow these steps:

1. **Tap the share icon, and then tap the Print command.**

The icon is shown in the margin.

2. **In the Printer Options bubble that appears, tap Select Printer to select a printer, which the iPad locates in short order.**

3. **Depending on the printer, specify the number of copies you want to print, the number of double-sided copies, and a range of pages to print.**

Graphics that appear may even show you how much ink the printer has left.

4. **When you're happy with your settings, tap Print.**

If you display the preview pages while a print job is underway, the Print Center icon appears with all your other recently used apps. A badge indicates how many documents are in the print queue, along with the currently printing document.

Proactive search

Using the Safari browser (see Chapter 4), you can search the web via Google, Yahoo!, Bing, or DuckDuckGo. If you've added a foreign language keyboard, other options may present themselves. For example, with a Chinese keyboard enabled, you can summon the Baidu search engine.

You can search also for people and programs across your iPad and within specific apps, using a combination of Search and Siri. We show you how to search within apps in the various chapters dedicated to Mail, Contacts, Calendar, and Music.

Searching across the iPad is based on the powerful Search feature familiar to Mac owners. Search can search for news and trending topics, local restaurants, movie times, and content in Apple's own iTunes Store, App Store, and iBooks Store.

Moreover, with Siri teaming up with the Search feature (familiar to Mac owners), you'll also see circled icons representing the contacts you engage with the most, the people you are next scheduled to meet, as well as nearby eateries, shops, and other nearby places of possible interest.

The searches are also proactive, meaning that the device gets to know you over time and makes suggestions accordingly. It attempts to read your mind. The tablet might surface the News app for example, if it learns that you turn to it every morning (while enjoying your coffee).

Or if you're in a particular area, you may see the news that's trending in your location.

Here's how the Search feature works:

1. **Swipe down from any screen to access Search.**

   A bar slides into view at the top of the screen.

2. **Tap the bar and use the virtual keyboard to enter your search query.**

   The iPad spits out results the moment you type a single character; the list narrows as you type additional characters.

   The results are pretty darn thorough. Say that you entered *Ring* as your search term. Contacts whose last names have *Ring* in them show up, along with friends who might have done a trapeze act in the now defunct Ringling Bros. circus. All the songs on your iPad by Ringo Starr show up too, as do such song titles as "Ring-A-Ling," from the Black-Eyed Peas if that happens to be in your library. The same goes for apps, videos, audiobooks, events, and notes with the word *Ring*. You'll see web and App Store references as well.

3. **Tap any listing to jump to the contact, ditty, or app you seek.**

TIP

At the bottom of the Search results list, you can tap to move your search query to the web (using your designated search engine). You can search the Maps app too.

You can enable Suggestions by choosing Settings ➪ Siri & Search to summon results from the web, iTunes, the App Store, movie showtimes, nearby locations, and more. A separate switch lets you enable Suggestions in Look Up when taking advantage of the Look Up feature.

The Incredible, Intelligent, and Virtual iPad Keyboard

As you know by now, instead of a physical keyboard, several soft, or virtual, English-language or (depending upon what you chose during setup) foreign-language keyboard layouts slide up from the bottom of the iPad screen, including variations on the alphabetical keyboard, the numeric and punctuation keyboard, the more punctuation and symbols keyboard, and the emoji keyboard.

Indeed, the beauty of a software keyboard is that you see only the keys that are pertinent to the task at hand. The layout you see depends on the app. The keyboards in Safari differ from the keyboards in Mail. For example, in Mail, you'll see a Return key (and the @ symbol when typing in an address field). The similarly placed key in Safari is labeled Go, as shown in Figure 2-8.

TIP

See the little gray letters and numbers at the top of most keys in Figure 2-8? They are new in iOS 11. If you swipe down on a key instead of tapping it, you'll get that second character instead of the main one.

FIGURE 2-8:
The keys on the Mail (top) and Safari (bottom) keyboards.

Before you consider how to *use* the keyboard, we want to share a bit of the philosophy behind its so-called *intelligence*. Knowing what makes this keyboard smart can help you make it even smarter when you use it. The keyboard

>> Has a built-in English dictionary that even includes words from today's popular culture. Dictionaries in other languages are automatically activated when you use a given international keyboard, as described in the sidebar "A keyboard for all borders," later in this chapter.

>> Adds your contacts to its dictionary automatically.

>> Uses complex analysis algorithms to predict the word you're trying to type.

>> Suggests corrections as you type. It then offers you the suggested word just below the misspelled word. When you decline a suggestion and the word you typed is *not* in the iPad dictionary, the iPad adds that word to its dictionary and offers it as a suggestion if you mistype a similar word in the future.

TIP

Actively decline incorrect suggestions by tapping the characters you typed as opposed to the suggested words that appear. This helps train your intelligent keyboard.

» Reduces the number of mistakes you make as you type by intelligently and dynamically resizing the touch zones for certain keys. The iPad increases the zones for keys it predicts might come next and decreases the zones for keys that are unlikely or impossible to come next. Cool!

Anticipating what comes next

The keyboard takes an educated stab at the next word you mean to type and presents what it surmises to be the best possible word choices front and center. Say you're in the Messages app and the last message you received was an invitation to lunch or dinner. Above the row of keys on the iPad keyboard, you'd see buttons with three word suggestions: *Dinner, Lunch,* and *Not sure* (as shown in Figure 2-9). If one of those was the appropriate response, you could tap the button to insert its text into your reply.

FIGURE 2-9:
The iPad keyboard predicts what you might want to type next.

If you wanted to respond with something different than the three options presented by Apple, you'd just type your response with the regular QWERTY keys. As you type additional letters and words, the three suggested word choices above the keyboard change in real time. For instance, if you start by typing *That's a* in your message, the new trio of word choice buttons that show up might be *great, good,* and *very.*

To exploit the predictive typing feature, make sure the Predictive setting is turned on (as it is by default). Go to Settings ➪ General ➪ Keyboard, and slide the Predictive switch to on.

Discovering the special-use keys

The iPad keyboard contains several keys that don't actually type a character. Here's the scoop on each of these keys:

 » **Shift:** If you're using the alphabetical keyboard, the shift key switches between uppercase and lowercase letters. You can tap the key to change the case, or hold down shift and slide to the letter you want to be capitalized.

 » **Typewriter:** Enable the Split Keyboard option (tap Settings ⇨ General ⇨ Keyboard), and you can split the keyboard in a thumb-typist-friendly manner, as shown in Figure 2-10. When you're ready to split your keyboard, press and hold down the typewriter icon key, and tap Split on the menu. From that menu you can also dock the keyboard to the bottom of the screen. When you want to bring the keyboard back together, press and hold down the typewriter icon key again and choose either Merge or Dock and Merge from the menu.

FIGURE 2-10: Press and hold down the typewriter icon key to split the keyboard.

 » **#+= or 123:** If you're using a keyboard that shows only numbers and symbols, the traditional shift key is replaced by a key labeled #+= or 123. Pressing that key toggles between keyboards that just have symbols and numbers.

» **Emoji:** Tap this key and you can punctuate your words by adding smiley faces and other emojis.

 » **International keyboard:** You see this key only if you've turned on an international (or third-party) keyboard, as explained in the nearby sidebar "A keyboard for all borders."

 » **Delete:** Tapping this key (otherwise known as the backspace key) erases the character immediately to the left of the cursor.

 » **Return:** This key moves the cursor to the beginning of the next line. You might find this key labeled Go or Search, depending on the app you're using.

 » **Dictation:** Tap the microphone icon and start talking. The iPad listens to what you have to say. Tap the key again, and the iPad attempts to convert your words into text. You can use this dictation feature in many of the instances in which you can summon the keyboard, including the built-in Notes and Mail apps, as well as many third-party apps. See Chapter 14 for more on dictation.

When you use dictation, the things you say are recorded and sent to Apple, which converts your words into text. Just make sure to proofread what you've said because the process isn't foolproof. Apple also collects other information, including your first name and nickname, the names and nicknames of folks in your contacts list, song names in Music, and more. Apple says it anonymizes this information, which helps the Dictation feature perform its duties. If any of this freaks you out, however, tap Settings ➪ General ➪ Keyboard and slide the Enable Dictation switch to off. You can also restrict the use of dictation in Settings, as explained in Chapter 15.

On the top row of the keyboards that pop up in certain apps — Mail and Notes, for instance — you'll find dedicated **B**, *I*, and U keys to the right of the three suggested word alternatives. These permit you to bold, italicize, or underline selected text. To the right of the **B**, *I*, and U keys are a camera icon, which lets you insert images from the Photos app, and a paperclip icon, which lets you choose files to add from iCloud Drive.

To the left of the three alternative word suggestions on various keyboards, you'll see icons for undoing or redoing your last steps, plus a third icon that pastes the last selected word or passage that you copied. Such options are visible in both images that make up Figure 2-8.

What you see also varies by what you do. For example, after you select text in the Mail app, a scissors icon appears on the top row of the virtual keyboard; when you tap the icon, it cuts the selected text.

Choosing an alternative keyboard

Good as the keyboards that Apple supplies to your iPad are, you can choose an alternative keyboard from a third-party app developer, a welcome change to the producers of the SwiftKey, Swype, and Fleksy keyboards, among others, which debuted on the rival Android mobile operating system. You can fetch new keyboards in the App Store. Some are free; some require a modest sum.

After you've downloaded a keyboard, visit Settings ➪ General ➪ Keyboard ➪ Keyboards ➪ Add New Keyboard and select the keyboard of choice. Then press and hold down on the international keyboard key (globe icon) on the iPad's own keyboard, and select your new keyboard from the list that appears. Alternatively, keep tapping the globe icon until the keyboard you want takes over.

Finger-typing on the virtual keyboards

The virtual keyboards in Apple's multitouch interface just might be considered a stroke of genius. Or they just might drive you nuts.

If you're patient and trusting, in a week or so, you'll get the hang of finger-typing — which is vital to moving forward, of course, because you rely on a virtual keyboard to tap a text field, enter notes, type the names of new contacts, and so on.

As we note earlier in this chapter, Apple has built intelligence into its virtual keyboard, so it can correct typing mistakes on the fly or provide helpful word choices by predicting what you're about to type next. The keyboard isn't exactly Nostradamus, but it does an excellent job of coming up with the words you have in mind. We've found that tapping one of the predictive buttons appears to speed things up as well as bolster our typing accuracy. Apple is also relying ever more deeply on deep neural network technology to improve accuracy even more.

A KEYBOARD FOR ALL BORDERS

Apple is expanding the iPad's reach globally with international keyboard layouts for dozens of languages. To access a keyboard that isn't customized for Americanized English, tap Settings ➪ General ➪ Keyboard ➪ Keyboards ➪ Add New Keyboard. Then flick through the list to select any keyboard you want to use. Up pops the list shown in the figure, with custom keyboards for German, Italian, Japanese, and so on. Apple even supplies four versions of French (including keyboards geared to Belgium, Canadian, and Swiss customers) and several keyboards for Chinese. Heck, you can even find Australian, Canadian, Indian, Singapore, and UK versions of English.

A note about the Chinese keyboards: You can use handwriting character recognition for simplified and traditional Chinese, as shown here. Just drag your finger in the box provided. We make apologies in advance for not knowing what the displayed characters here mean. (We neither speak nor read Chinese so can only assume what we've produced is gibberish.)

Have a multilingual household? You can select as many of these international keyboards as you might need by tapping the language in the list.

When you're in an app that summons a keyboard, tap the international keyboard key (globe icon) in the lower left until the keyboard you want to call on shows up. (The globe key sometimes shows up as an emoji key with a smiley face; you have to tap the emoji key to see the globe icon.) Tap again to choose the next keyboard in the corresponding list of international keyboards that you turned on in Settings. If you keep tapping, you come back to your original keyboard. Or press against the globe icon until you see the list of all the keyboards you've added. You'll also see the aforementioned Predictive switch above the list of keyboards that you've added to your iPad.

To remove a keyboard that you've already added to your list, tap the Edit button in the upper-right corner of the Settings screen showing your enabled keyboards and then tap the red circle with the white horizontal line that appears next to the language to which you want to say *adios.*

Meanwhile, your iPad keypad is even more fluent with iOS 11. You can now type in two languages at once, without switching keyboards. You can type with any pair of the following languages: English, French, German, Italian, Portuguese, and Spanish. This multilingual typing feature is also supported for English and Chinese.

TIP

As you start typing on the virtual keyboard, we think you'll find the following additional tips helpful:

>> **See what letter you're typing.** As you press your finger against a letter or number on the screen, the individual key you press darkens until you lift your finger, as shown in Figure 2-11. That way, you know that you struck the correct letter or number.

>> **Slide to the correct letter if you tap the wrong one.** No need to worry if you touched the wrong key. You can slide your finger to the correct key because the letter isn't recorded until you release your finger.

>> **Tap and hold down to access special accent marks, alternative punctuation, or URL endings.** Sending a message to an overseas pal? Keep your finger pressed against a letter, and a row of keys showing variations on the character for foreign alphabets pops up, as shown in Figure 2-12. This row lets you add the appropriate accent mark. Just slide your finger until you're pressing the key with the relevant accent mark and then lift your finger.

Meanwhile, if you press and hold down the .? key in Safari, it offers you the choice of .us, .org, .edu, .com, or .net with additional options if you also use international keyboards.

» **Tap the space bar to accept a suggested word, or tap the suggested word to decline the suggestion.** Alas, mistakes are common at first. Say that you meant to type a sentence in the Notes app that reads, "I am fixing an important . . ." But because of the way your fingers struck the virtual keys, you actually entered "I am fixing an *importsnt . . .*" Fortunately, Apple knows that the *a* you meant to press is next to the *s* that showed up on the keyboard, just as *t* and *y* and *e* and *r* are side by side. So the software determines that *important* was indeed the word you had in mind and, as Figure 2-13 reveals, places it front and center among the three predictive text buttons. Note that the suspect word is highlighted. To accept the suggested word, merely tap the space bar. And if for some reason you actually did mean to type *importsnt* or maybe *imports to,* tap those choices instead among the predictive buttons that appear.

FIGURE 2-11:
The ABCs of virtual typing.

FIGURE 2-12:
Accenting your letters.

If you don't appreciate these features, you can turn off Auto-Correction and Predictive in Settings. See Chapter 15 for details. Visit `www.wiley.com/extras/ipad` for autocorrection tricks.

TIP

Because Apple knows what you're up to, the virtual keyboard is fine-tuned for the task at hand, especially when you need to enter numbers, punctuation, or symbols. The following tips help you find common special characters or special keys that we know you'll want to use:

» **Putting the @ in an email address:** If you're composing an email message (see Chapter 5), a dedicated @ key pops up on the main Mail keyboard when you're in the To: field choosing whom to send a message to. That key disappears from the first view when you tap the body of the message to compose your words. You can still get to the @ by tapping the 123 key.

» **Switching from letters to numbers:** When you're typing notes or sending email and want to type a number, symbol, or punctuation mark, tap the 123 key to bring up an alternative virtual keyboard. Tap the ABC key to return to the first keyboard. This toggle isn't hard to get used to, but some may find it irritating. Meanwhile, after tapping the 123 key, the shift key shifts into a #+= key. Tap #+= to summon additional character and symbol keys.

FIGURE 2-13:
Fixing an *important* mistake.

» **Adding apostrophes and other punctuation shortcuts:** If you press and hold down the exclamation mark/comma key, a pop-up offers the apostrophe. If you press and hold down the question mark/period key, you'll see the option to type quotation marks.

TIP

If you buy the 12.9-inch iPad Pro or the 9.7-inch iPad, you'll likely want to consider purchasing the optional iPad Pro Smart Keyboard cover accessory. At $169 (12.9-inch iPad Pro) or $159 (10.5-inch iPad Pro), these are kind of pricey, but you just might be tempted to go with a physical keyboard. You'll be tempted also by the $99 accessory stylus know as Apple Pencil. For more on iPad accessories, let us direct you to Chapter 17.

Of course, we already mentioned that other iPads, unlike some tablets from the past (and a few in the present), eschew a pen or stylus. But sometimes you might want to call upon a digital pen, and third-party companies fill the bill. For example, Wacom sells various Bamboo Stylus models, starting around $10 and going well up from there. It's a potentially useful tool for those with too broad, oily, or greasy fingers, or those who sketch, draw, or jot notes. You can find lower-priced styluses as well.

Editing mistakes

We think typing with abandon, without getting hung up over mistyped characters, is a good idea. The self-correcting keyboard can fix many errors (and occasionally introduce errors of its own). That said, plenty of typos are likely to turn up, especially in the beginning, and you have to correct them manually.

TIP

A neat trick for doing so is to hold your finger against the screen to bring up the magnifying glass. Use the magnifying glass to position the pointer on the spot where you need to make the correction. Then use the delete key (also called the backspace key) to delete the error and press whatever keys you need to type the correct text.

And with that, you are hereby notified that you've survived basic training. The real fun is about to begin.

Chapter **3**

Synchronicity: Getting Stuff to and from Your iPad

We have good news and . . . more good news. The good news is that you can easily set up your iPad so that your contacts, appointments, reminders, events, mail settings, bookmarks, books, music, movies, TV shows, podcasts, and photos are synchronized between your computer and your iPad (or other iDevices). And the more good news is that after you set it up, your contacts, appointments, events, and everything else we just mentioned can be kept up to date automatically in multiple places — on one or more of your computers and iPad, iPhone, and iPod touch devices.

Here's more good news: Whenever you make a change in one place, it's reflected almost immediately in all the other places it occurs. So if you add or change an appointment, an event, or a contact on your iPad while you're out and about, the information is automatically updated on your computers and other iDevices. And if no Wi-Fi or cellular network is available at the time, the update synchronizes the next time your iPad encounters a wireless network, all with no additional effort on your part.

This communication between your iPad and computer is called *syncing* (short for *synchronizing*). Don't worry: It's easy, and we walk you through the entire process in this chapter.

But wait. We have even more good news. Items that you choose to manage on your computer, such as movies, TV shows, podcasts, and email account settings, are synchronized only one way — from your computer to your iPad. This is the way it should be so you can delete media from your iPad after you've watched it without removing it from your iTunes library or iCloud or both.

The information in this chapter is based on iTunes 12.7 and iOS 11, the latest and greatest when these words were written. If your screens don't look exactly like ours, you probably need to upgrade to iTunes 12.7 or higher (choose iTunes ⇨ Check for Updates), or iOS 11 or higher (on your iPad, tap Settings ⇨ General ⇨ Software Update), or both. Both upgrades — iTunes and iOS — are free, and offer useful new features not found in their predecessors.

WARNING

Because Apple updates iTunes and iOS often, having the latest and greatest version is a double-edged sword. Sometimes you'll see something in the book that looks different on your iPad because you're using a *newer* version of iOS than we had when we wrote this. If you encounter a figure or an instruction that conflicts with what you're seeing on your iPad (and you're certain you're using the latest and greatest versions of both iTunes and iOS), please drop us a note so that we can make any necessary changes; our email addresses appear at the end of this book's Introduction.

REMEMBER

iOS 11 does let you set up your iPad computer-free (and as such, you're not *required* to sync your iPad with a computer running iTunes). Turn to Chapter 2 if you really want to set up your iPad computer-free. But some things are easier with a computer than without.

In this chapter, you find out how to sync all the digital data your iPad can handle, right after this short interlude about Apple's iCloud service.

A Brief iCloud Primer

Apple's iCloud service is more than just a wireless hard drive in the sky. iCloud is a complete data synchronization and wireless storage solution. In a nutshell, iCloud stores and manages your digital stuff — your music, photos, contacts, events, and more — and makes it available to all your computers and iDevices automatically.

iCloud pushes information such as email, calendars, contacts, reminders, and bookmarks to and from your computer and to and from your iPad and other iDevices, and then keeps those items updated on all devices wirelessly and without any effort on your part. iCloud also includes nonsynchronizing options, such as photo stream and iCloud photo sharing (see Chapter 9) and email (see Chapter 5).

Your free iCloud account includes 5GB of storage, which is all many users will need. If you have several devices (including Macs and PCs) or like saving data in the cloud, you'll probably find yourself needing more storage; 50- and 200-gigabyte upgrades are available for $1 and $3 a month, respectively.

A nice touch is that music, apps, periodicals, movies, and TV shows purchased from the iTunes Store, as well as your photo stream and iTunes Match content (see Chapter 7), don't count against your 5GB of free storage. iBooks don't count against your 5GB either, but audiobooks do. You'll find that the things that do count — such as mail, documents, account information, settings, and other app data — don't use much space, so 5GB may last a long time.

Conversely, if you use iCloud photo library and take a lot of photos and videos with your iDevice cameras, you're going to fill up your free 5GB pretty fast.

REMEMBER

If you're not using iCloud photo library (described in loving detail in Chapter 9), you might want to sync your iPad photos with a computer every so often and then delete the photos from the iPad. Otherwise, over time, those photos will take up a lot of space and eventually fill up your iPad.

If you plan to go PC-free but still want to have your email, calendars, contacts, and bookmarks synchronized automatically and wirelessly (and believe us, you do) between your computers and other iDevices, here's how to enable iCloud syncing on your iPad:

1. **On your Home screen, tap Settings.**

2. **Tap the first item in the list of settings on the left: *yourname* with *Apple ID, iCloud, iTunes, & App Store* below it.**

3. **Tap iCloud, and provide your Apple ID and password (if you haven't provided it previously).**

4. **Tap Sign In.**

A list of apps and services appears on the right side of the screen. Tap any individual on/off switch to enable or disable iCloud sync for Mail, Contacts, Calendars, Reminders, Safari (Bookmarks), Home, Notes, and News.

In the same list are five items that don't have switches:

>> **Photos:** Enable or disable four iCloud services with the by now familiar on/off switches (see Chapter 9 for details). The options are:

- *iCloud Photo Library:* Automatically upload and store your entire photo library in iCloud. The benefit is that you can access all your photos and videos on all your Macs and iDevices. One possible downside: This option could put you over iCloud's free 5GB limit.

  If you enable iCloud photo library, a pair of mutually exclusive options appear. If you choose Optimize iPad Storage, whenever your iPad runs low on space, your full-resolution photos and videos will automatically be replaced with lower-resolution versions that use less space. Or if you choose Download and Keep Originals, your iPad will download full-resolution versions of every photo and video in your iCloud photo library.

- *Upload to My Photo Stream:* Automatically upload photos you shoot with your iPad camera and send them to all your devices when connected to Wi-Fi.

  When Upload to My Photo Stream is enabled, the Upload Burst Photos option appears. Enable it to upload all photos taken in burst mode; disable to upload only favorites from bursts.

- *iCloud Photo Sharing:* Create and share albums with other iCloud users, or subscribe to other iCloud users' shared albums.

>> **Keychain:** Keep passwords and credit card information you save up to date on all devices you approve. The info is encrypted and can't be read by Apple (or, we hope, by anyone else).

>> **Find My iPad:** Tap this option to reveal two choices. The first is Find My iPad, so you can locate, lock, or erase your iPad and prevent anyone else from erasing or reactivating it without your password. The second option, Send Last Location, tells the iPad to send its location when the battery gets critically low.

>> **iCloud Backup:** Enable or disable iCloud backup, which backs up your photo library, accounts, documents, and settings whenever your iPad is plugged in, locked, and connected to Wi-Fi. Tap the Back Up Now button to initiate a backup, well, now.

TIP

Tap Manage Storage (near the top of the screen) to manage iCloud storage or upgrade your storage plan. Tap Share with Family (near the top of the Storage screen) to add or remove family members and shared payment methods from your Family Sharing plan (which you read more about in Chapter 15).

You find out much more about iCloud in the rest of this chapter and several other chapters, so let's move on to syncing your iPad.

Syncing with iTunes

Synchronizing your iPad with iTunes on a Mac or PC provides three main benefits over computer-free iPad use:

>> Viewing and managing your media — your music, movies, TV Shows, and so on — are easier on a computer's large screen and real keyboard than on your iPad.

>> You can maintain backup copies of your media on your Mac or PC almost effortlessly.

>> You can transfer to your iPad content not stored in iTunes — ringtones, audio recordings, PDFs, and other documents — by dragging items onto your device in the iTunes sidebar.

>> Managing your iPad's contents with iTunes offers sorting and viewing options not available on your iPad.

Synchronizing your iPad with your computer is a lot like syncing an iPhone with your computer, so if you're an iPhone user, the process will be a piece of cake. But even if you've never used an iPhone or iTunes, the process isn't difficult. Follow these steps:

1. **Start by connecting your iPad to your computer with the Lightning-to-USB cable that came with your iPad.**

   When you connect your iPad to your computer, iTunes should launch automatically. If it doesn't, chances are that you plugged the cable into a USB port on your keyboard, monitor, or hub. Try plugging it into one of the USB ports on your computer instead. Why? Because USB ports on your computer supply more power to a connected device than USB ports on a keyboard, monitor, or most hubs, and the iPad requires a lot of that power — even more than an iPod or an iPhone.

   If iTunes still doesn't launch automatically, try launching it manually.

2. **If you see an alert asking whether you want iTunes to open automatically when you connect this iPad, click Yes or No, depending on your preference.**

   You can change this setting later, so don't give it too much thought.

3. **If this is the first time you've introduced your iPad to iTunes:**

   a. *When an alert will asks "Do you want to allow this computer to access information on this iPad?" click Continue.*

   b. *On your iPad screen, when you see an alert asking, "Trust this computer?" tap Trust. Enter your passcode if requested, put down the iPad, and go back to iTunes on your computer.*

4. **Click the iPad icon, shown in the margin and near the top left of the iTunes window.**

TIP

If you don't see the iPad icon and you're positive that it's connected to a USB port *on your computer* (not the keyboard, monitor, or hub), try restarting your computer.

5. **If you use more than one iDevice with this computer, select your iPad in the drop-down list of all your devices that appears when you click the iPad icon.**

The Welcome to Your New iPad screen appears.

6. **Click Set Up as New iPad or select a backup from the Restore from This Backup drop-down menu and then click Continue.**

REMEMBER

See Chapter 16 for the scoop on restoring from iCloud or iTunes backups. For this example, we tap Set Up as New.

The Sync with iTunes screen appears.

7. **Click the Get Started button.**

The iPad screen appears, as shown in Figure 3-1.

8. **Click Summary in the list on the left, as shown in Figure 3-1.**

If you don't see a Summary tab, make sure your iPad is still connected. If you don't see your iPad's name near the top-left corner of the iTunes window, as shown in Figure 3-1, go back to Step 1 and try again.

9. **(Optional) If you want to rename your iPad, click its name and type a new one.**

We renamed the one in Figure 3-1 hsbob's iPad.

FIGURE 3-1:
The Summary pane is relatively painless.

From the Summary pane, you can set any options that you want from the Options area:

>> **Open iTunes When This iPad Is Connected check box:** Select this option if you want iTunes to launch automatically whenever you connect your iPad to your computer. Why might you choose not to enable this option? If you intend to connect your iPad to your computer to charge it, for example, you might not want iTunes to launch every time you connect it. If you do choose to enable it, iTunes launches and synchronizes automatically every time you connect your iPad.

Don't worry about this setting too much right now. As usual, if you change your mind, you can always come back to the Summary pane and deselect the Open iTunes When This iPad Is Connected check box.

TIP

If you do select the Open iTunes When This iPad Is Connected check box but don't want your iPad to sync automatically every time it's connected, launch iTunes and choose iTunes ⇨ Preferences (Mac) or Edit ⇨ Preferences (PC). Click the Devices tab at the top of the window and select the Prevent iPods, iPhones, and iPads from Syncing Automatically check box. This method prevents your iPad from syncing automatically, even if the Open iTunes When This iPad Is Connected option is selected. If you choose this option, you can sync your iPad by clicking the Sync or Apply button that appears in the lower-right corner of the iTunes window when your iPad is selected in the sidebar.

>> **Sync with This iPad Over Wi-Fi:** If you want to sync automatically over your Wi-Fi connection, select this check box.

WARNING

If you choose to sync wirelessly, your iPad and computer must be on the same Wi-Fi network and your iPad must be plugged into a power source for syncing to occur.

You may need to scroll down to see the following options (which are not visible in Figure 3-1).

>> **Sync Only Checked Songs and Video:** If you want to sync only items that have check marks to the left of their names in your iTunes library, select this check box. If you choose to use Apple's iTunes Match cloud-based storage (described in Chapter 7), this option will appear dimmed and be unavailable.

>> **Prefer Standard Definition Videos:** If you want high-definition videos you import to be automatically converted into smaller standard-definition video files when you transfer them to your iPad, select this check box.

Standard-definition video files are significantly smaller than high-definition video files. You'll hardly notice the difference when you watch the video on your iPad (unless it's an iPad with a Retina display, in which case you'll almost certainly notice), but you can have more video files on your iPad because they take up less space.

WARNING

The conversion from HD to standard definition takes a *long* time, so be prepared for very long sync times when you sync new HD video and have this option selected.

If you plan to use Apple's digital AV adapter (choose the dock version or Lightning version, as appropriate) or Apple TV ($99) to display movies on an HDTV, consider going with high definition. Although the files will be bigger and your iPad will hold fewer videos, the HD versions look spectacular on a big-screen TV.

» **Convert Higher Bit Rate Songs to 128/192/256 Kbps AAC:** If you want songs with bit rates higher than 128, 192, or 256 Kbps converted into smaller AAC files when you transfer them to your iPad, select this check box and choose the lower bit rate from the drop-down menu (which reads 128 kbps in Figure 3-1).

A *higher* bit rate means that the song will have better sound quality but use a lot of storage space. Songs that you buy at the iTunes Store or on Amazon, for example, have bit rates of around 256 Kbps. So a four-minute song with a 256-Kbps bit rate is around 8MB; convert it to 128-Kbps AAC, and it's roughly half that size (that is, around 4MB) while sounding almost as good.

Most people don't notice much (if any) difference in audio quality when listening to music on most consumer audio gear. So unless you have your iPad hooked up to a great amplifier and superb speakers or headphones, you probably won't hear much difference, but your iPad can hold roughly twice as much music if you choose this option. Put another way, we're picky about our audio, and we both used to select this option to allow us to carry more music around with us on our iPads before we subscribed to iTunes Match and Apple Music. None of us has noticed the lower bit-rate songs sounding much different (or worse) with the types of headphones and speakers we use with our iPads. Finally, using higher bit rates may increase the time it takes to sync.

» **Manually Manage Videos:** To turn off automatic syncing in the Video panes, select this check box.

One more thing: If you decide to select the Prevent iPods, iPhones, and iPads from Syncing Automatically check box on the Devices tab in iTunes Preferences (that's iTunes ⇨ Preferences on a Mac and Edit ⇨ Preferences on a PC), you can still synchronize manually by clicking the Sync or Apply button in the lower-right corner of the window.

Why the Sync *or* Apply button? Glad you asked. If you've changed *any* sync settings since the last time you synchronized, the Sync button instead says Apply. When you click that button — regardless of its name — your iPad will start to sync.

Backing Up Your iPad

Whether you know it or not, your iPad backs up your settings, app data, photos and videos you shoot, and other information whenever you connect to a computer and use iTunes to sync with, update, or restore your iPad.

TIP

Every time you sync your iPad and computer, most (but not all) of your iPad content, including (but not limited to) photos in the Camera Roll album, text messages, notes, contact favorites, and sound settings is backed up to either your computer's hard drive or to iCloud before the sync begins. Most of your media, including songs, TV shows, and movies, *isn't* backed up during this process. This shouldn't be a problem; these files should be restored when you sync with iTunes again.

Backups are saved automatically and stored in iCloud by default, or you can choose to back up to your computer by clicking the appropriate button in the iTunes Summary pane.

To switch to backing up to your computer, follow these steps:

1. **Connect the iPad to the computer.**

   If iTunes doesn't launch automatically when you connect the iPad, launch it now.

2. **Click the iPad icon near the top of the window on the left.**

   If you use more than one iDevice with this computer, select the device from the drop-down list that appears when you click the iPad icon.

3. **On the left, click the Summary tab.**

4. **In the Automatically Back Up section, click iCloud.**

If anything goes wonky, or you get a new iPad, you can restore most (if not all) of your settings and files that aren't synced with iCloud or iTunes on your computer. Or, if you've backed up an iPhone, an iPod touch, or another iPad, you can restore the new iPad from the older device's backup.

Regardless of whether you back up locally or to iCloud, you should encrypt your backups. Unless you enable encryption, important data such as website and Wi-Fi passwords won't be backed up. Because backups to iCloud are encrypted by default with the Apple ID password associated with the account, you don't have to do anything else if you choose iCloud backups. But if you back up to your computer, encryption is turned off by default. So enable the Encrypt Local Backup check box (refer to Figure 3-1).

Trust us, you want your backups encrypted; just select the box, type a password (and don't forget it), and you'll never have to think about it again.

If you're using an iPad computer-free, here's how to enable backing up to iCloud from your iPad (if it's not already enabled), which we strongly suggest computer-free iPad users do without further delay:

1. **Tap Settings ⇨ iCloud.**

2. **Tap iCloud Backup.**

3. **Tap iCloud Backup to switch it on (green).**

WARNING

Choosing this option means your iPad no longer backs up automatically if you connect it to a computer.

If you are a computer-free iPad user, you don't care because you never connect your iPad to a computer. But if you sync your iPad with your computer like many folks do, give some thought to which option suits your needs. Restoring from a computer backup requires physical or Wi-Fi access to that computer, but you don't need Internet access. Restoring from iCloud requires Internet access — and can happen anywhere on Earth that has it.

Backups are good; select one or the other and move on.

TIP

One last thing: Many users maintain both types of backup: iCloud and computer. To do this, merely enable This Computer instead of iCloud (or iCloud instead of This Computer) and click the Back Up Now button. When the backup is finished, switch it back (or not). Either way, you now have a backup on your hard drive and a second backup in iCloud. Although your iCloud backups use up some of your iCloud space, redundancy in backups is a good thing.

Disconnecting the iPad

If your iPad is connected and syncing, you'll see the sync icon next to the device (as shown in Figure 3-2). At the same time, a message appears at the top of the iTunes window to inform you that your iPad is syncing, as shown at the top of Figure 3-2.

Sync icon   Click to cancel sync

FIGURE 3-2: During a sync, the eject icon turns into a sync icon; click the *x*-in-a-circle to cancel the sync.

When your iPad is connected and not syncing, you'll see the eject icon (shown in the margin) to the right of its name rather than the sync icon.

When the sync is finished, the sync icon in Figure 3-2 stops spinning and morphs back into an eject icon, and the message at the top of the window disappears.

WARNING

If you disconnect your iPad before the sync finishes, all or part of the sync may fail. Although early termination of a sync isn't usually a problem, it's safer to cancel the sync and let it finish gracefully than to yank the cable out while a sync is in progress. So just don't do that, okay?

To cancel a sync properly and disconnect your iPad *safely* from your Mac or PC, click the little *x*-in-a-circle to the left of the sync message in iTunes, as shown in Figure 3-2.

Synchronizing Your Data

Your next order of business is to tell iTunes what data you want to synchronize between your iPad and your computer.

To get started, first select your iPad by clicking the iPad icon (or the devices drop-down menu, if you have more than one iDevice) near the top left of the iTunes window. Then click the Info tab, which is the last tab in the Settings list on the left.

If you're using iCloud to sync contacts, calendars, bookmarks, or notes, you won't be able to enable these items in iTunes, as we're about to describe. Turn off iCloud syncing on your iPad (choose Settings ⇨ iCloud) for items you want to sync with your Mac or PC.

On some displays you may see only one or two sections at any time and have to scroll up or down to see the others.

The Info pane has these sections: Sync Contacts, Sync Calendars, and Advanced. The following sections look at them one by one. One last thing: To use your iPad with your Google or Yahoo! account, you must first create an account on your iPad, as described in Chapter 5. After you've created a Yahoo! or Google account on your iPad, you can enable contact or calendar syncing with it in the Settings app's Mail, Contacts, Calendars section.

Contacts

In Figure 3-3, note that the section is named Sync Contacts because this image was captured on a Mac. Contacts (formerly known as Address Book) is the Mac application that syncs with your iPad's Contacts app.

FIGURE 3-3:
Want to synchronize your contacts? This is where you set up things.

If you use a PC, you see a drop-down list that gives you the choices of Outlook, Google Contacts, Windows Address Book, or Yahoo! Address Book. Don't worry — the process works the same on either platform.

The iPad syncs with the following address book programs:

>> **Mac:** Contacts and other address books that sync with Contacts, such as Microsoft Outlook 2011 or the discontinued Microsoft Entourage

>> **PC:** Windows Contacts (Vista, Windows 7, or later), Windows Address Book (XP), Microsoft Outlook, and Microsoft Outlook Express

>> **Mac and PC:** Yahoo! Address Book and Google Contacts

You can sync contacts with multiple apps.

Here's what each option does:

>> **All Contacts:** One method is to synchronize all your contacts, as shown in Figure 3-3. This will synchronize every contact in your Mac or PC address book with your iPad's Contacts app.

>> **Selected Groups:** You can synchronize any or all groups of contacts you've created in your computer's address book program. Just select the appropriate check boxes in the Selected Groups list, and only those groups will be synchronized.

WARNING

If you sync with your employer's Microsoft Exchange calendar and contacts, it's possible that all personal contacts and calendars already on your iPad will be wiped out. You might want to check with the administrator of your Exchange server or other iPad users before you enable syncing with Exchange.

Calendars

The Sync Calendars section of the Info pane determines how synchronization is handled for your appointments, events, and reminders. You can synchronize all your calendars, as shown in Figure 3-4. Or you can synchronize any or all individual calendars you've created in your computer's calendar program. Just select the appropriate check boxes.

FIGURE 3-4:
Set up sync for your calendar events here.

The iPad syncs with the following calendar programs:

>> **Mac:** iCal or Calendar

>> **PC:** Microsoft Exchange and Outlook 2003, 2007, and 2010

>> **Mac and PC:** Google and Yahoo! Calendars

You can sync calendars with multiple apps.

Advanced

Every so often, the contacts, calendars, mail accounts, or bookmarks on your iPad get so screwed up that the easiest way to fix things is to erase that information from your iPad and replace it with information from your computer.

If that's the case, go to the Advanced section of the Info pane and click to select the Contacts or Calendars check boxes (or both). Then, the next time you sync, that information on your iPad will be replaced with the contacts or calendars from your computer.

REMEMBER

Because the Advanced section is at the bottom of the Info pane and you have to scroll down to see it, you can easily forget that the Advanced section is there. Although you probably won't need to use this feature very often (if ever), you'll be happy you remembered that it's there if you do need it.

One last thing: Check boxes in the Advanced section are disabled for items not selected. If you're using iCloud and you want to replace any of these items on your iPad, you must first enable that item as discussed in the previous sections of this chapter. In other words, to replace contacts or calendars we had to disable iCloud syncing before we could enable the check boxes to replace the Contacts and Calendars on this iPad.

Synchronizing Your Media

If you chose to let iTunes manage synchronizing your data automatically, welcome. This section looks at how you get your media — your music, podcasts, videos, and photos — from your computer to your iPad.

REMEMBER

Podcasts and videos (but not photos) from your computer are synced only one way: from your computer to your iPad. If you delete a podcast or a video that got onto your iPad via syncing, the podcast or video will not be deleted from your computer when you sync.

That said, if you buy or download any of the following items from the Apple iTunes, iBooks, or App Store *on your iPad*, the item *will* be copied back to your computer automatically when you sync:

>> Songs

>> Ringtones

>> Podcasts

- ❯❯ Videos

- ❯❯ iBooks, e-books, and audiobooks

- ❯❯ Playlists that you create on your iPad

And if you save pictures from email messages, the iPad camera, web pages (by pressing and holding down on an image and then tapping the Save Image button), or screen shots (which can be created by pressing the Home and sleep/wake buttons simultaneously), these too can be synced using your favorite photo application (as long as it's Photos, Aperture, or Adobe Photoshop Elements).

You use the Music, Movies, TV Shows, and Photos panes to specify the media that you want to copy from your computer to your iPad. The following sections explain the options you find in each pane.

To view any of these panes, make sure that your iPad is still selected and then click the appropriate tab in the list of Settings on the left.

The following sections focus only on syncing. If you need help acquiring apps, music, movies, podcasts, or anything else for your iPad, just flip to the most applicable chapter for help.

TIP

The last step in each section is "Click the Sync or Apply button in the lower-right corner of the window." You have to do this only when selecting that item for the first time and if you make any changes to the item after that.

Sharp-eyed readers may notice that we aren't covering syncing iPad *apps* in this chapter. Apps are so darn cool that we've given them an entire chapter, namely Chapter 11. In that chapter, you discover how to find, rearrange, review, and delete apps, and much, much more.

Music, music videos, and voice memos

To transfer music to your iPad, select the Sync Music check box in the Music pane. You can then select the option for Entire Music Library or Selected Playlists, Artists, and Genres. If you choose the latter, select the check boxes next to particular playlists, artists, and genres you want to transfer. You also can choose to include music videos or voice memos or both by selecting the appropriate check boxes at the top of the pane (see Figure 3-5).

If none of the options just mentioned sounds just right (pun intended), you may prefer using the On My Device tab, which is covered in some detail later in this chapter.

FIGURE 3-5:
Use the Music pane to copy music, music videos, and voice memos from your computer to your iPad.

WARNING

If you choose Entire Music Library and have more songs in your iTunes library than storage space on your iPad, you'll see an error message when you try to sync. You'll also see a yellow alert on the right side of the capacity chart at the bottom of the screen, along with how much over your iPad's capacity adding the entire music library would make you. To avoid such errors, select playlists, artists, and genres that total less than the free space on your iPad, which is also displayed in the capacity chart at the bottom of the iTunes screen.

HOW MUCH SPACE DID I USE?

If you're interested in knowing how much free space is available on your iPad, look near the bottom of the iTunes window while your iPad is connected. You'll see a chart that shows the contents of your iPad, color-coded for your convenience. As you can see in the figure, this iPad has a whopping 87.23GB of free space. Hover your cursor over any color to see a bubble with info on that category, as shown for Documents & Data in the figure.

You can find similar information about space used and space remaining on your iPad by tapping Settings ➪ General ➪ Storage & iCloud Usage. The iPad's display isn't as pretty as the one pictured here, but it is useful when you need that info and you're not near your computer.

Music, podcasts, and video are notorious for using massive amounts of storage space on your iPad. If you try to sync too much media content, you see lots of error messages. Forewarned is forearmed. (The Podcasts app allows you to stream episodes as well as download them, and streamed episodes do not take up storage space on your iPad.)

One solution is to create one or more iPad-specific playlists and sync only those. Or listen to podcasts with the Podcasts app, which can stream episodes (in addition to letting you download them).

Finally, if you select the Automatically Fill Free Space with Songs check box, iTunes fills any free space on your iPad with music. Think long and hard about enabling this option. We recommend against it because when it's enabled, you can easily run out of space for pictures and videos you shoot or documents you save (to name just a few of the possible consequences of filling your iPad with songs).

Movies

To transfer movies to your iPad, select the Sync Movies check box and then choose an option for movies you want to include automatically from the pop-up menu, as shown in Figure 3-6. If you choose an option other than All, you can optionally select individual movies and playlists by selecting the boxes in appropriate sections.

FIGURE 3-6:
Your choices in the Movies pane determine which movies are copied to your iPad.

TV shows

The procedure for syncing TV shows is slightly different from the procedure for syncing movies. First, select the Sync TV Shows check box to enable TV show syncing. Then choose how many episodes to include and whether you want all shows or only selected shows from the two pop-up menus, as shown in Figure 3-7. If you want to also include individual episodes or episodes on playlists, select the appropriate check boxes in the Shows, Episodes, and Include Episodes from Playlists sections of the TV Shows pane.

FIGURE 3-7:
These menus determine how TV shows are synced with your iPad.

TIP

Regardless of the choices you make in the pop-up menus, you can always select individual episodes by selecting their check boxes.

Podcasts and books

You can also sync podcasts and two types of books — e-books for reading and audiobooks for listening — and photos.

TIP

If you like to read e-books or watch or listen to podcasts or iTunes U courses, visit the App Store (see Chapter 11) and grab copies of Apple's free Podcasts, iBooks, and iTunes U apps. Audiobooks, on the other hand, don't require a special app; you can listen to them using the Music app (see Chapter 7).

Podcasts

To transfer podcasts to your iPad, select the Sync Podcasts check box in the Podcasts pane. Then you can automatically include however many podcasts you want by making selections from the two pop-up menus, the same way you did for TV Shows.

Books and Audiobooks

By now we're sure you know the drill: You can sync all your e-books and audiobooks as well as just sync selected titles by choosing the appropriate buttons and check boxes in the Books and Audiobooks panes.

TIP

To sync e-books, you need the free iBooks app; if you don't already have a copy on your iPad, you can download it from the App Store. For more information on apps and the App Store, read Chapter 11. To start using iBooks, see Chapter 10.

Photos

Syncing photos is a little different from syncing other media because your iPad has a built-in camera — two cameras, actually — and you may want to copy pictures or videos you take with the iPad to your computer, as well as copy pictures stored on your computer to your iPad.

You won't see syncing options if you've enabled iCloud photo library. But if you haven't, you can sync your iPad photos and videos with the following programs:

WARNING

>> **Mac:** Aperture version 3.2 or later, Photos version 1.2 or later, or Image Capture (included with Mac OS X), which can import photos only from your iPad to your Mac (and not from your Mac to your iPad).

Apple ended development of Aperture in 2014. Although you can't buy a new copy, if you already own Aperture, it still works. That said, it will probably stop working someday, so you might want to start thinking about a different solution.

>> **PC:** Adobe Photoshop Elements or Adobe Photoshop Album (or any other app that recognizes the iPad as a camera when you connect it).

You can also sync photos with any folder on your Mac or PC that contains images.

In the Photos pane, select the Sync Photos check box, and then choose an application or folder from the pop-up Copy Photos From menu (which says Photos in Figure 3-8).

FIGURE 3-8:
The Photos pane determines which photos will be synchronized with (or copied to) your iPad.

If you choose an application that supports photo albums (such as Photoshop Elements, Aperture, or Photos), projects (Aperture), events (Photos), facial recognition and places (Aperture or Photos), or any combination thereof, you can automatically include recent projects (Aperture), events (Photos), or faces (Aperture and Photos) by making a selection from the same pop-up menu.

Note that although Photoshop Elements includes features called Places and Faces, those features are not supported by your iPad.

TIP

You can also type a word or phrase in the search field (in the upper right) to search for a specific event or events.

If you choose a folder full of images instead of Photos or another app, you can create subfolders inside it that will appear as albums on your iPad. But if you choose an application that doesn't support albums or events, or a single folder full of images with no subfolders, you have to transfer all or nothing.

Because we selected Photos in the Copy Photos From menu, and Photos 1.2 (the version installed on our Mac) supports projects and faces in addition to albums and photos, we have the option of syncing any combination of photos, projects, albums, and faces.

If you've taken any photos with your iPad or saved images from a web page, an email, an MMS message, or an iMessage since the last time you synced, the appropriate program launches (or the appropriate folder is selected), and you have the option of uploading the pictures to your computer.

Manual Syncing

This chapter has focused on automatic syncing thus far. Automatic syncing is great; it selects items to sync based on criteria you've specified, such as genre, artist, playlist, and album. But it's not efficient for transferring a few items — songs, movies, podcasts, or other files — to your iPad.

The solution? Manual syncing. With automatic syncing, iTunes updates your iPad automatically to match your criteria. Changes to your iTunes library since your last sync are synced automatically to your iPad. With manual syncing, you merely drag individual items to your iPad.

TIP

Automatic and manual sync aren't mutually exclusive. If you've set up automatic syncing, you can still sync individual items manually.

You can manually sync music, movies, TV shows, podcasts, and iTunes U lessons but not photos and info such as contacts, calendars, and bookmarks.

To configure your iPad for manual syncing:

1. **Connect your iPad to your computer via USB or Wi-Fi.**

If iTunes doesn't open automatically, open it manually.

2. **Click the iPad icon.**

If you have more than one iDevice, the iPad icon becomes a drop-down menu listing all your connected iDevices. Click the icon to display the menu with your devices, and then select the device you want.

3. **(Optional) Click the Summary tab. In the Options section, select Manually Manage Music and Videos.**

This step disables automatic syncing for music and videos.

TIP

If you're happy with automatic syncing and just want to get some audio or video from your computer to your iPad, feel free to skip this step.

To add items from iTunes to your iPad without using the syncing controls or performing an actual sync, first click the back icon, and then choose the type of media you want to copy to your iPad — music, movies, or TV shows — from the pop-up menu near the top left of the iTunes window.

Now, just click the songs, albums, movies, TV shows, books, or other media you want to add to your iPad and drag them onto your device in the sidebar, as shown in Figure 3-9.

FIGURE 3-9:
Click the ellipsis to manually add media to your iPad.

And that's pretty much all you need to know to sync files automatically or manually. And if you haven't figured out how to watch movies or listen to audio on your iPad yet, it's only because you haven't read Part 3 on multimedia, where watching and listening to your iPad are made crystal clear.

The Internet iPad

2

Explore Safari, the best web browser to ever to grace a handheld device. Take advantage of links and bookmarks; discover how to pay for purchases securely with Apple Pay; and find out how to open multiple web pages at the same time. Plus: how to view every open web page on any of your other Apple devices in Safari on your iPad.

Set up email accounts and send and receive real honest-to-goodness email messages and attachments. And discover iOS 11's cool iMessage features.

Marvel at the Maps app's unerring capability to show you where you are. Discover the joys of step-by-step driving directions and real-time traffic info.

Chapter **4**

Going on a Mobile Safari

Y ou feel like you're holding the web right in the palm of your hand.

Sure, that's something Apple might say, but there's a lot of truth behind it. The spectacular Retina display, which was introduced with the third-generation iPad, in combination with Apple's snappy AX family of chips makes browsing on Apple's tablets an absolute delight. With the 64-bit A10X Fusion chip and embedded M10 coprocessor in the newest iPad Pro models, browsing on an iPad has never been better.

In this chapter, you discover the pleasures — and the few roadblocks — in navigating cyberspace on your iPad.

Surfin' Dude

The Apple Safari web browser is a major reason that the Internet on the iPad is very much like the Internet you've come to expect on a more traditional computer. Come to think of it, the Internet often looks a lot better on iPads with the striking Retina display. And the screens on iPad models without the Retina display aren't too shabby either. Safari for the Mac and for Windows are two of the very best web browsers in the business. In our view, Safari on the iPhone has no rival as a cellphone browser. Safari on the iPad is even more appealing.

Exploring the browser

We start our cyberexpedition with a quick tour of the Safari browser. Take a gander at Figure 4-1. Not all browser controls found on a Mac or a PC are present, but Safari on the iPad still has a familiar look and feel. We describe these controls and others throughout this chapter.

Blasting off into cyberspace

Surfing the web begins with a web address, of course.

TIP

Here are a few tips for using the keyboard in Safari (and see Chapter 2 for more help with using the virtual keyboard):

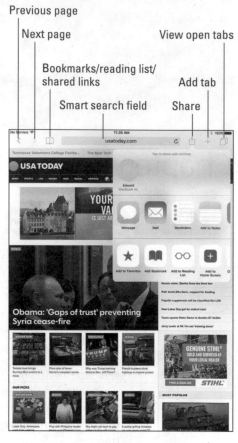

FIGURE 4-1:
The iPad's Safari browser.

>> Because so many web addresses end with the suffix .com (pronounced *dot com*), the virtual keyboard has a few shortcuts worth noting. Press and hold your finger against the .? key, and you'll see that .com option. You'll see other common web suffixes as well — .us, org, .edu, and .net. Some options appear only if you've selected an international keyboard (as discussed in Chapter 2).

>> The moment you tap a letter, you see a list of web addresses that match those letters. For example, if you tap the letter *E* (as we did in the example shown in Figure 4-2), you see web listings for eBay, ESPN, and others. Tapping *U* or *H* instead may display listings for *USA TODAY* or the *Houston Chronicle* (shameless plugs for the newspapers where Ed and Bob are columnists).

>> In iOS 11, each key on the virtual keyboard has two values. Tap, and you get the darker letter, number, or symbol. Swipe down on a key, and you get the letter, number, or symbol in gray, at the top of the key.

TIP

Siri can lend a hand, um, voice, as you surf. If you call upon Siri and ask the voice genie inside the iPad to open the Safari app, Siri obliges. If you mention a specific website to Siri — "ESPN.com," say — Siri opens the site or at the very least your designated search engine (Google, Bing, or Yahoo!), as discussed later in this chapter.

When you tap certain letters, the iPad has three ways to determine websites to suggest:

» **Bookmarks:** The iPad suggests websites you've bookmarked from the Safari or other browsers on your computer (and synchronized, as we describe in Chapter 3). More on bookmarks later in this chapter.

» **History:** The iPad suggests sites from the history list — those cyberdestinations where you recently hung your hat. Because history repeats itself, we also tackle that topic later in this chapter.

» **Smart search field:** When you type an address in the search field, you see icons for sites you frequent most often, and you can tap any of those icons to jump immediately to those sites.

FIGURE 4-2:
Web pages that match your search letter.

You might as well open your first web page now — and it's a full *HTML* page, to borrow from techie lingo:

1. **Tap the Safari icon docked at the bottom of the Home screen.**

If you haven't moved it, it's a member of the Fantastic Five on the dock (along with Messages, Mail, Music, and Files). Chapter 1 introduces the Home screen.

2. **Tap the smart search field (refer to Figure 4-1).**

3. **Begin typing the web address, or *URL*, on the virtual keyboard that slides up from the bottom of the screen.**

4. Do one of the following:

- *To accept one of the bookmarked (or other) sites that show up in the list, merely tap the name.*

  Safari automatically fills in the URL in the address field and takes you where you want to go.

- *Keep tapping the proper keyboard characters until you enter the complete web address for the site you have in mind and then tap the Go key on the right side of the keyboard.*

REMEMBER

You don't need to type **www** at the beginning of a URL. So if you want to visit www.theonion.com (for example), typing **theonion.com** is sufficient to transport you to the humor site. For that matter, Safari can take you to this site even if you type **theonion** without the .com. **Onion** alone might do it, too.

TECHNICAL STUFF

Because Safari on the iPad runs a variation of the iPhone mobile operating system, every so often you may run into a site that serves up the light, or mobile, version of a website, sometimes known as a *WAP site*. Graphics may be stripped down on these sites. Alas, the producers of these sites may be unwittingly discriminating against you for dropping in on them by using an iPad. In fact, you may be provided a choice of which site you want — the light or the full version. Bravo! If not, you have our permission to berate these site producers with letters, emails, and phone calls until they get with the program. Fortunately, such a scenario is increasingly rare.

Zoom, zoom, zoom

If you know how to open a web page (if you don't, read the preceding section in this chapter), we can show you how radically simple it is to zoom in on pages so that you can read what you want to read and see what you want to see, without enlisting a magnifying glass.

Try these neat tricks for starters:

>> **Double-tap the screen so that the area of the display that you make contact with fills the entire screen.** It takes just a second before the screen comes into focus. By way of example, check out Figure 4-3, which shows two views of the same USA TODAY.com web page. In the first view, you see what the page looks like when you first open it. In the second one, you see how the menu of stories box takes over much more of the screen after you double-tap it. The area of the screen you double-tapped is the area that swells. To return to the first view, double-tap the screen again.

>> **Pinch the page.** Sliding your thumb and index finger together and then spreading them apart (or, as we like to say, *unpinching*) also zooms in and out of a page. Again, wait just a moment for the screen to come into focus.

>> **Press down on a page and drag it in all directions, or flick through a page from top to bottom.** You're panning and scrolling, baby.

>> **Rotate the iPad to its side.** This action reorients from portrait view to a widescreen landscape view. The keyboard is also wider in this mode, making it a little easier to enter a new URL. However, this little bit of rotation magic won't happen if you set and enabled the screen orientation lock feature, which we describe in Chapter 1.

FIGURE 4-3:
Doing a double-tap dance zooms in and out.

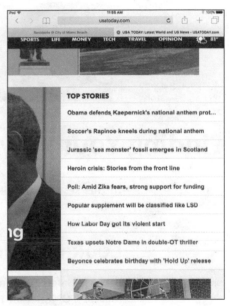

Reading clutter-free web pages with reader view

It's all too easy to get distracted reading web pages nowadays, what with ads, videos, and other clutter surrounding the stuff you want to take in. So pay attention to the horizontal lines that often appear in the smart search field, as shown in Figure 4-4 (left). Tap those lines to activate reader view to read the same article without the needless diversions, as shown in Figure 4-4 (right). Tap the lines again to return the standard web view.

Tap for clutter-free reading

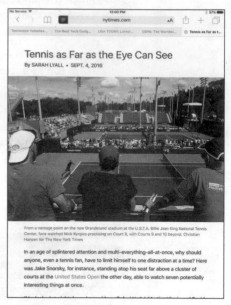

FIGURE 4-4:
Reducing
clutter when
reading a web
story.

Finding Your Way around Cyberspace

In this section, we discuss ways to navigate the Internet on your iPad by using links and tabs.

Looking at lovable links

Because Safari functions on the iPad the same way that browsers work on your Mac or PC, links on the device behave in much the same way. Text links that transport you from one site to another typically are underlined, are shown in blue, red, or bold type, or appear as items in a list. Tap the link to go directly to the site or page.

Tapping other links leads to different outcomes:

>> **Open a map:** Tapping an address may launch the Maps app that is, um, addressed in Chapter 6.

>> **Prepare an email:** Tap an email address, and the iPad opens the Mail program (see Chapter 5) and prepopulates the To field with that address. The virtual keyboard is also summoned so that you can add other email addresses and compose a subject line and message. Note that this shortcut doesn't always work.

TIP

To see the URL for a link, press your finger on the link and hold it there until a list of options appears (see Figure 4-5). Use this method also to determine whether a picture has a link. Just hold your finger down on the picture; if it's linked, you see the web address to which the link points.

As for the link options shown in Figure 4-5, here's what three of them do:

>> **Open:** Opens the page in this tab.

>> **Copy:** Copies the link's URL to your iPad's Clipboard so that you can paste it elsewhere.

>> **Share:** Tap to open the same sharing options that are presented when you tap the share icon.

| http://www.espn.com/nfl/team/_/name/phi/ philadelphia-eagles |
| Open |
| Open in New Tab |
| Add to Reading List |
| Copy |
| Share... |

FIGURE 4-5:
Press and hold down on a link to see these options.

You read more about the other options — Open in New Tab and Add to Reading List — a little later in this chapter.

Not every web link cooperates with the iPad because it doesn't support some common web standards — most notably, Adobe Flash video. If you see an incompatible link, nothing may happen — or a message may appear, asking you to install a plug-in.

This lack of support for Adobe Flash video is a void that is (frankly) unlikely to ever get addressed. Even Adobe is no longer embracing Flash for mobile devices. Apple does support the ever-popular HTML 5 standard for audio and video, which Adobe, too, is now backing.

Tabbed browsing

When we surf the web on a Mac or PC, we rarely go to a single web page and call it a day. In fact, we often have multiple web pages open at the same time. Sometimes we choose to hop around the web without closing the pages we visit. Sometimes a link automatically opens a new page without closing the old one. (If these additional pages are advertisements, this behavior isn't always welcome.)

Safari on the iPad lets you open multiple pages simultaneously by using a brilliant rendition of tabbed browsing similar to the desktop version of Safari (and other browsers).

After you have one page open, you have two ways to open additional web pages in Safari so that they appear on the tab bar at the top of the screen (rather than replace the page you're currently viewing):

>> **Tap the + icon (see Figure 4-6 near the top-right corner of the browser.** A tab named Favorites appears, as shown in Figure 4-6. Now type a URL, tap a bookmark or an icon for a favorite or frequently visited site, or initiate a search, and the result will appear in this tab.

FIGURE 4-6:
A new tab, ready to display any page you choose.

>> **Hold your finger on a link until a list of options appears (refer to Figure 4-5), and then tap Open in New Tab.**

To switch tabs, just tap the tab you want to view. To close a tab, tap the gray x-in-a-circle that appears on the left edge of the active tab.

You can manage tabs in one other way. Tap the view open tabs icon in the top-right corner of the browser (refer to Figure 4-1) to summon thumbnail views of your open web pages, as shown in Figure 4-7. You can tap the X on any thumbnail to close it. From here you can also go into private browsing mode (discussed later in this chapter) or check out iCloud tabs, the topic we're about to dive into.

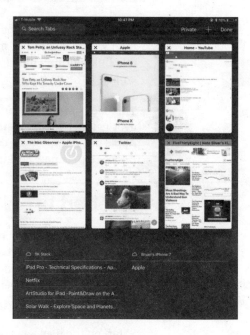

FIGURE 4-7:
A thumbnail view of all your open tabs.

iCloud tabs

Although the iPad is your likely traveling companion just about everywhere you go, we know that you also browse the web from your smartphone or personal computer. If that smartphone happens to be an iPhone and the computer is a Macintosh (or a Windows PC running Safari), you can take advantage of iCloud tabs, a feature that lets you resume reading web pages that you started looking at on those other devices.

The feature works with the iPod touch, too. If you read the preceding section, you already know how to access iCloud tabs: Tap the View Open Tabs icon to bring up tab view, which is shown in Figure 4-7. In this example, there are open tabs on Bryan's 5K Stack and on his iPhone. Tap a link to open the page on your tablet.

Doing the splits

When you rotate an iPad running iOS 10 or later in landscape mode, you have the option to display a split view in Safari, with two web pages each claiming half the screen. You can imagine all sorts of scenarios where such a dual view would be useful. Perhaps you're trying to decide between two cars. Or checking out two dress designs. Or exploring a couple of different places to go on vacation.

In typical Apple fashion, you can arrive at this split view in more than one way (works with iPad Air 2, all iPad Pros, iPad 9.7-inch, and iPad mini 4):

» Press and hold down on a link on a web page, and then tap Open in Split View.

» Two-finger tap on a link. It opens on the other side of the screen.

» Drag a tab to the right edge of the screen and release.

To exit split view, tap the x-in-a-circle at the top of one of the visible web pages. The other will take over the entire display.

Revisiting Web Pages Time and Again

Surfing the web would be a drag if you had to enter a URL every time you wanted to navigate from one page to another. So you can find those favorite websites in the future, the iPad provides bookmarks, web clips, reading lists, and history lists.

Book(mark) 'em, Dano

You already know how useful bookmarks are and how you can synchronize bookmarks from the browsers on your computer. It's equally simple to bookmark a web page directly on the iPad. Follow these steps:

1. **Make sure that the page you want to bookmark is open, and then tap the share icon (shown in the margin) at the top of the screen.**

   You have many options beyond bookmarking when you tap the share icon (refer to Figure 4-1, though not all the options are visible in the figure), as you discover later in this chapter.

2. **Tap Add Bookmark.**

A new Add Bookmark window opens with a default name for the bookmark, its web address, maybe a logo, and its folder location.

3. **Give it a name and folder location:**

- *Accept the default bookmark name and default bookmark folder:* Tap Save.

- *Change the default bookmark name:* Tap the *x*-in-a-circle next to the name, enter the new title (using the virtual keyboard), and then tap Save.

- *Change the location where the bookmark is saved:* Tap the suggested location field, which likely shows Favorites, tap the folder where you want the bookmark to be kept so that a check mark appears, and then tap Save.

To open a bookmarked page after you set it up, tap the bookmarks icon, which is to the left of the smart search field. (Refer to Figure 4-1.)

REMEMBER

If you don't see bookmarks right away after tapping the bookmarks icon, make sure the leftmost of the three tabs at the top of the bookmarks menu is high-lighted in blue. The other tabs are for the reading list and shared links — those shared by your contacts from selected social networks.

If the bookmark you have in mind is buried inside a folder, tap the folder name first and then tap the bookmark you want.

Altering bookmarks

If a bookmarked site is no longer meaningful, you can change or get rid of it:

TIP

» **To remove a bookmark (or folder),** tap the bookmarks icon and then tap Edit. Tap the red circle next to the bookmark you want to toss off the list, and then tap Delete.

To remove a single bookmark or folder, swipe its name from right to left and then tap the red Delete button.

» **To change a bookmark name or location,** tap Edit at the bottom-right corner of the Bookmarks window. Tap a given bookmark, and an Edit Bookmark window appears, with the name, URL, and location of the book-mark already filled in. Tap the fields you want to change. In the Name field, tap the gray *x*-in-a-circle and then use the keyboard to enter a new title. In the Location field, tap the location name and scroll up or down the list until you find a new home for your bookmark.

» **To create a new folder for your bookmarks,** tap Edit and then tap New Folder. Enter the name of the new folder, and choose where to put it.

>> **To move a bookmark up or down in a list,** tap Edit and then drag the three bars to the right of the bookmark's name to its new resting place.

REMEMBER

If you take advantage of iCloud, the web pages you've bookmarked on your Mac and on your other iOS devices will be available on the iPad, and vice versa.

Saving to your reading list

When you visit a web page you'd like to read, but just not now, the reading list feature is sure to come in handy, including when you're offline. Here's how it works:

>> **Saving a page for later:** Tap the share icon and then tap Add to Reading List. Or, if you see a link to a page you'd like to read later, press on the link until a list of options appears (refer to Figure 4-5) and then tap Add to Reading List.

>> **Reading a page on your reading list:** Tap the bookmarks icon and tap the page in the reading list, as shown in Figure 4-8.

>> **Keeping track of what you've read:** Tap Show Unread to display only those items that you haven't read yet. Tap Show All to show all the items in the reading list.

>> **Removing items from the reading list:** Swipe the item from right to left, and then tap its red Delete button. If you swipe a little farther to the left, you can tap Mark Read instead.

TIP

The reading list feature used to require an active Internet connection, which is why we always admired the superb save-to-read-later Instapaper app — and still do. It's now free in the App Store, though there are also premium subscription options that add functionality separate from the Safari reading list.

In Safari Settings, you can choose to use your cellular network (if available) to save reading list items from iCloud so you can read them offline.

FIGURE 4-8:
Tap a page in the reading list to read it.

Finally, don't forget that you can share your reading list (and bookmarks) among your computers and iOS devices with iCloud, as described in Chapter 3.

Clipping a web page

You frequent lots of websites, some way more than others. For example, perhaps you consult the train schedule several times during the day. In their infinite wisdom, the folks at Apple let you bestow special privileges on frequently visited sites, not just by bookmarking pages but also by affording them their unique Home screen icons. Apple used to call these *web clips,* and we still like the term. Creating one is dead simple. Follow these steps:

1. **Open the web page in question, and tap the share icon (shown in the margin).**

2. **Tap Add to Home Screen; you may have to scroll through the options to find it.**

    Apple creates an icon out of the area of the page that was displayed when you saved the clip, unless the page has its own custom icon.

3. **Type a new name for your web clip or leave the one that Apple suggests.**

4. **Tap Add.**

    The icon appears on your Home screen.

TIP

As with any icon, you can remove a web clip by pressing and holding down on its icon until it starts to wiggle. Tap the X in the corner of the icon, and then tap Delete. You can also move the web clip to a more preferred location on one of your Home screens or on the dock.

Letting history repeat itself

Sometimes you want to revisit a site that you failed to bookmark, but you can't remember the darn destination or what led you there in the first place. Good thing you can study the history books.

Safari records the pages you visit and keeps the logs on hand for several days. Here's how to access your history:

1. **Tap the bookmarks icon and then tap History.**

    The History option is near the top of the bookmarks list.

2. **Tap the day you think you hung out at the site.**

Sites are listed under such headings as "This Morning," "Thursday Evening," or "Thursday Morning," or segregated by a specific date.

3. **When you find the listing, tap it.**

You're about to make your triumphant return.

TIP

To clear your history so that no one can trace your steps, tap Clear at the bottom-right corner of the history list. You can clear the last hour, clear only the day that you tapped Clear, clear today and yesterday, or clear all your history. Alternatively, starting on the Home screen, tap Settings ⇨ Safari ⇨ Clear History and Website Data. In both instances, per usual, you have a chance to back out without wiping the slate clean.

WARNING

When you clear your history from settings, your history, cookies and browsing data will be removed from all the devices you have signed into iCloud. If that is not your intention, tap Cancel.

Saving web pictures

You can capture most pictures you come across on a website — but be mindful of any potential copyright violations, depending on what you plan to do with the images. To copy an image from a website, follow these steps:

1. **Press your finger against the image.**

2. **Tap the Save Image button that appears, as shown in Figure 4-9.**

Saved images end up in your Photos library in the All Photos album, from which they can be synced back to a computer.

FIGURE 4-9:
Hold your finger against a picture in Safari to save it to the iPad.

TIP

Tap Copy instead, and you can paste the image into an email or as a link in a program such as Notes.

In some cases, typically advertisements, you also see an Open button or an Open in New Tab button, which takes you to the ad image.

Sharing Your Web Experiences

 When you find a great website that you just must share, tap the share icon (shown in the margin) or tap Share after pressing down on a link, and you find these sharing options:

>> **AirDrop:** Share the page with other people who have compatible devices and AirDrop. You'll need to turn on AirDrop in Control Center (drag upward from the bottom of the screen). Then choose whether to make your iPad discoverable to everyone or only to people in your contacts. AirDrop works with only fourth-generation iPads or later — including the iPad Pro — the iPad mini, and some Mac computers with OS X Yosemite, OS X El Capitan, macOS Sierra, or macOS High Sierra.

>> **Message:** Send a link to the web page in a text or an iMessage.

>> **Mail:** The Mail program opens with a link for the page in the message and the name of the site or page in the Subject line.

>> **Add to Notes:** Sure you can bookmark pages. But sometimes it's even more convenient to reserve space in the Notes app for a web page you want to refer to later. Aren't you glad to know you can?

>> **Twitter:** The iPad adds a link for a web page to an outgoing tweet. You must fill in the rest of the actual post.

>> **Facebook:** Post the page — and whatever comments you choose to add — to the popular social network.

>> **Sina Weibo** and **Tencent Weibo:** If available, you can post via these Chinese blogging services. You need to activate a Chinese keyboard or language to see these options.

>> **Save PDF to iBooks:** To do just that, tap here.

>> **Reminders:** You can add a page to the Reminders app. If you tap Options, you can be reminded on a given day or at a location.

>> **Add to Favorites:** When you tap the + button to add a new tab, you see a page of icons representing your favorite websites (or at least those you frequent). Tap Add to Favorites and the site in question joins this most-favored-nation-status grouping.

>> **Open in News:** The News app on your iPad (see Chapter 10) is a repository of stories and articles from prominent news sources. Tap Open in News, and the web page you're reading opens in the News app.

- » **Copy:** Tap Copy to copy the page in question.

- » **Print:** The iPad searches for an AirPrint printer. If you have one, you can choose the number of copies you want. Tap Print to complete the job.

- » **Find on Page:** Tap this option and use the virtual keyboard that slides up to type in the field above the keyboard the word you want to find. Highlighted words appear in yellow. Use the up and down arrows to find each mention of the word. Tap Done when you're done.

- » **Request Desktop Site:** If such a page is available (and different from the mobile site), tapping here delivers that page.

- » **More:** Tap More to summon a list of activities. You can change the order of the activities by dragging the three horizontal lines to the right of each activity. (By pressing down on an icon, you can drag it to a new position without tapping More.)

Launching a Mobile Search Mission

Most of us spend a lot of time using search engines. And the ones we summon most often are Google, Yahoo!, and Microsoft's Bing, at least in the United States. If you're in China, chances are you search using Baidu. All these search options are available on the iPad, along with DuckDuckGo, a search engine that doesn't track your web footsteps.

Apple combines the address bar and search fields into a single, convenient, unified strip called the *smart search field*, following the path taken on most popular web browsers for PCs and Macs. Although you can certainly use the virtual keyboard to type *google.com*, *yahoo.com*, *bing.com*, or other search engines into this field, Apple doesn't require that tedious effort. Instead, just type your search query directly in the box.

To conduct a web search on the iPad, tap the smart search field. You immediately see icons for your favorite web destinations, with Apple betting on your frequent return visits. But when you start typing in the smart search field, a Google (or other) search mission commences, with top hits — an educated guess, really — shown at the top.

You see other search suggestions as you start tapping additional letters. In Figure 4-10, for example, typing the letters **ap** yields such suggestions as Applebees, Apple Store, and Apple Watch. Tap any search result that looks promising, or tap Go on the keyboard to immediately land on the top hit. Or keep tapping out letters until you generate the search result you want.

TIP

You can also find a search word or phrase on the web page you have on-screen. Just look in the list for On This Page. You're informed of the number of matches; if it's more than one, you can move back and forth through them with the up-pointing and down-pointing arrows, respectively, at the bottom of the screen.

FIGURE 4-10:
Running a search on the iPad.

TIP

To switch the search field from the current search engine to another search engine choice on your iPad, check out the "Smart Safari Settings" section, later in this chapter.

As mentioned earlier in this chapter, Siri can open Safari — all you have to do is ask. Of course, much of what Siri can do is web-centric. So now is as good a time as any to recommend Chapter 14, where you get an excellent sense of all that Siri can do.

TIP

You conduct a web search also by initiating a search. To summon the search field, swipe down from any screen. Type (or dictate) your search term and then scroll to the bottom of the list below any search results that point to the use of the term on the iPad itself (meaning inside messages, notes, apps, and so on). Tap Search Web to search the web with the term you entered. You can also tap Search Maps to, well, search maps.

Through the Search Engine Suggestions and Safari Suggestions features, you can get potentially useful information even if you don't explicitly search for it. If you search the name of a movie, for example, Safari will also provide showtimes at nearby theaters without being asked. If you're not comfortable with this feature, you can turn it off in Settings. And why wouldn't you be comfortable? When you use Safari Suggestions, your search queries and related data are shared with Apple. Speaking of which . . .

Private Browsing

Don't want to leave any tracks while you surf? Don't worry — we won't ask and we won't tell. Turn on private browsing for a "what happens in Safari stays in Safari" tool. Those truly bent on staying private will also want to tap Clear History, as we mention earlier in this chapter.

To go incognito, tap the view open tabs icon (refer to Figure 4-1), and then tap the Private button at the upper-right corner of the screen. After private browsing is on, any traces of your visit to nonono.com (or wherever) are nowhere to be found. Your history is wiped clean, open tabs don't appear in iCloud tabs, and your autofill information is not stored anywhere. To remind you that you're browsing privately, the Safari interface takes on a darker shade — a not-so-subtle message here, we suppose, that you might be engaging in a shady or naughty activity. We don't pass judgment.

To come out of hiding, tap the view open tabs icon again and then tap Private again to turn it off.

The history of pages you've visited can be useful and a huge timesaver, so don't forget to disable this option again when you're finished doing whatever it is you don't want people to know you're doing.

You can separately turn on a Do Not Track setting in Settings. Speaking of which, kindly move on to the next section.

Be mindful of your settings on other machines. If you run Safari on both an iPad and a Mac, but choose to go private only on Apple's tablet, your Mac browsing history will still show up in your history listings on the iPad. Safari browsers marked private on the iPad will still bring in sites from iPhones or Macs via iCloud. Mark things private across all devices to keep things really private.

Smart Safari Settings

Along with the riches galore found on the Internet are places in cyberspace where you're hassled. You might want to take action to protect your privacy and maintain your security.

To get started, tap the Settings icon on the Home screen and then tap Safari.

The following settings enable you to tell your iPad what you want to be private and how you want to set your security options:

>> **Search Engine:** Tap the search engine you desire — just as long as that search engine happens to be Google, Yahoo!, Bing, DuckDuckGo, or, if you've enabled a Chinese keyboard, Baidu. Other settings found here let you determine whether the iPad can make Search Engine Suggestions and Safari Suggestions, features touched on earlier in this chapter.

>> **AutoFill:** Safari can automatically fill out web forms by using your personal contact information, usernames, and passwords, or information from your other contacts. Tap AutoFill and then tap the on/off switch to enable or disable AutoFill.

- Tap Use Contact Info if you're comfortable using the information found about your contacts.

- Tap My Info to select yourself in your contacts so that Safari knows which address, phone numbers, email addresses, and other information to use when it fills in a form.

- Tap the Names and Passwords on/off switch to enable or disable, respectively, Safari's capability to remember usernames and passwords for websites. You also get to decide whether credit card information can be used and saved.

- Tap Credit Cards to manage and enter the credit card numbers you're comfortable sharing. Tap Saved Credit Cards to view the cards you've saved on your tablet or to add others.

WARNING

Turning on AutoFill can compromise your security if someone gets hold of your iPad. It can also affect security across all your iCloud-enabled devices.

>> **Open New Tabs in Background:** If you enable this setting, new tabs that you open in Safari will load even if you're reading a different page in another tab.

>> **Favorites:** Apple lets you quickly access favorite bookmarks when you enter an address, search, or create a tab. Tap the category of sites for which you'd like to see icons in that category (News, Business, Technology, whatever). A

check mark appears next to your selection. Or if you're cool with it, leave the default category setting as Favorites.

>> **Show Favorites Bar:** If you enable the Show Favorites Bar option, you'll be able to see Safari's bookmarks bar between the smart search field and tab bar.

>> **Show Tab Bar:** You can display the open tab buttons in a bar near the top of the Safari display or not, another matter of personal preference.

>> **Block Pop-ups:** *Pop-ups* are those web pages that appear whether or not you want them to. Often, they're annoying advertisements. But on some sites, you welcome the appearance of pop-ups, so remember to turn off blocking under such circumstances.

>> **Quick Website Search:** Determine whether or not to use website shortcuts when you're searching within a website. For example, you can type **wiki FDR** to show Wikipedia entries for Franklin Roosevelt.

>> **Preload Top Hit:** We talk about the smart search field throughout this chapter. Here you get to choose whether the iPad can preload the top hit in the background.

>> **Block Cookies:** We're not talking about crumbs you may have accidentally dropped on the iPad. *Cookies* are tiny bits of information that a website places on the iPad when you visit so that the site recognizes you when you return. You need not assume the worst; most cookies are benign.

If this concept wigs you out, take action and block cookies from third parties and advertisers: Tap the Always Block option, and you will theoretically never again receive cookies on the iPad. Or choose to accept cookies only from the website you're currently visiting or only from the websites you happen to visit. You can also tap Always to accept cookies from all sites. Tap Safari to return to the main Safari Settings page.

If you set the iPad so that it doesn't accept cookies, certain web pages won't load properly, and other sites such as Amazon won't recognize you or make any of your preferred settings or recommendations available.

REMEMBER

>> **Do Not Track:** As the name suggests, if you turn this setting on, the iPad will not trace your cyberfootsteps.

>> **Clear History and Website Data:** You met this option earlier. Tap it to erase everything in Safari's history, leaving nary a trace of the pages you've visited.

>> **Fraudulent Website Warning:** Safari can warn you when you land on a site whose producers have sinister intentions. The protection is better than nothing, but don't let down your guard because the Fraud Warning feature isn't foolproof. The setting is on by default.

>> **Check for Apple Pay:** If you come to a website that accepts Apple Pay (Apple's mobile payments service), the site can check whether you have Apple Pay enabled on your tablet. Make sure this switch is off if you're not comfortable with this idea.

>> **JavaScript:** Programmers use JavaScript to add various kinds of functionality to web pages, from displaying the date and time to changing images when you drag over them. However, some security risks have also been associated with JavaScript. If you do turn it off, though, some things might not work as you expect. But this setting is found under the Advanced topic for a reason, meaning that Apple doesn't think too many of us should mess with this setting. We generally leave things as they are, but go with whatever makes you comfortable.

Although the Advanced settings are indeed advanced, you might want to drop by if you're curious about how much data you're consuming at different sites. Developers might also want to check out Advanced settings to turn on a Web Inspector feature that most readers need not concern themselves with.

IN THIS CHAPTER

» Reading and managing email
messages

» Sending email messages

» Using the Messages app

» Jazzing up IMessages

Chapter 5

The Email Must Get Through

On any computing device, emails come and go with a variety of emotions. Messages may be amusing or sad, frivolous or serious. Electronic missives on the iPad are almost always touching.

The reason, of course, is that you're touching the display to compose and read messages. Okay, so we're having a little fun with language. But the truth is, the bundled Mail app on the iPad is a modern program designed not only to send and receive text email messages but also to handle rich HTML email messages — formatted with font and type styles and embedded graphics. If someone sends you mail with a picture, it's quite likely that the picture is visible right in the body of the message.

Furthermore, your iPad can read several types of file attachments, including (but not limited to) PDFs, JPG images, Microsoft Word documents, PowerPoint slides, and Excel spreadsheets, as well as stuff produced through Apple's own productivity software, notably Pages, Keynote, and Numbers. Better still, all this sending and receiving of text, graphics, and documents can happen in the background, so you can surf the web or play a game while your iPad quietly and efficiently handles your email behind the scenes.

Apple even lets you grant VIP status to important senders so that there's almost no chance you'll miss mail from the people who matter most.

And before we're finished with this chapter, we delve into the iPad's Messages app, home to the ever more expressive iMessages messaging service.

Prep Work: Setting Up Your Accounts

First things first. To use Mail, you need an email address. If you have broadband Internet access (that is, a cable modem, FiOS, or DSL), you may have received one or more email addresses when you signed up. If you're one of the handful of readers who doesn't already have an email account, you can get one for free from Google (http://mail.google.com), Microsoft Outlook (http://www.microsoft. com/en-us/outlook-com/), AOL (www.aol.com), or numerous other service providers.

Or you can get a free premium email account (for example, *yourname*@iCloud. com) from Apple as part of iCloud. From your Home screen, just tap Settings ➪ Accounts & Passwords ➪ Add Account ➪ iCloud.

TIP

Many free email providers add a bit of advertising at the end of your outgoing messages. If you'd rather not be a billboard for your email provider, use Apple's excellent iCloud email, the address(es) that came with your broadband Internet access (*yourname*@comcast.net or *yourname*@att.net, for example), or pay a few dollars a month for a premium email account that doesn't tack advertising (or anything else) onto your messages.

Finally, while the rest of the chapter focuses on the Mail app, you can also use Safari to access most email systems, if that's your preference. You can also install separate Gmail, Outlook, and other dedicated email apps.

Setting up your account the easy way

Chapter 3 explains the option of automatically syncing the email accounts on your Mac or Windows PC with your iPad. If you chose that option, your email accounts should be configured already on your iPad. And if you signed in with an iCloud account while setting up your iPad (read Chapter 2), you should already be good to go with your iCloud email account. If so, you may proceed directly to the later section "See Me, Read Me, File Me, Delete Me: Working with Messages."

TIP

If you haven't yet chosen that option but want to set up your account the easy way now, go to Chapter 3, read about syncing email accounts, and then sync your iPad with your Mac or PC. Then you, too, can proceed directly to the section "See Me, Read Me, File Me, Delete Me: Working with Messages," later in this chapter.

Remember that syncing email accounts doesn't have any effect on your email messages; it merely synchronizes the *settings* for email accounts so you don't have to set them up manually on your iPad.

Setting up your account the less-easy way

If you don't want to sync the email accounts on your Mac or PC, you can set up an email account on your iPad manually. It's not quite as easy as clicking a box and syncing your iPad, but it's not rocket science either. Here's how you get started:

» **If you have no email accounts on your iPad:** The first time you launch Mail, you see the Welcome to Mail screen. Your choices are iCloud, Microsoft Exchange (business email), Google (Gmail), Yahoo!, AOL, Microsoft Outlook. com, and Other.

Merely tap the account type you want to add to the iPad and follow the steps in the upcoming "Setting up an account with another provider" or "Setting up corporate email" section.

» **If you have one or more email accounts on your iPad and want to add a new account manually:** Tap Settings on the Home screen and then tap Accounts & Passwords ⇨ Add Account.

You see an Add Account screen, shown in Figure 5-1, with the same account options that appear on the Welcome to Mail screen. Proceed to one of the next three sections, depending on the type of email account you selected.

FIGURE 5-1:
Tap a button to set up an account.

Setting up an email account with iCloud, Gmail, Yahoo!, AOL, or Microsoft Outlook

If your account is with iCloud, Gmail (Google), Yahoo!, AOL, or Outlook, follow these steps:

1. **Tap the appropriate button on the Welcome to Mail screen (refer to Figure 5-1).**

2. **Enter your name, email address, password, and optional description, as shown in Figure 5-2.**

   If you don't add a description (such as Work or Personal), the field fills in automatically with the contents of the Address field. Some accounts don't have space for a description or even your name. In other words, all that is required is an email address and password.

FIGURE 5-2: Just fill 'em in and tap Next, and you're ready to rock.

3. **Tap the Next button in the upper-right corner of the screen.**

   That's all there is to setting up your account. You can now proceed to "See Me, Read Me, File Me, Delete Me: Working with Messages."

Setting up an account with another provider

If your email account is with a provider other than iCloud, Microsoft Outlook, Gmail (Google), Yahoo!, or AOL, you have a bit more work ahead of you. You need a bunch of information about your email account you may not know or have handy.

We suggest that you scan the following instructions, note the items you don't know, and go find the answers before you continue. To find the answers, look at the documentation you received when you signed up for your email account or visit the account provider's website and search there.

Here's how you set up an account:

1. **Starting at the Home screen, tap Settings ⇨ Accounts & Passwords ⇨ Add Account ⇨ Other.**

2. **Under Mail, tap Add Mail Account.**

   Those of you more technically oriented might note another option here to add a macOS Server Account instead.

3. **Fill in the name, address, password, and description in the appropriate fields, and then tap Next.**

   With any luck, that's all you'll have to do. The iPad will look up and retrieve your account settings. If that doesn't happen, continue with Step 4.

4. **Tap the button at the top of the screen that denotes the type of email server this account uses, IMAP or POP, as shown in Figure 5-3.**

5. **Fill in the Internet hostname for your incoming mail server, which looks something like mail.*providername*.com.**

6. **Fill in your username and password.**

7. **Enter the Internet hostname for your outgoing mail server, which looks something like smtp.*providername*.com.**

8. **Enter your username and password in the appropriate fields.**

9. **Tap the Next button in the upper-right corner to create the account.**

   You're now ready to begin using your account. See the section "See Me, Read Me, File Me, Delete Me: Working with Messages."

FIGURE 5-3:
If you set up an IMAP or a POP email account, you may have a few more fields to fill in before you can rock.

TIP

Rarely, outgoing mail servers don't need your username and password. The fields for these items on your iPad note that they're optional. Still, we suggest you fill them in anyway. Doing so saves you from having to add them later if your outgoing mail server does require an account name and a password, which almost all do these days.

Setting up corporate email

The iPad makes nice with the Microsoft Exchange servers that are a staple in large enterprises, as well as many smaller businesses.

What's more, if your company supports Microsoft Exchange ActiveSync, you can exploit push email so that messages arrive pronto on the iPad, just as they do on your other computers. (To keep everything up to date, the iPad also supports push calendars and push contacts.) For push to work with an Exchange Server, your company must support one of the last several iterations of Microsoft Exchange ActiveSync (most companies are). If you run into a problem, ask your company's IT or tech department.

Setting up Exchange email isn't particularly taxing, but you might have to consult your employer's techie-types for certain settings.

Start setting up your corporate email on your iPad by following these steps:

1. **Tap the Exchange listing on the Welcome to Mail or Add Account screen. (Refer to Figure 5-1.)**

2. **Fill in what you can: your email address, domain, username (sometimes domain\user), and password. Or call on your IT staff for assistance. Tap Next when you're done.**

3. **On the next screen, as shown in Figure 5-4, enter the Server email address, assuming the Microsoft Autodiscover service didn't already find it. Tap Next when you're done.**

   That server address may begin with exchange.*company*.com.

4. **Choose which information you want to synchronize through Exchange by tapping each item you want.**

   You can choose Mail, Contacts, Calendars, Reminders, and Notes. When one of these switches is turned on, it turns green, as in Figure 5-5; otherwise, what you see appears dimmed.

5. **Tap Save.**

FIGURE 5-4:
You're on your way to a corporate email account.

WARNING

The company you work for doesn't want just anybody having access to your email — heaven forbid your iPad is lost or stolen — so your bosses may insist you change the passcode lock in Settings on your iPad. (The passcode lock is different than your email account password.) On iPads with Touch ID, you may use your

FIGURE 5-5:
Keeping your mail, contacts, calendars, and reminders in sync.

fingerprint in lieu of a passcode. Skip over to Chapter 15 for instructions on adding or changing a passcode. Now if your iPad ends up in the wrong hands, your company can remotely wipe the contents clean.

You can choose how long you want the iPad to keep email in certain accounts synchronized. Head to Settings; tap Mail; and then tap an email account that presents this option. Tap Mail Days to Sync, and tap No Limit or choose another time frame (1 day, 3 days, 1 week, 2 weeks, or 1 month).

If you're moonlighting at a second job, you can configure more than one Exchange ActiveSync account on your iPad; there used to be a limit of just one such account per device.

See Me, Read Me, File Me, Delete Me: Working with Messages

Now that your email accounts are all set up, it's time to figure out how to receive and read the stuff. Fortunately, you've already done most of the heavy lifting when you set up your email accounts. Getting and reading your mail is a piece of cake.

You can tell when you have unread mail by looking at the Mail icon at the bottom of your Home screen. The cumulative number of unread messages across all your email inboxes appears in a little red badge in the upper right of the icon.

The badge display is the default behavior. If you don't care for it, turn it off in Settings ➾ Notifications.

In the following sections, you find out how to read messages and attached files and send messages to the trash, or maybe a folder, when you've read them. Or, if you can't find a message, check out the section on searching your email messages. Reading email on an iPad versus a desktop or notebook computer is similar, except you have the advantage of the iPad's touchscreen.

Reading messages

To read your mail, tap the Mail icon on the Home screen. Remember that what appears on-screen depends on whether you're holding the iPad in landscape or portrait mode as well as what was on the screen the last time you opened the Mail app:

>> **Landscape:** With the iPad in landscape mode, you see All Inboxes at the top of the Mailboxes section (see Figure 5-6), which, as its name suggests, is a repository for

all the messages across all your accounts. The number to the right of All Inboxes (64,136 in Figure 5-6) matches the number on the Mail icon on your home page. Again, it's the cumulative tally of unread messages across all your accounts.

Below the All Inboxes listing are the inboxes for your individual accounts. The number to the right of them, as you'd expect, is the number of unread messages in those accounts (981 in iCloud and 63,155 in Gmail, in the example shown in Figure 5-6).

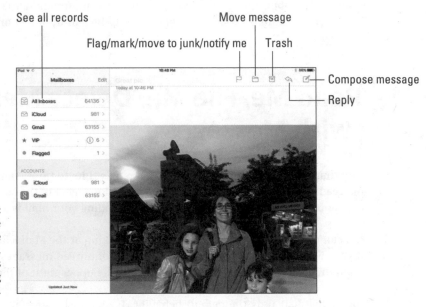

See all records

Move message

Flag/mark/move to junk/notify me   Trash

Compose message

Reply

FIGURE 5-6: When you're holding the iPad sideways, Mail looks something like this.

If you tap an account, you see the available subfolders for that account (Drafts, Sent Mail, Trash, and so on).

One of these accounts is the VIP mailbox. The VIP mailbox lists all the messages from senders you deem most important. We tell you how to give someone VIP status in the later section, "More things you can do with messages."

REMEMBER

Depending on the last time the Mail app was open, you may alternatively see previews of the messages in your inbox in the left panel. Previews show the name of the sender, the time the message arrived, the subject header, and the first two lines of the message. (In Settings, you can change the number of lines shown in the preview from one line to five or to no preview lines.)

>> **Portrait:** When you hold the iPad in portrait mode, as shown in Figure 5-7, the last incoming message fills the entire screen. You have to tap the Inbox button (in the upper-left corner of the screen) to summon a panel that displays other accounts or message previews. You can summon the panel also by swiping

from the left edge of the screen to the right. The panel overlays the message that otherwise fills the screen.

Messages are displayed in *threads*, or conversations, making them easy to follow, but you can still view accounts individually. To read your email:

1. **If the email mailbox you want to see isn't front and center, tap the Mailboxes button in the upper-left corner of the screen to summon the appropriate one.**

   Again, this button may say All Inboxes, Mailboxes, or some other folder name, or it may say the name of the email account that is currently open. Within an email account, you can see the number of unread messages in each mailbox.

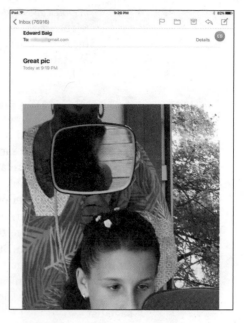

2. **(Optional) To summon new messages, swipe down the left panel that lists your accounts or mailboxes and immediately release.**

   If you see a spinning gear, the iPad is searching for new mail.

3. **Swipe down one of the inboxes or accounts to refresh that specific mailbox. To summon the unified inbox, tap All Inboxes instead.**

   If a blue dot appears next to a message, the message hasn't been read.

4. **Tap a message to read it.**

5. **When you've finished reading, tap the Mailboxes button in the upper-left corner of the message.**

   The button carries a different name, depending on which account you have open. For example, it may say Exchange, Inbox, or something else.

6. **Read additional messages.**

   When a message is on-screen, the buttons for managing incoming messages appear at the top, most of which you're already familiar with.

   - *In portrait mode:* If the message list pane isn't visible, drag from the left edge of the screen to the right, and then scroll up or down until you see the message you want to read. Tap the message so that it takes over the entire screen.

- *In landscape mode (and from within an account):* Tap a preview listing to the left of a message to read the next or previous message or any other visible message. Scroll up or down to find other messages you may want to read, and tap the appropriate message.

Threading messages

Apple lets you *thread* messages by related missives. The beauty of this arrangement is that you can easily trace an email conversation. When you organize messages by thread, the related messages appear as a single entry in the preview pane mailbox, with a double right-pointing arrow cluing you in that the message is indeed part of a larger ongoing exchange. When you tap that listing, all messages that make up the threaded conversation appear in the larger pane on the right, though you may have to have to scroll up or down to see them all. Figure 5-8 (left) shows that Bob, Susan, and Ed are hanging together by a thread. If you tap an individual message from the thread in the pane on the right, you can swipe to quickly reply to the message, forward it, or mark it unread, as Figure 5-8 (right) shows. These are the same options you see when you swipe a preview in the message list.

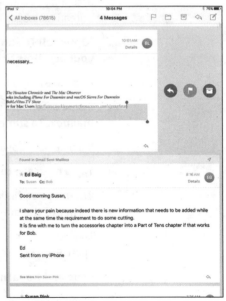

FIGURE 5-8: Your emails are hanging together by a thread.

When you look at a message that's part of a thread, the number at the top of the screen tells you how many individual messages make up the entire conversation.

To turn on threading, go to the Home screen and tap Settings ⇨ Mail, and then tap on Organize by Thread so that green is visible, as shown in Figure 5-9. You can also choose whether to display the most recent message in a thread on top, and whether to complete the thread so that all messages in the conversation are shown, even if you subsequently moved some messages to other mailboxes.

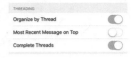

FIGURE 5-9:
Organize by Thread keeps related messages together.

Managing messages

Managing messages typically involves either moving the messages to a folder or deleting them. To herd your messages into folders, you have the following options:

» **To create a folder to organize messages you want to keep:** Open the Mail app and rotate your iPad to its side in landscape mode. In the column of mailboxes on the left side of the screen, tap Edit. Then tap New Mailbox at the bottom. Type a name for the mailbox and choose a location for it.

» **To file a message in another folder:** Tap the move message icon (labeled in Figure 5-6). When the list of mailboxes appears, tap the folder where you want to file the message. Watching the message fly and land in the designated new folder is cool.

» **To read a message that you've filed:** Tap the folder where the message now resides and then tap the header or preview for the message in question.

» **To delete, move, or mark multiple messages:** Tap Edit. In both portrait and landscape, Edit appears at the top of your inbox or another mailbox when those mail folders are selected. Tap Edit, and it becomes a Cancel button, and Mark All, Move, and Trash buttons appear at the bottom of the list. Tap each message you want to select so that a check mark appears; Mark All becomes Mark, Move All becomes Move, and Trash All becomes Trash:

- *Tap Trash* to delete all selected messages.

- *Tap Move* to move all selected messages to another folder in the same or another Mail account, and then tap the new folder or mailbox (or both) in which you want those messages to hang out.

- *Tap Mark* to mark all selected messages as Read (and Unread) and Flagged (and Unflagged) or to Move messages to a junk folder.

» **To delete a single message:** Tap the delete message (trash can) icon. In case you tap the delete message icon by mistake, you have a chance to cancel, provided the Ask Before Deleting switch is turned on in Settings ⇨ Mail.

» **To delete a single message without opening it:** Swipe one finger to the left across the message in the mailbox list, and then tap the red Trash button that appears to the right of the message. You'll also see a Flag option and a More button. Tapping More gives you, well, more options: reply, forward, mark it as unread, move it to junk or elsewhere, or have the iPad send a notification when someone replies to the message or thread.

TIP

In certain Mail accounts, Gmail being one, the Trash option may be replaced by an Archive option, depending on your preference. That means you're not getting rid of a message but stashing it, or to be precise, saving the message in your All Mail folder. If the Archive message option does present itself, you can turn the feature on or off in Settings ⇨ Mail.

Searching emails

With Search, you can quickly and easily search through a bunch of messages to find the one you want to read — such as that can't-miss stock tip from your broker. In the search box at the top of a mailbox preview pane, type *stock* or whichever search term seems relevant. You'll notice a couple of things right off the bat. You can confine your query to just the current mailbox or widen the search to include all your mailboxes, as Figure 5-10 shows. What's more, Apple has helpfully organized the search results, so that senders who have *stock* as part of their name are separated from the subject headings of email messages that include the search term.

FIGURE 5-10:
Stock up on your search skills.

Next, for a more granular search, tap Search for "Stock," which is below the search field and is preceded by a magnifying glass (refer to Figure 5-10). You have the option of searching for *stock* in the body or subject of email messages. (For more on Search, see Chapter 2.)

Search within Mail is quite powerful. For example, you can search by time frame by typing something along the lines of *March meetings.* You can also search to find just flagged messages from your VIPs (*flag unread VIP*).

Siri can also find emails on your behalf. For example, ask her to find all the emails from a particular person in a particular month, or have Siri run a search similar to the stock example we just used.

If you're using Exchange, iCloud, or certain IMAP-type email accounts, you may even be able to search messages stored on the server.

Don't grow too attached to attachments

Your iPad can receive email messages with attachments in a wide variety of popular file formats. Which file formats does the iPad support? Glad you asked:

- **Images:** .jpg, .tiff, .gif, .png
- **Microsoft Word:** .doc, .docx
- **Microsoft PowerPoint:** .ppt, .pptx
- **Microsoft Excel:** .xls, .xlsx
- **Web pages:** .htm, .html
- **Apple Keynote:** .key
- **Apple Numbers:** .numbers
- **Apple Pages:** .pages
- **Preview and Adobe Acrobat:** .pdf
- **Rich Text:** .rtf
- **Text:** .txt
- **Contact information:** .vcf

If the attachment is a file format the iPad doesn't support (for example, an Adobe Photoshop .psd file), you see the name of the file in your email, but you can't open it on your iPad, at least not without an assist from a third-party app that you may have installed.

Here's how to read a supported attachment:

1. **Open the email that contains the attachment, which you can identify by a little paper clip icon.**

   Another option is to conduct a search for Messages with Attachments.

2. **Tap the attachment.**

   The attachment typically appears at the bottom of the message, so you might need to scroll down to see it.

In some cases, the attachment downloads to your iPad and opens automatically. In other instances, you may have to tap the button representing the attachment to download it.

3. **Read or (in the case of a picture) eyeball the attachment.**

    Tap the attachment (in the case of a document), and you can likely read it immediately. Tap Done to return to the message text.

TIP

Alternatively, tap and hold down on the attachment in the email, and then tap the app from the presented options. Among the possible choices: Tap Quick Look for a quick peek at the attachment, or tap Markup and Reply to add your comments to a document before whisking it back to the sender. You can also add the attachment to iCloud Drive or Notes, or import it to Apple's Pages word processor should that app resides on your tablet. Third-party apps you added to your iPad may also become available as a destination for said attachment.

More things you can do with messages

Wait! You can do even more with your incoming email messages:

TIP

>> **To see all recipients of a message:** Tap Details, which appears to the right of the recipients' names, assuming you cannot already see all the names of the people receiving the message.

    If all recipients are displayed, you'll see Hide instead of Details; tap Hide to hide all names except the sender's.

>> **To add an email recipient or sender to your contacts:** Tap the name or email address at the top of the message and then tap Create New Contact or Add to Existing Contact.

>> **To make a sender a VIP:** Tap the name or email address at the top of the message and then tap Add to VIP. You may want to give VIP status to important people in your life, such as your significant other, family members, boss, or doctor. A star appears next to any incoming messages from a VIP. You can summon mail from all your VIPs by tapping the VIP folder in the list of Mailboxes. To demote a VIP to an NVIP (not very important person), tap the name or email at the top of the message and then tap Remove from VIP.

>> **To mark a message as unread, flag it, move it to junk, or arrange to receive a notification when someone replies:** Tap the flag icon at the top of a message. These options appear:

    • *Mark as Unread:* Choose Mark as Unread for messages that you may want to revisit at some point but which don't necessarily have special significance. The message is again included in the unread message count on the Mail icon on your Home screen, and its mailbox again has a blue dot next to it in the message list for that mailbox. You can tap Mark as Read if the message loses its significance. As an alternative, you can mark a message as unread by swiping from left to right in the preview pane.

- *Flag:* Choose Flag for those messages that deserve special status or that you want to find again in a hurry. Alternatively, swipe from right to left in the preview pane and tap Flag. Yet another option will get you to the flag option, albeit with what we reckon are too many added steps: Swipe from right to left in the preview pane and then tap More, tap Mark, and then tap Flag.

- *Move to Junk:* We all get crap email. This option moves those messages to your junk pile. You can also swipe from right to left in the preview pane, tap More, and then tap Move to Junk.

- *Notify Me:* Tap to receive notifications whenever anyone replies to this email thread. Or again, swipe from right to left in the preview pane, tap More, and then tap Notify Me.

>> **To zoom in on and out of a message:** Use the pinch and unpinch gestures, at which we suspect you now excel. See Chapter 2 if you need help with your touchscreen moves.

>> **To follow a link in a message:** Tap the link. Links are typically displayed in blue, but they sometimes appear in other colors, or underlined, or both. If the link is a URL, Safari opens and displays the web page. If the link is a phone number, the iPad gives you the chance to add it to your contacts, copy it, call it using FaceTime Audio or your iPhone (through a Handoff feature), or send a message. If the link is an address, the Maps app opens and displays the location. If you tap a date, you can create an event on that date or show it in Calendar. And, last but not least, if the link is an email address, a new pread-dressed blank email message is created.

TIP

>> If the link opens Safari, Contacts, or Maps and you want to return to your email, tap Mail in the upper-left corner of the display. Or press the Home button on the front of your iPad and then tap the Mail icon. Or double-press the Home button and select the Mail icon from the app switcher.

Darling, You Send Me (Email)

Sending email on your iPad is a breeze. You'll encounter several subspecies of messages: pure text, text with a photo, a partially finished message (a *draft*) that you want to save and complete later, or a reply to an incoming message. You can also forward an incoming message to someone else — and in some instances print messages. The following sections examine these message types one at a time.

Sending an all-text message

To compose a new email message, tap Mail on the Home screen. As before, what you see next depends on how you're holding your iPad. In landscape mode, your email accounts or email folders are listed in a panel along the left side of the screen, with the actual message filling the larger window on the right.

Now, to create a message, follow these steps:

1. **Tap the compose new message icon (labeled in Figure 5-6).**

The New Message screen appears, like the one shown in Figure 5-11.

2. **Type the names or email addresses of the recipients in the To field, or tap the + symbol to the right of the To field to choose a contact(s) from your iPad's contacts list.**

TIP

If you start typing an email address, email addresses that match what you typed appear in a list below the To or Cc field. If the correct one is in the list, tap it to use it.

As part of the intelligent and proactive iOS operating system, your iPad may suggest people that you typically include when starting to address a message.

3. **(Optional) Tap the field labeled Cc/Bcc, From.**

Doing so breaks the field into separate Cc, Bcc, and From fields (refer to Figure 5-11).

The Cc/Bcc label stands for *carbon copy/blind carbon copy. Carbon copy* (a throwback term from another era) is kind of an FYI to a recipient. It's like saying, "We figure you'd appreciate knowing this, but you don't need to respond."

When using Bcc, you can include a recipient on the message, but other recipients can't see that this recipient has been included. Bcc is great for those secret agent emails! Tap the respective Cc or Bcc field to type names. Or tap the + symbol that appears in those fields to add a contact.

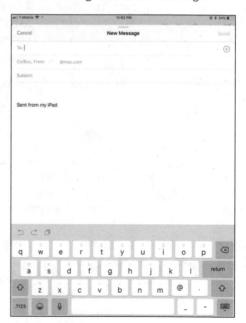

FIGURE 5-11:
The New Message screen is ready for you to start typing.

4. **(Optional) If you tap From, you can choose any of your email accounts on the fly — assuming you have more than one account set up on the iPad.**

5. **In the subject field, type a subject.**

   The subject is optional, but it's considered poor form to send an email without one.

6. **In the message area, type your message.**

   The message area is immediately below the Subject field. You have ample space to get your message across.

7. **Tap the Send button in the upper-right corner of the screen.**

   Your message wings its way to its recipients almost immediately. If you aren't in range of a Wi-Fi network or a cellular network when you tap Send, the message is sent the next time you're in range of one of these networks.

Formatting text in an email

One of the goodies in Mail is the capability to format email text by underlining, bolding, or italicizing it. First you select the text by pressing your finger against the screen until you see the options to select some or all of the text. After making your selection, you'll have various other options: Cut, Copy, Paste, BIU, Replace, Look Up, Share, Quote Level, Insert Photo or Video, or Add Attachment. To format text, tap the BIU button. Then apply whichever style (bold, italics, underline) suits your fancy.

If you tap Quote Level (if you don't immediately see it, tap the right-pointing arrow after selecting a word), you can quote a portion of a message you're responding to. *Note:* Increase Quote Level must be turned on in Mail Settings. You can also increase or decrease the indentation in your outgoing message.

If you tap Replace, you are provided with alternative word choices to the word that you selected. Tap one of the alternative options to select it.

If you tap Look Up, you can summon a definition from the *New Oxford Dictionary* or another available dictionary, as well as see suggestions, if appropriate, from iTunes, the App Store, nearby locations, movie showtimes, and more.

Sending a photo with an email message

Sometimes a picture is worth a thousand words. When that's the case, follow these steps to send an email message with a photo attached:

1. **Tap the Photos icon on the Home screen.**

2. **Find the photo you want to send.**

3. **Tap the share icon at the top of the screen (and shown in the margin).**

4. **Tap the Mail button.**

   An email message appears on-screen with the photo already attached. The image may appear to be embedded in the body of the message, but the recipient receives it as a regular email attachment.

   On the Cc/Bcc line of your outgoing message, you see the size of the attached image. If you tap the size of the image shown, a new line appears, giving you the option to choose an alternative size among Small, Medium, Large, or Actual Size. Your choice affects both the visible dimensions and file size of the photo (with the actual size of the file as measured in kilobytes or megabytes reported for each possible choice).

5. **Choose what size photo you want to send.**

6. **Address the message and type whatever text you like, as you did for an all-text message previously, and then tap the Send button.**

You have an alternative way of inserting pictures (or videos) into your outgoing mail messages. In the preceding "Formatting text in an email" section, we mention an Insert Photo or Video option that appears after you press your finger against the body of a message that you're composing. Tap Insert Photo or Video, tap the album in which the photo (or video) you want to send exists, and then tap that photo or video. Tap Use to embed the image and proceed with composing.

Adding attachments

You've seen how you can attach photos and videos to your outgoing messages. Apple supplies another way to add an attachment. Press your finger against the body of the message in the same way you just did to format text. Tap the arrow to the right of Quote Level and tap the new Add Attachment option. You're immediately ushered to an iCloud Drive screen, where you can choose the attachment you would like to add from the likes of the Pages app, Keynote, Preview, QuickTime Player, TextEdit, and the Documents folder. Tap the file to add it to the body of your soon-to-be sent email.

You can also select among other options, depending on the apps you have installed on your iPad.

Marking up attachments

If you're attaching a photo or a PDF document, you can take advantage of a Markup feature. With the picture attachment or PDF embedded in your outgoing message, tap and hold down or double-tap the attachment, and from the share menu that appears, tap Markup.

You can summon the Markup feature also when you receive a PDF or picture attachment. Tap on the attachment and then tap the briefcase icon accompanied by the words Markup and Reply in the share sheet that appears. Or choose Markup as one of the options in the same bar you've seen earlier in this chapter with such choices as Select, Select All, Paste, and Quote Level.

Now that you're in markup mode, you can draw on that image or PDF, tapping the simple annotation tools just below. The tools are represented by icons: one for a pen tool (your finger will be that pen unless you use an Apple Pencil with an iPad Pro or another optional stylus on other iPad models), one for a magnification loupe so you can zoom in on the document or pic, one for writing text (you can summon the keyboard), and one for drawing your signature, which we get to shortly.

If you draw a shape such as an arrow and the iPad recognizes that that was the shape you had in mind, it will give you the option to draw it for you. You can leave your own imperfect arrow (or other symbol) if you prefer to use that one instead of Apple's. One piece of advice on that arrow business that we discovered: Draw with a single stroke and do not lift your finger.

Within Markup, you have the option to change the color and thickness of the lines and symbols that you draw and change the fonts and text size.

Lastly, you can write your signature in script, a potential boon for lawyers or folks needing to get a John Hancock on a contract or lease. Just choose the fourth icon at the bottom of the Markup screen and tap Add or Remove Signature. Then tap the + and sign your name with your finger.

Saving an email to send later

Sometimes you start an email message but don't have time to finish it. When that happens, you can save it as a draft and finish it some other time. Here's how:

1. **Start an email message, as described in one of the previous sections.**

2. **When you're ready to save the message as a draft, tap the Cancel button in the upper-left corner of the screen.**

3. **Tap the Save Draft button if you want to save this message as a draft and complete it another time.**

   If you tap the Delete Draft button, the message disappears immediately without a second chance. Don't tap Delete Draft unless you mean it.

To work on the message again, tap the Drafts mailbox. A list of all messages you saved as drafts appears. Tap the draft you want to work on, and it reappears on the screen. When you're finished, you can tap Send to send it or tap Cancel to save it as a draft again.

REMEMBER

The number of drafts appears to the right of the Drafts folder, the same way that the number of unread messages appears to the right of other mail folders, such as your inbox.

Replying to, forwarding, or printing an email message

When you receive a message and want to reply to it, open the message and then tap the reply icon (the curved arrow at the upper-right corner of the screen, as shown in Figure 5-12). Then tap Reply, Reply All, Forward, or Print, as described next:

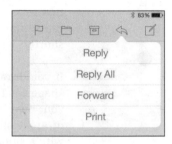

FIGURE 5-12:
Reading and managing an email message.

>> **Reply and Reply All:** The Reply button creates an email message addressed to the sender of the original message, with the content of that original message embedded in your reply. The Reply All button creates an email message addressed to the sender and all other recipients of the original message, plus Ccs. (The Reply All option appears only if more than one recipient was on the original email.) In both cases, the subject is retained with a *Re:* prefix added. So if the original subject were *iPad Tips*, the reply's subject would be *Re: iPad Tips*.

>> **Forward:** Tapping the Forward button creates an unaddressed email message that contains the text of the original message. Add the email address(es) of the person or people you want to forward the message to, and then tap Send. In this case, rather than a *Re:* prefix, the subject is preceded by *Fwd:*. So this time, the subject would be *Fwd: iPad Tips*. If the email you're forwarding has an attachment, you'll be given the option to forward the attachment along with the message.

>> **Print:** Tap Print if you want to print using an AirPrint-capable printer.

TIP

It's considered good form to leave the subject lines alone (with the *Re:* or *Fwd:* prefix intact), but you may want to change them sometimes. You can edit the subject line of a reply or a forwarded message or edit the body text of a forwarded message the same way you'd edit any other text. Worth noting: When the Re:

is modified, a new email thread is created and the modified message won't be included in the old thread listing.

To send your reply or forwarded message, tap the Send button as usual.

Settings for sending email

You can customize the mail you send and receive in lots of ways. In this section, we explore settings for sending email. Later in this chapter, we show you settings that affect the way you receive and read messages. In each instance, start by tapping Settings on the Home screen.

You can customize your mail in the following ways:

REMEMBER

>> **To hear an alert when you successfully send a message:** From the main Settings screen, tap Sounds. Make sure that the Sent Mail setting is turned on. You'll know because you'll see a sound type listed (among alert sounds and ringtones), Swoosh by default. If you tap Sent Mail in Settings, you can select another sound besides Swoosh or choose None if going silent is your preference.

If you want to change other settings, tap the Sounds button at the top of the screen. If you're finished setting the settings, tap the Home button on the front of your iPad.

>> No matter what setting you've just accessed, if you want to continue using Settings, tap whichever left-pointing button appears at the top of the right Settings pane — General, Mail, or something else. After you return to the previous screen, you can change other settings. Similarly, you can tap the Home button on the front of your iPad when you're finished setting any setting. That action always saves the changes you just made and returns to the Home screen.

>> **To add a signature line, phrase, or block of text to every email message you send:** Tap Settings ⇨ Mail, and then tap Signature in the right pane. The default signature is *Sent from my iPad*. You can add text before or after it, or delete it and type something else. Your signature is affixed to the end of all your outgoing email. You can choose a signature that is the same across all your accounts or select different signatures for each account.

>> **To have your iPad send you a copy of every message you send:** Tap Settings ⇨ Mail, and then turn on the Always Bcc Myself setting. This step isn't usually necessary because your Sent folder typically captures all such messages.

>> **To set the default email account for initiating email from outside the Mail application:** Tap the Settings icon on the Home screen and then tap Mail ⇨ Default Account. Tap the account you want to use as the default.

This designated email account is the one that's used when you want to email a picture directly from the Photos app, for example. Note that this setting applies only if you have more than one email account on your iPad. Also, if you choose one default account, you can dispatch mail from another account at send time.

Setting Your Message and Account Settings

This final discussion of Mail involves more settings that deal with your various email accounts.

Checking and viewing email settings

Several settings affect the way you can check and view email. You might want to modify one or more, so we describe what they do and where to find them:

>> **To specify how often the iPad checks for new messages:** Tap the Settings icon on the Home screen, and then tap Accounts & Passwords ➪ Fetch New Data. You're entering the world of *fetching* or *pushing*. Check out Figure 5-13 to glance at your options. If your email program (or, more precisely, the email server behind it) supports push and the Push setting is enabled on your iPad, fresh messages are sent to your iPad automatically as soon as they hit the server. If you turned off push or your email program doesn't support it, the iPad fetches data instead. Choices for fetching are Every 15 Minutes, Every 30 Minutes, Hourly, Manually, and Automatically. Tap the one you prefer. With push email, messages can show up on the lock screen and in Notification Center.

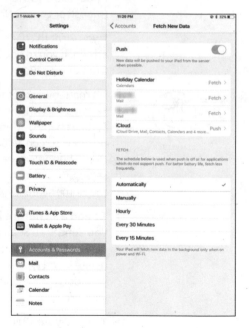

FIGURE 5-13:
Fetch or push? It's your call.

>> **To hear an alert sound when you receive a new message:** Tap Sounds on the main Settings screen and then tap the New Mail setting. The Ding sound is there

by default. Do nothing if you're satisfied with the Ding you hear each time a new message arrives. If you aren't satisfied, tap New Mail and select an alternative sound from the list, or tap None if you don't want to hear any such alert.

>> **To set the number of lines of each message to be displayed in the message list:** From the main Settings screen, tap Mail ⇨ Preview; then choose a number. Your choices are None, 1, 2, 3, 4, and 5 lines of text. The more lines of text you display in the list, the fewer messages you can see at a time without scrolling. Think before you choose 4 or 5.

>> **To specify whether the iPad shows the To and Cc labels in message lists:** From the main Settings screen, tap Mail, and then turn on or off the Show To/Cc Label setting.

>> **To turn on or off the Ask before Deleting warning:** From the main Settings screen and then tap Mail. Next, turn on or off the Ask before Deleting setting. If this setting is turned on, you need to tap the trash icon at the bottom of the screen and then tap the red Delete button to confirm the deletion. When the setting is turned off, tapping the trash icon deletes the message, and you never see a red Delete button.

>> **To change swipe options:** From the main Settings screen, tap Mail and then tap Swipe Options. You can choose whether swiping left (on the preview pane) flags messages and whether swiping right marks messages as unread.

>> **To change the flag style from a color to a shape:** Tap Settings ⇨ Mail ⇨ Flag Style and make your determination.

>> **To mark email addresses that originate or are received from a designated mail server:** Tap Settings ⇨ Mail ⇨ Mark Addresses and flip the switch on. Enter the email address from your company (or wherever) that you do *not* want marked. From then on, when you're composing a message, all email addresses sent to or from that specified address will appear in blue, while all other mail addresses will be shaded red. Why do this? The idea is that you can more easily identify mail dispatched to addresses outside your organization, alerting you to a potential security risk if you're exchanging, say, sensitive information.

>> **To specify whether the iPad will automatically display images that are embedded in an email:** Tap Mail and then tap Load Remote Images in the right pane so that the switch is on. If it's off, you can still manually load remote images. Security risks are associated with loading remote images, and they can also hog bandwidth.

>> **To organize your mail by thread:** Tap Organize by Thread so that the setting is on. Then, as mentioned, you can choose whether to show the most recent message on top and whether to show all messages in a thread, even those since moved to other mailboxes.

Altering account settings

The last group of email settings we explore in this chapter deals with your email accounts. You most likely will never need most of these settings, but we'd be remiss if we didn't at least mention them briefly. So here they are, whether you need 'em or not:

TIP

>> **To stop using an email account:** Tap the Settings icon on the Home screen, tap Accounts & Passwords ⇨ *account name,* and then flip the switch for Mail off. As a reminder, when Mail is on, you see green by the Mail switch. Otherwise, the switch is gray.

   This setting doesn't delete the account; it only hides it from view and stops it from sending or checking email until you turn it on again. (You can repeat this step to turn off calendars, contacts, reminders, and notes in a given account.)

>> **To delete an email account:** Tap the Settings icon on the Home screen; tap Accounts & Passwords ⇨ *account name* ⇨ Delete Account ⇨ Delete. Tap Cancel if you change your mind and don't want your account blown away, or tap Delete to proceed.

WARNING

   In iOS 11, you can only sign out of your iCloud account; you can't delete it. But when you sign out, all of your iCloud account data, including mail, will be deleted.

WARNING

   Deleting an email account will also remove calendar entries, contact names, and notes from the given account.

You can find still more advanced Mail settings, reached the same way: Tap the Settings ⇨ Accounts & Passwords ⇨ Account ⇨ Advanced.

REMEMBER

The settings you see under Advanced (sometimes shown as Advanced Settings under a specific email account) and how they appear vary by account. This list describes some of the settings you might see:

>> **Specify how long until deleted messages are removed permanently from your iPad:** In iCloud Mail, your choices are Never, After One Day, After One Week, and After One Month. Tap the choice you prefer. Other mail accounts may give you different time frame options or not present this setting.

>> **Choose whether drafts, sent messages, archived, and deleted messages are stored on your iPad or on your mail server:** Tap Advanced and then choose the setting under Mailbox Behaviors. You can decide for drafts, sent messages, and trash. If you choose to store any or all of them on the server, you can't see them unless you have an Internet connection (Wi-Fi or cellular). If you choose to store them on your iPad, they're always available, even if you don't have Internet access. Under Mailbox Behaviors, in certain circumstances, you also get to determine whether to delete or archive discarded messages.

WARNING

We strongly recommend that you don't change the next two items unless you know exactly what you're doing and why. If you're having problems with sending or receiving mail, start by contacting your ISP (Internet service provider), email provider, or corporate IT person or tech department. Then change these settings only if they tell you to. Again, these settings and exactly where and how they appear vary by account.

>> **Reconfigure mail server settings:** In the Incoming Mail Server or Outgoing Mail Server section of the account settings screen, tap Host Name, User Name, or Password and make your changes.

>> **Adjust SSL, Authentication, or IMAP Path Settings, or Server Port:** Tap Advanced and then tap the appropriate item and make the necessary changes.

And that, as they say in baseball, retires the side. You're now fully qualified to set up email accounts and send and receive email on your iPad. But, as the late Apple cofounder Steve Jobs was wont to say, there is one more thing . . .

Getting the iMessage

The Messages app lets you exchange iMessages, pictures, contacts, videos, audio recordings, and locations with anyone using an Apple iDevice with iOS 5 or higher or with a Mac running OS X Mountain Lion or later. In the following sections, find out how each of the iMessages features works.

Sending iMessages

To start a new message, tap the Messages icon on the Home screen to launch the Messages app and then tap the compose new message icon, the little pencil-and-paper icon in the left pane of the screen (on the Messages list).

At this point, with the To field active and awaiting your input, you can do three things:

TIP

>> **If the recipient *is* in your contacts list, type the first few letters of the name.** A list of matching contacts appears. Scroll through it if necessary and tap the name of the contact.

The more letters you type, the shorter the list becomes. And after you've tapped the name of a contact, you can begin typing another name so that you can send this message to multiple recipients at once.

>> **Tap the blue circled + icon on the right side of the To field to select a name from your contacts list.**

>> **If the recipient *isn't* in your contacts list, type his or her phone number or email address.**

You have a fourth option if you want to compose the message first and address it later. Tap inside the text-entry field (the narrow rectangular area just above the keyboard and to the left of the Send button or microphone icon) to activate the field and then type or dictate your message. When you've finished typing, tap the To field and use one of the preceding techniques to address your message.

TIP

You aren't limited to sending an iMessage to a single person. To initiate a group message, type the names or phones numbers of everyone you want to include in the To field.

When you've finished addressing and composing, tap the Send button to send your message on its merry way. And that's all there is to it.

REMEMBER

You can communicate with people who don't have iMessage on their phones, tablets, or computers; messages will be exchanged through either SMS text messages or MMS multimedia-type missives. If you're involved in an SMS schmooze-fest, the messaging bubbles will be green. If you're indeed exchanging iMessages with others, those bubbles will be blue. The distinction is important because most of the fancy multimedia tricks we tell you about in this chapter won't work outside the iMessage environment.

Group messages

The Messages app on your iPad is all-inclusive — that is, an iMessage need not be one to one. Instead, a group of folks can communicate. Start by preparing a message with a single recipient, and then tap the circled + in the To field to add people to the conversation from your contacts or manually. After pressing + you can also tap Groups to select any previous groups you've set up.

Adding voice to an iMessage

You can record an audio message and send it along to a recipient. Apple calls this Tap to Talk and here's how to take advantage of it. Press and hold down the microphone icon to the right of the text-entry field (not the microphone icon on the iPad keyboard) and start speaking. Your voice appears as a waveform at the bottom of the screen, as shown in Figure 5-14. When you've finished speaking, keep your finger pressed down and swipe up to send the message. You can listen to the audio before sending it by tapping the play icon, which appears after you release the button you held down to record. If you're not thrilled with what you've just recorded, swipe left instead to cancel.

The recipient of your recorded iMessage will be able to tap a Play button to listen to what you had to say. But in some cases, he or she had best listen right away because you can set things (in Settings) so that audio messages expire after two minutes. Your only other option is for the message to never expire.

Keep in mind that the microphone icon that lets you record your voice will be enabled only if you're sending an iMessage to a chat partner.

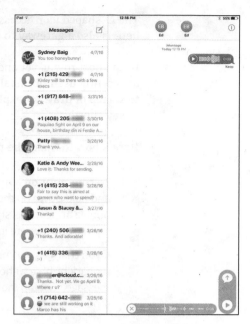

FIGURE 5-14:
Lending your voice to an iMessage.

Massive multimedia effects overhaul

iOS 11 includes the biggest batch of Messages effects and features since, well, Apple got into the messaging game. You'll find a gaggle of bubble and screen effects, handwriting, annotation, Digital Touch, plus the fastest and easiest way we've ever seen to replace words with emojis. You can also tap a message to offer a quick reaction to the sender, via what Apple refers to as *tapback*.

The Messages app in iOS 11 includes an open architecture and built-in App Store for third-party add-ons, including stickers and additional emojis.

Let's plunge right in. Follow the previous instructions and choose a recipient or group that you want to engage with, and then tap the right-pointing arrow button just to left of the iMessage text box. The two adjacent icons shown in Figure 5-15 appear, with a row of recent apps.

FIGURE 5-15:
When sending an iMessage, you can add a picture, sketch, visit a dedicated App Store, or choose from installed sticker packs.

You can probably guess what tapping the camera icon does. Yes, it accesses your camera so you can snap a new picture (or video) for your outgoing message or cherry-pick other images from your Photos library.

The A–shaped icon accesses the iMessage App Store for stickers and such. Tapping here is also a gateway to sharing music you're listening to in iTunes.

In the next row is yet another App Store icon, a heart with two fingers, and a row of recently used or installed iMessage apps. The heart icon brings you to an area to sketch or draw, or exploit Apple's Digital Touch effects, of which we have more to say shortly.

Here's how to make the most out the Messages app:

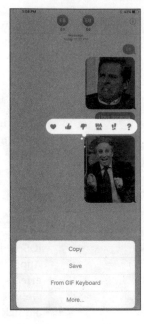

>> **To comment on a message with a tapback:** Press and hold down on the message until the tapback bubble appears, as shown in Figure 5-16, and then tap the appropriate icon.

If you change your mind and want to dismiss the tapback bubble without adding a tapback icon to the message, just tap the screen anywhere *outside* the tapback bubble.

Tapback works only with other devices running iOS 10, iOS 11, macOS Sierra, or macOS High Sierra. If the recipients are using any other operating system, they won't see any cute balloons, just plain old text that reads, "*Your-name-here* Loved/Liked/Disliked/ Laughed At/Emphasized/Questioned *item-name-here.*"

>> **To replace text with an emoji:** Type your message and then tap the emoji keyboard icon. As soon as you do, words that have associated emojis turn orange; tap an orange word to replace it with a possible emoji. If the word is associated with more than one emoji, you'll see multiple emojis in a bubble; tap the one you want and it replaces the word. Figure 5-17 illustrates to your messaging friends how much you love bananas.

FIGURE 5-16:
Tap a tapback icon to send a quick reaction to the message sender.

FIGURE 5-17:
Tap the orange words (left) to employ emojis to illustrate how much you love bananas.

» **To add bubble or screen effects:** Prepare your message as usual but rather than tapping the little up-arrow-in-a-blue-circle to send it, press and hold down on it for several seconds and the Bubble and Screen Effects screen appears. Tap the Bubble tab at the top to select Slam, Loud, Gentle, or Invisible Ink as the bubble effect for your message (meaning the recipient will have to swipe across the message to read it). Or tap the Screen tab and swipe left or right to select Balloons, Confetti, Lasers, Fireworks, or Shooting Star as the screen effect for this message.

If you change your mind and don't want to add an effect, tap the *x*-in-a-circle to dismiss the Bubble and Screen Effects screen.

» **To send a handwritten message:** Sometimes nothing but a handwritten note will do. Tap the handwriting icon in the lower-right corner of the keyboard (and shown in the margin). You'll be whisked off to a white area where you can write your message, using your finger, an Apple Pencil accessory (for iPad Pro models), or a third-party stylus. Tap > if you need more space.

If you prefer choose a preset handwritten message — Ed concedes with far more legible penmanship than his own — tap the tiny clock icon at the bottom-left corner of the white writing area and then tap Thinking of You, Congratulations, I'm Sorry, or any of the other selections shown in Figure 5-18.

FIGURE 5-18:
Choosing a handwritten preset.

» **To send Digital Touch effects:** Digital Touch effects were introduced on the Apple Watch and have spread to the Messages app. To use them, tap the Digital Touch icon to the left of the text field (and shown in the margin) to reveal the Digital Touch interface shown in Figure 5-19.

And here's how it works:

- **To expand the Digital Touch interface to full screen:** Tap the caret (^) near the lower-right corner.

- **To sketch:** Draw with one finger.

- **To send a pulsing circle:** Tap with one finger.

- **To send a fireball:** Press with two fingers.

- **To send a kiss:** Tap with two fingers.

- **To send a heartbeat:** Tap and hold down with two fingers.

- **To send a broken heart:** Tap and hold down with two fingers, and then drag down.

- **To switch ink colors:** Tap one of circles on the left. If you see only one hue option, tap the colored circle to reveal other choices.

- **To add a picture or video to your Digital Touch effect:** Tap the camera icon on the left.

Digital Touch messages are sent automatically, so don't tap or press the screen in Digital Touch mode unless you really mean it.

WARNING

 Last but not least, Messages has a built-in app store so you can buy (or download for free) sticker packs, new effects, and who knows what else. To get some free stickers and see what other third-party add-ons are avail-able, tap the app icon to the left of the text field then tap the four-dotted icon at the bottom left corner of the display (shown in the margin), and tap the + to enter the store.

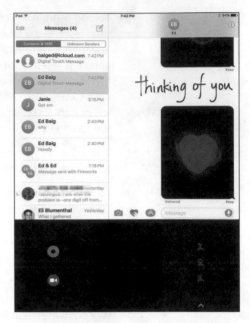

FIGURE 5-19:
We just sent a heartbeat through the Digital Touch interface.

Once you've acquired apps, this is also where you access them. So, for example, to send a sticker from a sticker pack you've downloaded, you'd tap the App Store icon, and again tap the four-dotted icon. The sticker packs and apps you used most recently appear in a tray next to the App Store icon.

Being a golden receiver: Receiving iMessages

When determining your settings for receiving iMessages, first things first. Decide whether you want to hear an alert when you receive a message:

>> **If you want to hear an alert sound when you receive a message:** Tap the Settings icon on your Home screen, tap Sounds ➪ Text Tone, and then tap an available sound. You can audition the sounds by tapping them. You can create your own tones in GarageBand for iPad.

REMEMBER

You hear the sounds when you audition them in the Settings app, even if the ring/silent switch is set to Silent. After you exit the Settings app, however, you *won't* hear a sound when a message arrives if the ring/silent switch is set to Silent.

>> **If you *don't* want to hear an alert when a message arrives:** Instead of tapping one of the listed sounds, tap None, which is the first item in the list of alert tones.

>> **If you don't want any messages:** Turn off iMessage. If you won't want iMessage (or other interruptions) for a designated period, consider the Do Not Disturb feature. It lives up to its name. Turn on the feature in Settings, and you'll see a moon icon in the status bar. Even easier, turn on Do Not Disturb in Control Center, and you won't be inundated with messages. You can also tap the *i*-in-a-circle in a given message thread to summon a Details pane and turn on Do Not Disturb, which mutes notifications for this particular conversation. For more about the Do Not Disturb feature and other settings, head to Chapter 15.

The following pointers explain what you can do with iMessages that you receive:

>> **When your iPad is asleep:** All or part of the text and the name of the sender appear on the unlock screen. Slide to the right to reply to a specific message (you'll have to get past any passcodes first).

>> **When your iPad is awake and unlocked:** All or part of the message and the name of the sender appear at the top of the screen in front of whatever's already there.

TIP

These notifications are on by default; turn them off in the Settings app's Notifications pane if you don't care for them. You'll also see any notifications for messages you've received in Notification Center.

>> **Reading or replying to a message:** Tap the Messages icon on your Home screen, swipe downward from the top of the screen to display Notification Center, or tap the notification if you can be quick (the notification fades away in a few seconds).

>> **Following the conversation:** Each conversation you have is saved as a series of text bubbles. Your messages appear on the right side of the screen in blue bubbles; the other person's messages appear in gray ones. When your message has been delivered, that fact will be noted just below the last bubble in your exchange. If there was a problem delivering the message, you'll see Not Delivered instead. If at first you don't succeed, try again.

>> **Forwarding a conversation:** If you want to forward all or part of a conversation to another iMessage user, press against a text bubble and tap the More button, which shows up at the bottom of the screen along with a Copy option. (You'll also see the aforementioned tapback icons.) Tap additional text, photo, or video bubbles that you want to forward (the one you pressed to summon the More button is already selected) so that a check mark appears in a circle to the left of each. Then tap the forward (curved arrow) icon at the lower right of the screen. The contents of the selected text bubbles are copied to a new text message; specify a recipient and then tap Send.

>> **Deleting part of a single conversation thread:** Press against a text bubble and tap More. Tap each text bubble that you want to delete; a check mark appears in the circle next to each one. Then tap the delete (trash can) icon at the bottom of the pane, and tap Delete Message(s). Or, to delete the entire conversation in one fell swoop, tap the Delete All button at the top of the screen and then tap Delete Conversation.

>> **Deleting an entire conversation thread:** Tap the Edit button at the upper left of the Messages list, tap the circle that appears to the left of the person's name, and then tap the Delete button at the bottom of the pane. Or swipe from right to left on the message in the Messages pane and then tap the red Delete button.

Sending pix and vids in a message

To send a picture or video in a message, follow the instructions for sending a text message and then tap the camera icon to the left of the text-entry field at the bottom of the screen. You'll have the option of using an existing picture or video or taking a new one. You can also add text to photos or videos. When you're finished, tap the Send button.

If you *receive* a picture or video in a message, it appears in a bubble just like text. Tap the play icon to play it right in Messages. Tap again to have the video take over the full screen.

In full-screen mode, tap the share icon in the upper-right corner of a received video or picture for additional options, such as sharing the image on Facebook or Twitter, assigning it to a contact, or more. If you don't see the icon, tap the picture or video once, and the icon will magically appear.

Meantime, in Messages Settings, you have the option to enable a Low Quality Image Mode switch. The setting applies to the images you send and will help you conserve data.

Smart messaging tricks

Here are some more things you can do with messages:

>> **Search your messages for a word or phrase.** Type the word or phrase in the search field at the top left of the Messages listing pane.

>> **Send Read Receipts to allow others to be notified when you have read their missives.** Tap Settings ⇨ Messages, and slide the switch so that Send Read Receipts is on.

TIP

In iMessages, you can see when your own message has been delivered and read, and when the other person is readying a response. You can also tap the *i*-in-a-circle (Details) button and then tap Send Read Receipts.

>> **Use a Bluetooth keyboard for typing instead of the on-screen keyboard.** Follow the instructions in Chapter 15 to pair your Bluetooth keyboard with your iPad.

>> **Dictate a message (third-generation iPads or later).** Tap the microphone key on your keyboard and start talking. Tap the microphone key again when you're done. This method isn't as quick or as much fun as Tap to Talk, but it works.

>> **Open a URL included in an iMessage.** Tap the URL to open that web page in Safari.

>> **Send an email to an address included in an iMessage, or call or FaceTime the person.** Tap the circled picture or initials representing the person you are communicating with and tap his or her email address to open a preaddressed email message in Mail, or tap the FaceTime or Call icon to communicate that way instead.

>> **See an address included in an iMessage.** Tap the address to see it on a map in Maps.

>> **Choose how you can be reached via iMessage.** Tap Settings ⇨ Messages ⇨ Send & Receive. Then add another email address or remove any existing addresses. You can also select the email address (or phone number) from which to start new conversations.

>> **Show the Subject field.** Flip the switch to show a Subject field with your messages.

>> **Filter Unknown Senders.** Flip this switch to turn off notifications for iMessages from folks who are not among your contacts. You can sort such unknown senders into a separate list.

>> **Block a sender.** Block someone who is harassing you or has left your good graces. Tap Settings ➪ Messages ➪ Blocked and select a name from your contacts. You will no longer receive messages or FaceTime calls from this person.

>> **Share your location.** Meeting a recipient in an unfamiliar place? In the middle of your conversation, you can share your location on a map. Tap the *i*-in-a-circle (Details) button at the upper-right corner and then tap either Send My Current Location or Share My Location. Choosing the latter gives you the option to share your whereabouts indefinitely, until the end of the day or for one hour. You can monitor how much time is left before your location will no longer be shared.

>> **See all the message attachments at once.** Tap the *i*-in-a-circle (Details) button and you can browse in one place all the photos and videos from your conversation.

>> **Keep Messages history.** You can keep your entire Messages history on the iPad permanently, for one year, or for 30 days. Tap Settings ➪ Messages ➪ Keep Messages and make your choice.

You are now a certified iMessage — and email — maven.

Chapter **6**

Maps Are Where It's At

With Maps on the iPad, you can quickly and easily discover exactly where you are, find nearby restaurants and businesses, get turn-by-turn driving instructions from any address to any other address, and see real-time traffic information and a photographic street view of many locations as well.

Apple says Maps is "beautifully designed from the ground up (and the sky down)," and we have to agree. But beyond its good looks, zooming in and out is faster than ever, and the spoken turn-by-turn navigation with real-time traffic updates actually works in most places. Plus it has a cool 3D flyover view.

Maps offers directions for public transit in numerous US and Chinese cities, with more cities promised. The free Google Maps app (available in the iTunes App Store), on the other hand, has directions for using public transportation in more cities than Apple Maps, at least for now. We keep both apps on our iPhones and iPads; you might want to do so as well.

REMEMBER

You can't use the Maps app unless you're connected to the Internet via Wi-Fi, 3G, or 4G. See Chapter 2 to find out how to connect.

Finding Your Current Location with Maps

We start with something supremely simple yet extremely useful — determining your current location. At the risk of sounding like self-help gurus, here's how to find yourself:

1. **Tap the Maps icon on your Home screen.**

2. **Tap the Location Services icon in the upper-right corner of the screen.**

   If you haven't used Maps previously, an alert will ask if you want to allow Maps to access your location while you use the app. You do, so tap Allow. (Tapping the other option, Don't Allow, renders Maps all but useless.)

   The icon turns dark blue, as shown in the margin, which assures you that Location Services is doing its thing and you'll see a blue circle on the map (see Figure 6-1), which indicates your approximate location.

REMEMBER

If you tap, drag the map, or zoom in or out, your iPad continues to update your location, but it doesn't continue to center the marker. When you tap the Location Services icon, it turns dark blue (refer to Figure 6-1) to indicate that your current location is in the middle of the screen. If you tap, drag, rotate, or zoom the map (that is, do anything that moves the current location indicator from the center of the screen), the icon turns white with a blue outline. So, if the icon is all blue, your current location is currently in the middle of the screen; if the icon is white with a blue outline, your current location is anywhere except the middle of the screen.

FIGURE 6-1:
A blue marker shows your GPS location.

REMEMBER

Unless, that is, you're using the satellite view, in which case you'll see gray instead of blue. You find out more about these views shortly.

HOW DOES MAPS DO THAT?

Maps uses iPad's Location Services to determine your approximate location using available information from your wireless data network. Wi-Fi–only models use local Wi-Fi networks; iPad Wi-Fi + 3G and 4G models use assisted GPS plus cellular data. If you're not using Location Services, turning it off conserves the battery. (To turn it off, tap Settings ➪ General ➪ Location Services.) Don't worry if Location Services is turned off when you tap the arrow icon — you're prompted to turn Location Services on. Keep in mind that it may not be available in all areas at all times.

Searching

The Maps app wouldn't be very useful if you couldn't use it to find things. In the following sections, we show you how to search for places you want to go and people you want to see — including people stored as contacts.

Finding a person, place, or thing

To find a person, place, or thing with Maps, follow these steps:

1. **Tap the search field at the top-left of the screen to make the keyboard appear, and then type what you're looking for.**

   You can search for addresses, zip codes, intersections, towns, landmarks, and businesses by category and by name, or in combinations such as *New York, NY 10022; pizza 60645;* or even *BBQ Lockhart TX.*

2. **If the letters you type match names in your contacts list, the matching contacts appear in a list below the search field; tap a name to see a map of that contact's location.**

   Maps is smart about it, too; it displays only the names of contacts that have a street address. See the section "Connecting maps and contacts," later in this chapter, for details.

3. **When you finish typing, tap Search.**

   After a few seconds, a map appears. If you searched for a single location, it's marked with a pushpin. If you searched for a category (*BBQ Lockhart TX,* for example), you see multiple pushpins, one for each matching location, as shown in Figure 6-2.

TIP

When you tap the search field, a handy drop-down list shows the search terms you've used recently. Tap any item in the list to search for it again.

Connecting maps and contacts

Maps and contacts go together like peanut butter and jelly. In this section, you discover two helpful tasks that illustrate maps and contacts at work.

To see a map of a contact's street address, follow these steps:

1. Tap in the search field, and begin typing the contact's name.

The list of matching contacts and locations is updated as you type.

2. Tap the contact's name whose address you want to see on the map.

A pin appears on the map at that contact's address.

FIGURE 6-2:
If you search for BBQ Lockhart TX, you see pushpins for all BBQ joints near Lockhart, Texas.

If you find a location by typing an actual street address in the search field, you can add that location to one of your contacts or create a contact with a location you've found. To do either one, follow these steps:

1. Tap the location's pushpin on the map.

That location's info appears as an overlay, as shown in Figure 6-3.

2. Scroll to the bottom of the info overlay and tap Create New Contact or Add to Existing Contact, whichever is applicable.

3. Fill in the new contact information and tap Done. Or select an existing contact from the list that appears and tap Done.

REMEMBER

You work with your contacts by tapping the Contacts icon on your Home screen. Go to Chapter 12 to find out more about the Contacts app.

Don't forget that you can swipe across your iPad screen with four or five fingers to switch apps. So if you're in Contacts, a four- or five-finger swipe from right to left should bring you back to the Maps app. If you have a lot of open apps, you might need more than one swipe to get back to the Maps app.

And don't forget that you can also use a four-finger swipe upward or double-press the Home button to reveal the multitasking screen and switch between Contacts and Maps (or any open apps, for that matter).

TIP

If nothing happens when you swipe with four or five fingers, tap Settings ⇨ General, scroll down to the Multitasking Gestures On/Off switch, and make sure it's on.

You can also use the Slide Over or Split Screen feature with Maps, to see two apps at once on iPads that support those features.

FIGURE 6-3:
The info screen for Black's Barbecue appears as an overlay.

Viewing, Zooming, and Panning

The preceding section talks about how to find just about anything with Maps. Now here's a look at some ways that you can use what you find. First, you need to know how to work with what you see on the screen. Three views are available at any time: standard, transit, and satellite. Select a view by tapping the little *i*-in-a-circle in the upper-right corner of the screen; an overlay appears with the view buttons and several other options, as shown in Figure 6-4.

FIGURE 6-4:
Tap the little *i*-in-a-circle to see these options.

In standard, transit, or satellite view, you can zoom to see either more or less of the map — or scroll (pan) to see what's above, below, or to the left or right of the current screen, as follows:

>> **Zoom out:** Pinch the map or tap using *two* fingers. To zoom out even more, pinch or tap using two fingers again.

The two-finger tap may be new to you. Simply tap with two fingers touching the screen simultaneously (rather than the usual one finger).

REMEMBER

>> **Zoom in:** Unpinch the map or double-tap (the usual way — with just one finger) the spot you want to zoom in on. Unpinch or double-tap with one finger again to zoom in even more. An *unpinch* (some people refer to this gesture as a *spread*) is the opposite of a pinch. Start with your thumb and a finger together and then spread them apart.

TIP

You can unpinch also with two hands (using two fingers or two thumbs), but you'll probably find that a single-handed pinch and unpinch are handier.

>> **Scroll:** Flick or drag up, down, left, or right to pan your view of the map.

Drag with two fingers to see the map from a three-dimensional bird's-eye view (not available in all locations).

Saving Time with Favorites, Categories, and Recents

In Maps, three tools can save you from typing the same locations repeatedly: favorites, recents, and contacts. You access them on the overlay displayed when you tap in the search field at the top of the screen. The following sections give you the lowdown on these tools.

Favorites

Favorites in the Maps app work like bookmarks in Safari. When you have a location you want to save as a favorite so that you can reuse it later without typing a single character, follow these steps:

1. **Tap the location's name or pushpin.**

   The info overlay for that location appears. (Refer to Figure 6-3.)

2. **Tap the Add to Favorites button near the bottom of the overlay.**

After you add a favorite, you can recall it at any time. To do so, tap the search field as though you were going to search for a location, and then tap Favorites at the bottom of the overlay. You can then tap the favorite's name to see it on the map.

TIP

The first things you should make favorites are your home and work addresses and their zip codes. You'll use these all the time with Maps, so you might as well add them to Favorites now to avoid typing them over and over.

TIP

Use zip code favorites to find nearby businesses. Choose the zip code favorite, and then type what you're looking for, such as *78729 pizza*, *60645 gas station*, or *90201 Starbucks*.

To delete a favorite from the Favorites list: Tap the – sign in a red circle to the left of the favorite's name and then tap the red Delete button.

When you've finished using Favorites, tap Cancel or the little x in the search field to return to the category buttons and recents list.

By the way, you can drop a pushpin anywhere on a map even if you don't know an exact address or zip code. Think of a *pushpin* as a temporary favorite.

Dropping a pushpin is simple: Press the location where you want the pin to appear, and hold down for two or three seconds until the pin appears with either *Dropped Pin,* the street address, or both. Press and drag the pin to move it to a new location.

To save a dropped pin as a favorite, tap the Add to Favorites button at the bottom of its info overlay.

To share a location, tap the share icon (shown in the margin) to send this location to others via AirDrop, Messages, Mail, FaceBook, and more.

Finally, to remove a marked location pin, tap the Edit Location button in its info overlay and then tap Remove Marker.

Categories & Recents

When you tap inside the search field, eight category buttons — Food, Drinks, Shopping, Travel, Services, Fun, Health, and Transport — appear below the search field. Tap one to find nearby attractions of that type.

Maps automatically remembers locations you've searched for and directions you've viewed in its recents list, which appears below the category buttons. To see a recent item on the map, tap the item's name.

To clear a recent item, swipe it from right to left and then tap the Remove button that appears.

You can no longer clear the entire list. Beginning with iOS 10, you can clear only individual items from the list, one at a time.

Smart Map tricks

The Maps app has more tricks up its sleeve. Here are a few nifty features that you may find useful.

Getting route maps and driving directions

You can get route maps and driving directions to any location from any location (within reason; a former tech editor tried to get driving directions from 1600 Pennsylvania Ave. in Washington, DC, to 10 Downing Street in London, but that didn't work). Just follow these steps:

1. **Tell your iPad to get directions for you.**

   Do one of the following:

   - Tap the big blue Directions button in any location's info overlay.

   - Just ask Siri by pressing and holding down the Home button, and saying, "How do I get to *(fill in the blank)*?" This method, of course, works only if your iPad includes Siri. (See Chapter 14 for more on Siri.)

2. **Tap the From or To field if you need to change the starting or ending point of your trip.**

3. **(Optional) If you need to swap the starting and ending locations, tap the little up-and-down arrows button between the Start and End fields.**

4. **When the start and end locations are correct, tap the Route button in the upper-right corner of the Directions overlay.**

   Suggested routes appear on the map, as shown in Figure 6-5.

If multiple routes exist, Maps shows you up to three, as in Figure 6-5. To switch routes, just tap the route you want to switch to. Note that the text at the bottom of the list on the left updates to tell you the time and distance of the selected route (38 minutes – 30 miles – US Highway 183 S in Figure 6-5).

5. **(Optional) Tap the Drive, Walk, or Transit tab (bottom) to choose driving, walking, or public transportation directions.**

   The transit view, not shown, is just the map view with added information about bus and train routes and stations. At present, it's available in only a handful of cities in the US and China, with the promise of additional cities soon.

6. **If Maps suggests several routes, select one by tapping its light blue line or balloon on the map or by tapping it in the list.**

   In Figure 6-5, the second 38-minute route is selected.

TIP

   Tap the little *i*-in-a-circle in the upper-right corner of the map and then tap the Show Traffic button to help you decide which route will be most expedient.

FIGURE 6-5:
Three routing options for travel from the State Capitol in Austin, Texas, to Black's Barbecue in Lockhart, Texas.

7. **Tap the Go button for the route you want.**

When you tap the Go button, a series of stark white-on-black road signs appear in the top-left corner of the map, one for each step in the directions, as shown in Figure 6-6.

8. **Navigate your directions by swiping the road signs to the left or right or by choosing from a list:**

- *Road signs:* Swipe right or left on the road signs to see the next or previous step in your route. Or just drive, and the map directions will update automatically as you proceed. The gray and white dots at the bottom indicate that this is the 6th of 11 steps.

- *List:* If you prefer to see your driving directions displayed as a list, swipe upward on the gray bar at the top of the button that says To Black's Barbec. . . in Figure 6-6 and the steps will appear in an overlay, as shown in Figure 6-7.

FIGURE 6-6:
The road signs show you each step of your route.

FIGURE 6-7:
Step-by-step driving directions displayed as a list.

Tap any step in the list to see that leg of the trip displayed on the map. Tap outside the list to return to the map.

NEW

iOS 11 introduces lane guidance to Maps navigation. When you're approaching a multilane interchange, lane-guidance arrows will appear at the top of the screen, as shown in Figure 6-8, to help you avoid missing your turn or exit. (As mentioned previously, Maps is less useful on Wi-Fi–only models.)

Getting traffic info in real time

You can find out the traffic conditions for the map you're viewing by tapping the little *i*-in-a-circle in the lower-right corner of the map and then tapping Show Traffic. If it says Hide Traffic, don't tap — the option is already on.

Major roadways are color-coded to inform you of the current traffic speed, as shown in Figure 6-9. Here's the key: Orange dots show slowdowns, and red dashes show stop-and-go traffic.

To see an incident report, tap a red minus-sign marker.

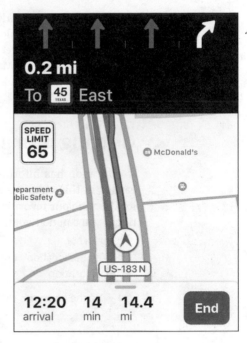

FIGURE 6-8:
The new lane-guidance arrows help you avoid missing your turn or exit.

FIGURE 6-9:
Downtown Los Angeles at 2:08 p.m. on a Saturday has more traffic than most cities at the peak of rush hour.

Traffic info doesn't work in every location. The only way to find out is to give it a try and see whether color codes appear. And because Maps works only when you have a network connection, you won't see traffic info if you're not connected. You might try Google Maps or Waze if Maps doesn't provide what you need in a particular location; we keep all three — Maps, Google Maps, and Waze — on all our iDevices.

Getting more info about a location

If a location has information available, it appears in the overlay. As we explain earlier in this chapter, you can get directions to or from that location, add the location to your favorites or contacts, or create a contact from it. With some locations, you can do two more things from the location's info overlay:

>> Tap the location's email address to launch the Mail app and send an email to the location.

>> Tap the location's URL to launch Safari and view the location's website.

3

The Multimedia iPad

Enjoy listening to music, podcasts, and audiobooks, plus get tips and hints for making your listening even more enjoyable.

Learn how to capture good video with your iPad, watch video on your iPad, and share video with others with (what else?) your iPad.

Find out how to shoot photos with your iPad, store them, sync them, and do all kinds of other interesting things with them.

Join the e-book craze: Download and read a good book right on your iPad with the nifty iBooks app and store.

Chapter **7**

Get in Tune(s): Audio on Your iPad

Your iPad is one of the best media players ever — and it's superb for playing audio and video. In this chapter, we show you how to use your iPad to listen to music and other audio content; in Chapter 8, we cover video.

We start with a quick tour of the iPad's Music app. Then we look at how to listen to music on your iPad. After you're nice and comfy with using it this way, we show you how to customize your listening experience so that it's just the way you like it. Then we offer a few tips to help you get the most out of using your iPad as an audio player. Finally, we show you how to use the iTunes app to buy music, audiobooks, videos, and more, and how to download free content.

We assume that you already synced your iPad with your computer or with iCloud and that your iPad contains audio content — songs, podcasts, or audiobooks. If you don't have any audio on your iPad yet, we humbly suggest that you get some (flip to Chapter 3 and follow the instructions for syncing, or launch the iTunes Store app and buy a song or download a free podcast) before you read the rest of this chapter.

Okay, now that you have some audio content on your iPad to play with, are you ready to rock?

Introducing Your iPad's Music Player

To use your iPad to listen to music, just tap the Music icon on the Home screen. Then, at the bottom of the screen that appears, you should see four (non–Apple Music subscribers) or five (Apple Music subscribers) icons, as described in the next section.

If you don't see these icons, tap the back icon in the upper-left corner of the screen (the one that looks like an angle bracket pointing to the left, as shown in the margin).

Before we can tell you about the Music app, you need to know about Apple Music and iTunes Match subscription services, because almost everything in the Music app works differently if you subscribe to one or both. So, to avoid confusion, read the nearby "Apple Music and iTunes Match Rock" sidebar before you do anything else.

APPLE MUSIC AND ITUNES MATCH ROCK

iTunes Match and Apple Music are a pair of subscription music services offered by Apple.

iTunes Match is the older of the two, designed to let you store all your music in iCloud so you can stream all your songs to any Mac, PC, or iDevice. It performs its magic by first determining which songs in your iTunes library are available in iCloud. And because tens of millions of songs are up there already, chances are that most of your music is already in iCloud. Then, iTunes proceeds to upload a copy of every song it *can't* match (which is much faster than uploading your entire music library). The result is that you can stream any song in your iTunes library on any of your Macs, PCs, or iDevices, regardless of whether the song files are available on the particular device.

As a bonus, all the music that iTunes matches plays back from iCloud at 256-Kbps AAC DRM-free quality even if your original copy was lower quality. (You can even replace your lower bit-rate copies by downloading higher-quality versions.)

You can store up to 100,000 songs in iCloud — songs you purchased from the iTunes Store don't count. The result is that only tracks or albums you specify are stored locally on your devices, saving gigabytes of precious storage space.

At just $24.99 a year, iTunes Match is a bargain, but Apple Music, introduced in early 2015, may be a better (albeit more expensive) option. It's a subscription music service that provides access to more than 40 million songs on demand for just $9.99 a month ($14.99 a month for you and up to five family members) or only $4.99 a month if you're a student.

That's good, but what's even better is that Siri now knows more about music than most people. Of course she can play songs, albums, artists, or genres by name, but you can also ask her to play things such as the number-one song in October of 1958 or music by a particular artist; in a few seconds, you'll be listening to whatever your heart desires.

Both services require Internet access, but as long as you're connected you can have access to your entire music library (up to 100,000 tracks with iTunes Match) or access to over 40 million songs (with Apple Music) on your iPad or other device. Either one means you won't have to worry about filling up your iDevice with music.

We'd be remiss if we didn't warn you that unless you have an unlimited data plan (on your cellular-equipped iPad), you might want to disable iTunes Match and Apple Music over cellular by tapping Settings ➪ Music, and then turning off the Use Cellular Data switch. Both subscription services are reasonably priced, but data surcharges could cost you a lot if you're not careful. And if you decide to partake in one or both services, it's a good idea to back up your media collection first, just in case.

Finally, here's our favorite tip for subscribers to either service: Before you go off the grid — say, on a plane flight or a cruise — tap the iCloud download button next to all the songs, albums, and playlists you want to have available when you're at 30,000 feet or out on the ocean.

You're welcome.

It's music, just not YOUR music

Before we look at managing and listening to *your* music, let's take a quick look at the other tabs in the Music app.

If you're not an Apple Music subscriber, you'll see four tabs: Library, Connect, Radio, and Search. If you're an Apple Music subscriber, you'll see Library, Radio, and Search, as well as Browse and For You, both of which are filled with music that's *not* technically yours, though you can listen to it as much as you care to for $9.99 ($14.99 for a family up to six people) per month.

TIP

Apple Music subscribers can listen to (almost) any song, album, or playlist that they discover; nonsubscribers can listen to a preview and purchase (almost) any song, album, or playlist they discover.

Here's a quick rundown of all the tabs:

>> **Library:** The Library tab displays the music available on this iPad organized in a variety of ways. Tap Library in the upper-left corner to choose Recently Added,

Playlists, Artists, Albums, Songs, or Home Sharing. You'll then see your music organized accordingly.

Or tap Edit at the top of the Library menu to display additional criteria (Music Video, Genres, Compilations, and Composers); tap to add them to the Library menu.

» **Connect (non-Apple Music subscribers):** This tab offers news and gossip direct from artists you choose to follow (by tapping the Follow button on their artist page). Or tap the See Who You're Following link near the top of the page to enable Automatically Follow Artists (when you add their songs to your music library). Not every artist "connects" at this time, but new artists appear regularly. If you can't connect with your favorite artist now, try again in a few weeks or months.

» **Radio:** If you've ever listened to the radio, you will grok the Radio tab immediately.

» **Search:** Find tracks, artists, composers, and albums that you can then add to your library (subscribers) or audition and purchase (non-subscribers).

» **Browse (Apple Music subscribers only):** Here you'll find the latest releases, plus song and album charts for dozens of musical genres as well as curated playlists featuring new songs and artists. Again, you'll see this tab only if Show Apple Music is enabled in Settings ⇨ Music.

» **For You (Apple Music subscribers only):** Many would say this tab — For You — is the best thing about the Music app, and we have to agree. Here you'll find music that iTunes thinks you'll enjoy: playlists, albums, artists, and songs that (mostly) aren't part of your iTunes library. It's scary how often iTunes suggests music we enjoy; these days we listen to the For You tab more than we listen to the music we already own. Remember, you see this tab only if Show Apple Music is enabled in Settings ⇨ Music.

The Radio, Connect, For You, and Browse tabs all operate in the same fashion; each is a long page filled with content. Scroll down to see more, and then tap any item to see additional information.

While you're browsing these tabs, you'll encounter several small icons; here's what each of them does:

» Tap the + icon to add this song, album, or playlist to the library (available only to Apple Music subscribers).

» Tap the heart icon to tell iTunes you love this artist, song, album, or playlist, which helps the For You tab suggest music it thinks you'll enjoy.

» Tap the ellipsis icon to see additional options, which may include Play Next, Play Later, Add to a Playlist, Create Station, Download, and Share.

» Tap the Play icon to listen to this song, album, or playlist.

By now we're sure you're ready to start listening to some music. We begin with some radio because we know every one of you has Radio (and some of you may *not* have anything in your Library tab yet).

To get started, tap the Music icon on your Home screen and then tap the Radio icon at the bottom of the screen.

The first thing you see at the top of the screen is Beats 1, Apple's live radio station. It's on the air worldwide 24 hours a day, 7 days a week, with world-class programming, interviews, and music. To listen, tap the Play Now button.

If Beats 1 isn't your cup of tea and you're an Apple Music subscriber, tap the Radio Stations button to see additional radio stations organized by the following:

» **Featured Stations:** This handful of stations has been handpicked for your enjoyment by the nice folks at Apple. Tap one to listen to it.

» **All Genres:** These stations are organized by genre, as shown in Figure 7-1. Tap a genre to see stations that play that type of music.

Did we mention that a limited number of iTunes Radio stations are available on your iPhone, iPad, iPod touch, Mac, PC, and Apple TV for free? You'll hear the occasional ad, but if you hate ads, you can listen without 'em if you subscribe to Apple Music.

So that's how you find a station; tap a station to start listening to it.

When a station is playing, the name of the current song appears near the

FIGURE 7-1:
Scroll down past Featured Stations to find stations organized by genre.

bottom of the screen (*"Louie Louie"* in Figure 7-1); tap it for additional options, as shown in Figure 7-2.

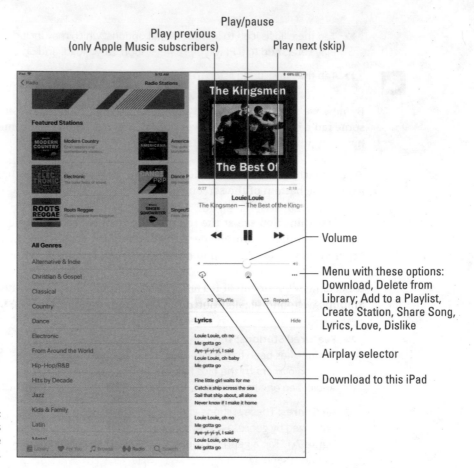

Play/pause

Play previous
(only Apple Music subscribers)

Play next (skip)

Volume

Menu with these options:
Download, Delete from
Library; Add to a Playlist,
Create Station, Share Song,
Lyrics, Love, Dislike

Airplay selector

Download to this iPad

FIGURE 7-2:
Tap the song's
name to see
these options.

If you want stations to play more (or fewer) songs you'll like, tap the ellipsis (. . .) and then tap the Love (heart) or Dislike (heart with a slash) icon whenever a song you love is playing. The more you do this, the better the suggestions in the For You tab will be.

And that, friends, is pretty much all you need to know to use and enjoy radio stations in the Music app.

Your Music Library

Moving right along, let's look at how to listen to music you already own, which is to say the music in your iTunes library. If you haven't already launched the Music app, do so now, and then tap Library at the bottom of the screen.

A library without library cards

Music in the Library tab becomes available by subscribing to iTunes Match, subscribing to Apple Music, buying music as described near the end of this chapter, syncing with iTunes (as described in Chapter 3), or any combination of the four.

 Note that if you're an iTunes Match or Apple Music subscriber, a music file doesn't have to be actually *stored* on your iPad to be available on the Library tab. As long as you have Internet access, you can stream songs that aren't on your device over the air. But if you want to ensure that you'll be able to listen to a song, an album, or a playlist anytime you like, with or without an Internet connection, you'll have to tap the download button (shown in the margin). And you can always download music you purchased, regardless of whether you subscribe to anything.

Readers with older devices surely remember previous versions of the Music app, which served up Artist, Album, Song, and Playlist buttons at the bottom of the main screen. You'll be happy to know that those useful features and many more are right here in the library, albeit somewhat hidden in the Library drop-down menu at the top left of the screen.

The drop-down menu at the top-left corner of the screen lets you view your music organized in various ways, including Recently Added, Playlists, Artists, Albums, Songs, Downloaded Music, and Home Sharing by default.

TIP

Tap the Edit button at the top of this menu to add Music Videos, Genres, Compilations, or Composers, or to hide one or more of the default items.

Tap Songs, as shown in Figure 7-3, to view your songs in alphabetical order.

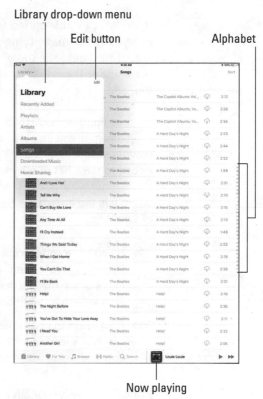

Library drop-down menu

Edit button

Alphabet

Now playing

FIGURE 7-3:
To see more of the songs or albums you've listened to lately, tap Recently Added.

If the list is longer than one screen (which it probably is), flick upward to scroll down or flick downward to scroll up. An easier way to find a song is to tap one of the little letters on the right side of the screen to jump directly to artists whose names start with that letter. In Figure 7-3, for example, that letter is B. The letters on the right are extremely small, so unless you have tiny fingers, you may have to settle for a letter close to the one you want or tap several times until you select the correct one.

TIP

Our technical editor for older editions, the late Dennis Cohen, suggested that using a stylus instead of your finger may help. He was probably right.

But there's an even easier way to find an artist — or a song, an album, or a music compilation, for that matter. Tell Siri what you want to hear. All you have to do is ask (see "Using your voice to control your music," later in this chapter, for details).

If Siri isn't a viable option for you, you can achieve the same effect by typing your query. Tap the magnifying glass at the bottom of the screen and then tap in the search field near the top of the screen to activate the virtual keyboard. Now type the name of the artist (or song or album) you're looking for, tap the Search button, and enjoy.

So choosing Songs, Artists, Albums, or Playlists, or Downloaded Music from the drop-down menu displays a list of your songs, artists, albums, playlists, or songs downloaded to this iPad. Tap any item in the list to hear it. Or choose Recently Added to see a list of albums that contain songs you've added recently.

When you tap an artist's name in the main list (or in a list of search results), one of two things occurs:

» **If you have songs from more than one album by an artist in your music library:** A list of albums and the songs they contain appears. Tap a song to play it or tap the first item in the list of songs on a particular album — Shuffle — to hear all songs on that album at random.

» **If all songs in your music library by that artist are on the same album or aren't associated with a specific album:** A list of all songs by that artist appears.

Either way, tap a song and the music starts.

Now for the good news: All the other items that may appear in the pop-up menu — Albums, Genres, Composers, and Compilations — work just like Artists. And, of course, Songs is nothing more than a long list of every song in your library. So you now know how to display and browse your library seven ways!

Play it again, list

Choose Playlists from the drop-down menu at the top of the screen to view your playlists. If you don't have any playlists on your iPad, or don't know what a playlist is, don't sweat it. If you had any, you'd find them here; if you don't know what they are, let us tell you.

Playlists let you create and organize collections of songs around a particular theme or mood: opera arias, romantic ballads, British invasion, or whatever. Or you can make playlists of your favorite albums, favorite songs of all times, or greatest hits collections. (Younger folks sometimes call playlists *mixes*; older folks think of them as the digital equivalent of a *mix tape*.)

Tap a playlist and a list of the songs it contains appears. If the list is longer than one screen, flick upward to scroll down. Tap a song in the list and it plays. Or tap Shuffle (above the list of songs) to hear a song at random from the playlist; all subsequent songs will then play at random.

That's all there is to selecting and playing songs from your playlists.

TIP

It's easier to create playlists in iTunes on your computer than in the Music app on your iPad.

As you see in Chapter 3, you can sync playlists with iTunes on your computer. Or if you're an Apple Music subscriber, all your playlists are always available on all your devices.

Although it may be easier to create playlists in iTunes on your computer, this is an iPad book, so here's how to create playlists in the Music app on your iPad:

1. **Tap the Music icon.**

2. **Tap the Library icon at the bottom of the screen.**

3. **Choose Playlists from the Library drop-down menu at the top left.**

4. **Tap New at the top of the screen on the right.**

5. **Tap the Playlist Name field and type a name for your new playlist.**

6. **Tap Add Music.**

   The Add Songs overlay appears.

7. **Tap Playlists, Artists, Albums, Songs, Videos, Genres, Composers, Compilations, or Downloaded Music in the overlay to begin choosing songs for this playlist.**

   If you chose Songs, an alphabetical list of songs appears.

If you chose any of the other options, a list of whatever you selected — Genres, Composers, Albums, and such — appears. You need to tap an album, genre, composer, or whatever before you see a list of songs.

If you scroll down past the last item on the list — Downloaded Music — you'll see a selection of recently added items you can choose to add to this playlist.

Or tap the Search Music field and type the name of the song, artist, album, or whatever.

Finally, note the little + that appears to the right of each song in every list.

8. **Tap the + next to a song name to add the song to your playlist.**

Repeat this process until you've added all the songs you want on this playlist.

9. **Tap the Done button in the upper-right corner.**

If you create a playlist on your iPad and then sync with your computer, that playlist remains on the iPad and will also appear in iTunes on your computer. Or if you're an Apple Music subscriber, the playlist will appear on all your other devices within a few minutes.

The playlists remain until you delete them — in iTunes or on your iPad. To remove a playlist in iTunes, select the playlist's name in the source list and then press Delete or Backspace. To remove a playlist on your iPad, long-press it and then choose Delete from Library. An alert warns that the playlist will be deleted from all your devices; tap Delete Playlist to axe it.

You can also edit playlists on your iPad. To do so, tap the playlist you want to edit and then tap the Edit button near the top-right corner of the screen to do any (or all) of the following:

>> **Move a song up or down in the playlist:** A little icon with three gray bars appears to the right of each song, as shown in Figure 7-4. Drag the icon up to move the song higher in the list or drag down to move the song lower in the list.

>> **Add more songs to the playlist:** Tap the + Add Songs button above the list.

>> **Delete a song from the playlist:** Tap the – sign to the left of the song name. Note that deleting a song from the playlist doesn't remove the song from your iPad or your iTunes library; it removes it only from this particular playlist.

When you finish editing, tap the Done button in the top-right corner of the screen. That's all there is to creating and managing playlists on your iPad.

Share and share alike

Two of our favorite features on the iPad have always been Home Sharing and Family Sharing. The former lets you use your iPad to stream music, movies, TV shows, and other media content from the iTunes library on your Mac or PC. The latter lets you share purchases from iTunes, iBooks, and the App Store with up to five more people in your family without having to share account information. Now you can pay for family purchases with the same credit card and approve kids' spending right from your iPad or iPhone.

Here's the scoop on both types of sharing: Home and Family.

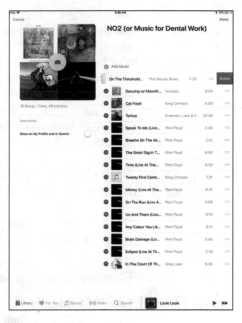

FIGURE 7-4:
Tap the red – sign and then tap the red Delete button to remove a song.

Home Sharing feature

Turn on Home Sharing to stream music, movies, TV shows, and other media from your computer to your iPad. The big gotcha here is that Home Sharing is only available *if your iPad and your computer are on the same Wi-Fi network and use the same Apple ID.*

To make Home Sharing work for you, first enable it on your computer, and then enable it on your iPad. To set up Home Sharing on your computer, launch iTunes and then Choose File ⇨ Home Sharing ⇨ Turn on Home Sharing. Type your Apple ID and password in the appropriate fields and click the Turn On Home Sharing button. From now on, as long as iTunes is open, your iTunes library will be available for Home Sharing on your Wi-Fi network.

Once Home Sharing is enabled on your computer (and your iPad and computer are on the same Wi-Fi network), enable Home Sharing on your iPad by tapping Library at the bottom of the screen, tapping the Library drop-down menu, and then tapping the last item, Home Sharing. If any shared libraries are available, you'll see them listed; tap one or more to make their contents available on your iPad for as long as you're connected to this Wi-Fi network.

Here's where it gets cool: Now, when you look at Library, rather than just seeing the playlists, artists, and songs you've synced with your iPad (and your Apple Music), you'll now see all the playlists, artists, songs, albums, and everything else in the iTunes libraries on the Home Sharing computers as well. And you'll continue to see the shared content in your Music app as long as your iPad remains connected to this Wi-Fi network.

To switch back to seeing just your music, reverse the process and disable Home Sharing for all other libraries.

Movies and TV shows shared via Home Sharing don't appear in the Music app. Look for them in the Videos app, as described in Chapter 8.

Home Sharing is simple, elegant, and free. If you've never used this feature, what are you waiting for?

Family Sharing feature

Family Sharing lets up to six members of the same family share everything they buy at the iTunes, iBooks, and App Stores. It also provides sharing of family photos and a family calendar, location sharing, and more. Finally, if you have a family subscription to Apple Music, up to five additional family members can use Apple Music at no additional cost.

To set up Family Sharing, one adult in the household (known as the family organizer) invites up to five family members to join and agrees to pay for all iTunes, iBooks, and App Store purchases those family members initiate while part of Family Sharing.

When any family member buys an app, a song, an album, a movie, or an iBook, it is billed directly to the family organizer's account. The item is then added to the purchaser's account and shared with the rest of the family. The organizer can turn on Ask to Buy for any family member to require approval for any purchase. When a purchase is initiated, a notification is sent to the family organizer, who can review the item and approve or decline the request from his or her iPad.

To become the family organizer, open Settings, tap iCloud, and then tap Set Up Family Sharing.

After you enable Family Sharing and invite your family members to join, everyone will have immediate access to other members' music, movies, TV shows, books, and apps, so you can download whatever you want to your iPad with a tap anytime you like without having to share an Apple ID or password.

The fine print says: You can be part of only one family group at a time and may switch to a different family group only twice per year. The features of Family Sharing may vary based on country and content eligibility.

Family Sharing requires iCloud, a personal Apple ID signed in to iCloud and iTunes, and iOS 8 or later and OS X Yosemite or later (Mac) or Windows 7 or later (PC).

Taking Control of Your Tunes

Now that you have the basics down, take a look at some other things you can do with the Music app, starting with the controls you see when a song is playing.

REMEMBER

If you don't see the controls when a song is playing, tap the song name near the bottom of the screen.

Now, here's how to use those controls:

>> **Back:** Tap to return to whichever list you used last — Playlists, Artists, Songs, and so on.

>> **Playhead and scrubber bar:** Drag the gray dot (the playhead) along the scrubber bar to skip to any point within the song. Note that the dot is near the left end of the bar in Figure 7-5, which means the person has heard roughly 5 percent of the song so far.

>> **Time elapsed and remaining:** Just below the scrubber bar on the left is the amount of time this song has played already (0:27 in Figure 7-5) and how much of this song remains to be played (-2:06 in the figure).

>> **Song name, artist, and album:** Near the top of the screen, you can see the name of the currently playing song, artist, and album.

>> **Restart/previous track/rewind icon:** Tap once to go to the beginning of the track. Tap twice to go to the start of the preceding track in the list. Touch and hold down this icon to rewind the song at double speed.

>> **Play/pause icon:** Tap to play or pause the song.

>> **Next track/fast forward icon:** Tap to skip to the next track in the list. Touch and hold down this icon to fast-forward through the song at double speed.

>> **Volume control:** Drag the little dot left or right to reduce or increase, respectively, the volume level.

>> **AirPlay selector icon:** You may or may not see the AirPlay selector icon (shown in the margin and visible in Figure 7-5). AirPlay lets you stream content

wirelessly over Wi-Fi from your iPad to any AirPlay-enabled device. Check out the "Playing with AirPlay" sidebar for the details.

>> **Shuffle button:** Tap once to shuffle songs and play them in random order. The letters become white and the background becomes red when shuffling is enabled, as shown in Figure 7-5. Tap the button again to play songs in order again and the icon returns to its original color (red letters) on a white background.

TIP

You can also shuffle tracks in any list of songs — such as playlists or albums — by tapping Shuffle, which appears at the top of the list.

FIGURE 7-5: These are the controls that appear when a song is playing.

- » **Repeat button:** Tap this button to hear the song, album, or playlist that's currently playing again when it finishes.

- » **More Options (. . .) icon:** Tap this icon to download this item to your iPad, delete it from your library, add it to a playlist, create a radio station based on it, share it, or love or dislike it. If you love this song, tapping the Love (heart) or Dislike (heart with a slash) icon will help the Music app choose more appropriate tracks in the For You tab.

TIP

If you're using the headset included with an iPhone or most headsets with inline controls, you can squeeze the mic to pause, and squeeze it again to play. You can also squeeze it twice in rapid succession to skip to the next song. Sweet!

And that, gentle reader, is all you need to know to enjoy listening to music (and podcasts and audiobooks) on your iPad. But wait! There's more! Although you now know all you need to know about listening to music, you can customize your listening experience to make it even better.

PLAYING WITH AIRPLAY

AirPlay is a wicked cool bit of technology baked into every copy of iOS. It enables you to wirelessly stream music, photos, and video to AirPlay-enabled devices such as Apple's AirPort Express Wi-Fi base station and second-generation (and later) Apple TVs, plus many third-party devices that have AirPlay technology, including (but not limited to) speakers and receivers.

The AirPlay selector icon (shown here), which is available in some apps and Control Center, can be quite shy. It will appear only if your iPad detects an AirPlay-enabled device on the same Wi-Fi network. Bob has two Apple TVs at his house, so he sees both when he taps his AirPlay selector icon.

Tapping one Apple TV or the other sends whatever is playing on the Music app to that Apple TV. The Apple TV, in turn, is connected to an HDTV via HDMI (an optical audio cable would suffice if you want to stream only audio, not video).

But wait — there's more! If you use an Apple TV as your AirPlay-enabled device, in addition to streaming music, video, or photos from your iPad to your HDTV, you can also stream from your Mac, PC, iPad, or iPod touch. Bob just loves his Apple TV and says it is one of his favorite Apple inventions and would be a bargain at twice the price.

Customizing Your Audio Experience

In this section, we cover some Music features designed to make your listening experience more enjoyable.

Setting preferences

You can change a few preference settings to customize your iPad-as-an-iPod experience.

Play all songs at the same volume level

The iTunes Sound Check option automatically adjusts the level of songs so that they play at the same volume relative to each other. That way, one song never blasts out your ears even if the recording level is much louder than that of the song before or after it. To tell the iPad to use these volume settings, you first have to turn on the feature in iTunes on your computer. Here's how to do that:

1. **Choose iTunes ⇨ Preferences (Mac) or Edit ⇨ Preferences (PC).**
2. **Click the Playback tab.**
3. **Select the Sound Check check box to enable it.**

Now, to tell the iPad to use the Sound Check settings from iTunes: On the iPad's Home screen, tap Settings ⇨ Music ⇨ Sound Check.

Choose an equalizer setting

An *equalizer* increases or decreases the relative levels of specific frequencies to enhance the sound you hear. Some equalizer settings emphasize the bass (low end) notes in a song; other equalizer settings make the higher frequencies more apparent. The iPad has more than a dozen equalizer presets, with names such as Acoustic, Bass Booster, Bass Reducer, Dance, Electronic, Pop, and Rock. Each one is ostensibly tailored to a specific type of music.

The way to find out whether you prefer using equalization is to listen to music while trying out different settings. To do that, first start listening to a song you like. Then, while the song is playing, follow these steps:

1. **On the Home screen, tap Settings ⇨ Music ⇨ EQ.**
2. **Tap different EQ presets (Pop, Rock, R&B, or Dance, for example), and listen carefully to the way they change how the song sounds.**

3. **When you find an equalizer preset that you think sounds good, press the Home button and you're finished.**

If you don't like any of the presets, tap Off at the top of the EQ list to turn off the equalizer.

WARNING

According to Apple's iPad battery information page (`www.apple.com/batteries/ipad.html`), applying an equalizer setting to song playback on your iPad can decrease battery life. So you need to decide which is more important to you: using equalization or maximizing battery life.

Set a volume limit for music (and videos)

You can instruct your iPad to limit the loudest listening level for audio or video. To do so, here's the drill:

1. **On the Home screen, tap Settings ⇨ Music ⇨ Volume Limit.**

2. **Drag the slider to adjust the maximum volume level to your liking.**

WARNING

The Volume Limit setting limits the volume of only music and videos. It doesn't apply to podcasts or audiobooks. And, although the setting works with any headset, headphones, or speakers plugged into the headset jack on your iPad, it doesn't affect sound played on your iPad's internal speaker.

Setting a sleep timer

If you like to fall asleep with music playing but don't want to leave your iPad playing music all night long, you can turn on its sleep timer.

Here's how:

1. **On the Home screen, tap the Clock icon.**

2. **In the lower-right corner, tap the Timer icon.**

3. **Set the number of hours and minutes you want music to play, and then tap the When Timer Ends button.**

4. **Tap the last item in the list, Stop Playing.**

TIP

If you don't see the Stop Playing item, don't be alarmed (semi-clever wordplay intended). You're simply looking at the middle (or the beginning) of the list of available alert sounds. To scroll to the bottom of the list and find the elusive Stop Playing item, flick upward on the list a few times.

5. **In the lower-right corner, tap the Start button.**

That's it! If you have music playing already, you're finished. If not, press the Home button, tap the Music icon, and select the music you want to listen to as you fall asleep. When the specified time period elapses, the music stops playing and your iPad goes to sleep. By then, we hope you're in slumberland as well.

Using your voice to control your music

Here's something cool: You can boss around your music by using nothing but your voice. Just press and hold down the Home button (or the equivalent button on a headset) and, after you hear the tone, you can:

>> **Play an album, an artist, or a playlist:** Say "Play" and then say "album," "artist," or "playlist," and the name of the album, artist, or playlist, respectively. You can issue these voice commands at any time except when you're on a phone call or having a FaceTime video chat. In other words, you don't have to have music playing for these voice commands to work.

>> **Shuffle the current playlist:** Say "Shuffle." This voice command works only if you're listening to a playlist.

>> **Find out more about the song that's playing:** Ask "What's playing?" "What song is this?" "Who sings this song?" or "Who is this song by?" Again, these commands work only if you're already listening to music.

>> **Get creative:** Siri has a much better grasp on music than before, so try asking her to do things like these:

- Play songs popular in 1973.

- Play music by The Beatles.

- Play the playlist "Music I Love."

- Play James Taylor's first album.

- Play some classic rock.

Siri can usually interpret commands such as these, and within seconds you'll be listening to exactly what you want to hear. Plus, if you're an Apple Music subscriber, you can ask Siri to play virtually any song in the iTunes Store (40 million plus at last count). Finally, because you're listening to this music on your iPad, you won't look stupid when you're talking to it!

WARNING

Although we found that controlling your music by speaking works most of the time, in noisy environments the iPad may mishear your verbal request and start playing the wrong song or artist or try to call someone on the phone. Using the wired headset helps. And syntax counts, so remember to use the exact wording in the list.

TIP

Siri can also identify songs playing in the background, just like the Shazam app we rave about in Chapter 18. Just ask Siri, "What song is playing?" and let her listen for a moment. She'll identify the song if she can — and she even has a sense of humor about it. When we asked her to identify "Come Together" by The Beatles, she replied, "This is The Beatles playing 'Come Together.' Right now."

By the way, Siri's song-identification prowess is powered by Shazam but doesn't require you to install the Shazam app. That said, we like all the other bells and whistles that the Shazam app brings to the party enough that we still recommend it.

Shopping with the iTunes Store App

Last but certainly not least, the iTunes Store app lets you use your iPad to download, buy, or rent just about anything you can download, buy, or rent with the iTunes application on your Mac or PC, including music, audiobooks, and videos. And, if you're fortunate enough to have an iTunes gift card or gift certificate in hand, you can redeem it directly from your iPad.

If you want to do any of those tasks, however, you must first sign in to your iTunes Store account. Tap Settings ➪ iTunes & App Store ➪ Sign In. Type your username and password, and then tap OK. Or, in the unlikely event that you don't have an iTunes Store account, tap Settings ➪ Store ➪ Create New Account, and follow the on-screen instructions.

After the iTunes Store knows who you are (and, more importantly, knows your credit card number, gift card balance, or PayPal info), tap the iTunes Store icon on your Home screen and shop until you drop.

Chapter **8**

iPad Videography

Picture this scene: The smell of popcorn permeates the room as you and your family congregate to watch the latest Hollywood blockbuster. A motion picture soundtrack swells up. The images on the screen are stunning. And all eyes are fixed on the iPad.

Okay, here comes the reality check. The iPad is not going to replace a wall-sized high-definition television as the centerpiece of your home theater, even if you have the comparatively mammoth 12.9-inch Retina display on the larger model iPad Pro. Then again, it's going to take a 4K TV to get a higher resolution in your living room than the gorgeous Retina displays on third-generation and later iPads and iPad Pros. Even the displays in the older iPad 2 look terrific. And now that the more recent iPad minis have also graduated to a Retina display, even a small-screen iPad is going to grab your attention.

Meantime, as you will discover, you can watch material that originates on the iPad on the bigger screen TV, too.

Bottom line: No matter which iPad you own, watching movies and other videos on Apple's prized tablet is a cinematic treat. What's more, you have front (FaceTime) and rear cameras that can help turn you into a filmmaker — right from the device.

And video on the iPad ventures into another area: video chat. You can keep in touch with friends and loved ones by gazing into each other's pupils. It's all done through *FaceTime*, a clever video chat program that comes with your iPad. In the interest of equal time, we'd also like to point out that you can do video chats on your iPad by downloading a popular third-party app such as Skype, among others.

We get to FaceTime later in this chapter. For now, and without any further ado, let's get on with the show!

Finding Stuff to Watch

iOS 11 brought a lot of changes to video. The biggest change is that the old Videos app is gone. In its place, Apple gave us the TV app, where you can find almost all of the streaming content available on your iPad, as well as movies and TV shows from the iTunes Store and anything shared from iTunes on your Mac or PC. (If you haven't done so yet, now is as good a time as any to read Chapter 3 for all the details on syncing.) Plus, you can watch streaming video from a host of third-party apps.

Apple offers videos on the iPad through the TV app, the iTunes Store, podcasts, courseware, and videos you've created. We describe all these options next.

Watching shows with the TV app

NEW

When you first launch the TV app, it opens on the Watch Now tab, alongside tabs for Library, Store, and Search. All of these tabs are designed for content from iTunes, third-party apps, and videos you've loaded onto your iPad through iTunes (or shared from iTunes). Videos you've made on your iPad are in the Photos app, which we get to later.

The Watch Now tab is the main point of the TV app. It allows you to find TV shows and movies, no matter where they are. It's almost like having an Apple TV box inside your iPad. For instance, at the time of this writing, Seth McFarland's new comedy *The Orville* is being offered under the What to Watch section of the TV app. Tap that show, and you get a new page with a description, an episode list, and a Play in FOX NOW button. Tap that button, and if the app is not already installed, you get a new screen inviting you to Get the Free FOX NOW app, as shown in Figure 8-1. A quick download later, and FOX NOW launches.

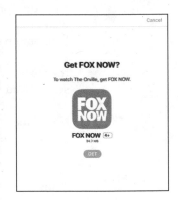

FIGURE 8-1:
Want to watch *The Orville?* The FOX NOW app is a tap away!

And that's the secret of the TV app. You don't need to know which network or service a given TV show is on to find it. The TV app acts as a centralized location for finding shows available in your region, be they on Netflix, ABC, NBC, CBS, Fox, HBO, iTunes, and many other services, including streaming services in other markets. When a show is available in two places, say iTunes and Netflix, you can choose which source you want to get it from.

TIP

Some streaming services, such as Netflix and HBO NOW, require subscriptions. Others, such as the ABC app, show commercials during streams. Still others, like HBO GO, rely on your cable or satellite subscription.

You can browse the TV app by genre, hits, trending movies, trending TV shows, and a list of recently watched shows.

NEW

In the Library tab at the bottom of the app, you find all the shows you've purchased or rented from iTunes as well as other videos. Tap the Library button in the upper-left corner of the screen, as shown in Figure 8-2, and you get options for Recently Added, TV Shows, Movies, Home Videos, Downloaded, and your shared iTunes Library, if you've turned on Home Sharing in iTunes on your Mac or PC.

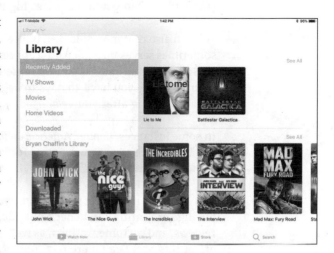

FIGURE 8-2:
The Library tab in the TV app is the new home for movies, TV shows, and downloaded videos.

The Store tab is a store for TV apps. Think of it as a sort of mini App Store with nothing but streaming video apps. Tap on one, say ABC, and it takes you to the App Store page for that app — even if you already have the app installed. We aren't sure why Apple did this, and we hope it gets smarter in the future.

Apple's new TV app is a one-stop shop for all your streaming needs. You can still choose to use any given streaming app on its own — you don't have to go through the TV app — but the TV app can be a great way of finding shows you're looking for and discovering new shows you didn't even know you wanted to watch.

Renting and buying at the iTunes Store

Although you can find all movies and TV shows on iTunes by using the TV app, you can also browse in iTunes itself. iTunes features dedicated sections for purchasing or renting episodes of TV shows and for buying or renting movies, as shown in Figure 8-3.

Pricing varies, but it's not atypical (as of this writing) to fork over $1.99 to pick up an episode of a popular TV show in standard definition or $2.99 for a high-def version. And a few shows are free. You can also purchase a complete season of a favorite show — prices are usually about $24.99 for standard-def and $29.99 to $39.99 for high-def or 4K, when available.

A new release feature film typically costs $19.99 in high definition or $14.99 in standard def, but you'll see prices higher and lower.

You can also rent many movies, typically for $2.99, $3.99, or $4.99, though Apple sometimes serves up a juicy 99-cent rental as well, and we've seen rentals as high as $6.99. Not all movies can be rented, and we're not wild about current rental restrictions — you have 30 days to begin watching a rented flick and 48 hours to finish watching after you've started.

In some instances, *Captain America: Civil War* is one example, purchasing a movie in HD also affords you iTunes Extras for your Mac or PC, featuring the kind of bonus content sometimes reserved for DVDs or Blu-rays.

Tap a movie listing in iTunes, and you can generally preview a trailer before buying (or renting) and check out additional tidbits: the plot summary, credits, reviews, and customer ratings, as well as other movies that appealed to other buyers of this one. See Figure 8-3. And you can search films by genre or top charts (the ones other people are buying or renting), or rely on the Apple Genius feature for recommendations based on stuff you've already watched. (Genius works for movies and TV much the way it works for music, as we explain in Chapter 7.) Apple also groups movies by various themes — Kids Movies and Notable Indies are two examples.

Perusing podcasts and courseware

NEW

In iOS 11, Apple features both podcasts and content that used to be called iTunes U collections, all inside the Podcasts app. Podcasts are like Internet radio, although instead of listening to live streams, you download files to your Mac, PC, iPod, iPhone, or iPad. Lots of audio podcasts are available, but the focus here is on video. You can watch free episodes that cover *Sesame Street,* sports, investing, political shows, news, technology, and much more.

There's also a stand-alone iTunes U app, for taking iTunes U courses at Harvard, Stanford, and other prestigious institutions, as shown in Figure 8-4. iTunes U boasts more than 1 million free lectures and other educational resources from around the world, many of them videos. And iTunes U now has content for younger students too, from K–12.

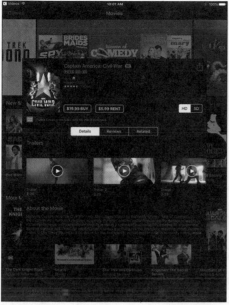

FIGURE 8-3:
Bone up on a movie before buying or renting it.

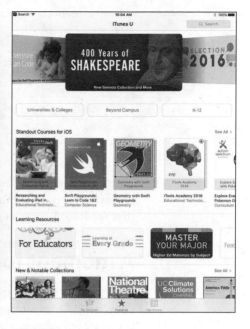

FIGURE 8-4:
Get smart. iTunes U offers a slew of lectures on diverse topics.

Some teachers even add homework and grade you (though that's still not typical). You might also have private discussions with your professor through the app, which is amazing. And here's unqualified good news: there's no tuition.

Watching your own videos

You can find videos you've created using the rear- or front-facing camera in your Photos Library, whether they're raw videos you filmed with your iPad or edited videos you created in iMovie. Check out the "Shooting Your Own Videos" section, later in this chapter, for direction on creating movies with the iPad.

TIP

For a somewhat technical work-around without potential conversion hassles, try the $5.99 Air Video HD app from Bit Cave Ltd. The utility app can deliver AVI, DivX, MKV, and other videos that wouldn't ordinarily play on your iPad. You have to download the free Air Video Server software to your Mac or PC to stream content to your iPad, even across the Internet. Or, for converting from a broader range of formats, try the excellent (and free) HandBrake app from http://handbrake.fr/.

For more on compatibility, check out the nearby "Are we compatible?" sidebar (but read it at your own risk).

A moment for HEVC

One of iOS's big under-the-hood improvements is the High-Efficiency Video Codec (HEVC) for storing video. HEVC's claim to fame is smaller video files with the same or higher quality as before.

So far, the new file format is used only internally by the Photos app on your Mac and the Camera and Photos apps on your iPad running iOS 11. You can't currently export files in the HEVC format, and iOS 11 intelligently exports using more common file formats. In other words, you don't need to worry about HEVC; it's just something Apple is using to make videos take up less space. We expect this to change over time, as HEVC is an industry standard like its predecessor, H.264.

Playing Video

Now that you know what you want to watch, it's time to find out how to watch it. For these steps, we walk you through watching a movie, but the steps for TV shows and downloaded videos are similar:

1. **On the Home screen, tap the TV icon.**

   You see a tabbed interface for Watch Now, Libraries, Store, and Search.

2. **Tap the Library tab.**

   As Figure 8-5 shows, you see poster thumbnails for any movies you previously purchased through iTunes — even for those movies you haven't downloaded yet.

3. **Tap the poster that represents the movie or other video you want to watch.**

FIGURE 8-5:
Choosing the movie, TV show, or music video to watch.

   You're taken to a movie summary page that reveals a larger movie poster, a description, the genre, the run time, and a play icon. If you haven't downloaded the movie, you can tap the iCloud icon to do so or tap play and stream it from Apple's servers.

4. **To start playing a movie (or resume playing from where you left off), tap the play icon.**

5. **(Optional) Rotate your iPad to landscape mode to maximize a video's view.**

Finding and Working the Video Controls

While a video is playing, tap the screen to display the controls shown in Figure 8-6. Here's how to work the controls:

» **To play or pause the video:** Tap the play/pause icon.

» **To adjust the volume:** Drag the volume slider to the right to raise the volume and to the left to lower it. The volume adjusts relative to how the physical Volume buttons are controlling audio levels.

» **To restart or go back:** Tap the restart/rewind icon to restart the video, or tap and hold down the same icon to rewind.

» **To skip forward:** Tap and hold down the fast forward icon to advance the video. Or skip ahead by dragging the playhead along the scrubber bar.

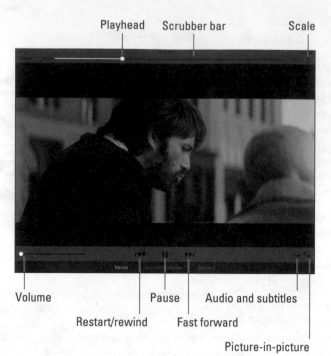

Playhead   Scrubber bar   Scale

Volume   Pause   Audio and subtitles

FIGURE 8-6:
Controlling
video.   Restart/rewind   Fast forward

Picture-in-picture

>> **To set how the video fills the screen:** Tap the scale icon, which toggles between filling the entire screen with video and fitting the video to the screen. Alternatively, you can double-tap the video to go back and forth between fitting and filling the screen.

Fitting the video to the screen displays the film in its theatrical aspect ratio. *Filling* the entire screen with the video may crop or trim the sides or top of the picture, so you don't see the complete scene that the director shot.

>> **To select subtitle settings:** Tap the audio and subtitles icon. You see options to select a different language, turn on or hide subtitles, and turn on or hide closed captioning. The control appears only if the movie supports any of these features. You can change certain subtitle styles by visiting Settings ⇨ General ⇨ Accessibility ⇨ Subtitles & Captioning and then turning on the Closed Captions + SDH switch.

>> **To take advantage of the picture-in-picture feature:** Tap the picture-in-picture icon (labeled in Figure 8-6) to continue to watch the video in a small window, which you can drag around the screen while using a separate app on your tablet. Alternately, if you're watching a video when you close the TV app, the movie will automatically go into picture-in-picture mode.

>> **To make the controls go away:** Tap the screen again (or just wait for them to go away on their own).

>> **To access bonus features in some commercial movies:** Tap the Extras button. In earlier versions of iOS, it was called Special Features, which is shown at the bottom of Figure 8-6. You won't see this button in every movie.

>> **To tell your iPad you've finished watching a video:** Tap Done. You return to the last videos screen that was visible before you started watching the movie.

Watching Video on a Big TV

We love watching movies on the iPad, but we also recognize the limitations of a smaller screen, even one as stunning as the Retina display. Friends won't crowd around to watch with you, as good as it is, so Apple offers two ways to display video from your iPad to a TV:

>> **AirPlay:** Through AirPlay, you can wirelessly stream videos as well as photos and music from the iPad to an Apple TV box connected to an HDTV. Start watching the movie on the iPad and tap the AirPlay/Screen Mirroring button in Control Center. Summon Control Center by swiping up from the bottom of the screen; then tap the Screen Mirroring button. You can watch only one screen at a time. Tap Apple TV to stream to the TV through the Apple TV box. Tap iPad to watch on the iPad.

You can multitask while streaming a video. Therefore, while the kids are watching a flick on the TV, you can surf the web or catch up on email.

REMEMBER

Although you can stream from an iPad to an Apple TV and switch screens between the two, you can't stream a rented movie that you started watching on Apple TV to the iPad.

>> **AV adapter cables:** Apple and others sell a variety of adapters and cables for connecting the iPad to the TV. For instance, Apple sells a Lightning–to–digital AV adapter for $49 that lets you connect an HDMI cable (which you'll have to supply) from the tablet to the TV. It also lets you *mirror* the iPad screen on the connected TV or projector. So you can not only watch a movie or video but also view anything else that's on the iPad's screen: your Home screens, web pages, games, other apps, you name it. You can also mirror what's on the screen through AirPlay.

Restricting Video Usage

If you've given an iPad to your kid or someone who works for you, you may not want that person spending time watching movies or television. You might want him or her to do something more productive, such as homework or the quarterly budget. That's where parental restrictions come in. Please note that the use of this iron-fist tool can make you unpopular.

Tap Settings ⇨ General ⇨ Restrictions ⇨ Enable Restrictions. You're asked to establish or enter a previously established passcode. Twice. Having done so, you can set restrictions based on movie ratings (PG, R, and so on) and regulate access to TV shows, also based on ratings. You can also restrict FaceTime usage or use of the camera (which when turned off also turns off FaceTime). For more on restrictions, flip to Chapter 15, where we explain the settings for controlling (and loosening) access to iPad features.

Deleting Video from Your iPad

Video takes up space — lots of space. After the closing credits roll and you no longer want to keep a video on your iPad, here's what you need to know about deleting it:

REMEMBER

>> To remove a downloaded video from the device — the flick remains in iCloud — tap Edit from the main Movies or TV Shows list screen, and tap the *x*-in-a-circle that appears on top of the movie poster. When Apple asks whether you're sure you want to delete the video, tap Delete. (If you change your mind, tap Cancel.) To delete episodes of a TV series that you've watched, swipe from right to left on the episode name and then tap the red Delete button.

Shooting Your Own Videos

The iPad 2 was the first iPad with a camera — um, two cameras, to be precise. Apple subsequently equipped later iPads with even better cameras. The 12-megapixel camera on iPad Pro takes terrific stills (see Chapter 9) and lets you capture 1080p high-definition or 4K videos. Another bonus is that the camera has built-in video stabilization, which helps compensate for slightly jittery videographers.

Meanwhile, the rear camera on the 9.7-inch iPad Pro, 10.5-inch iPad Pro, and second-generation 12.9-inch iPad Pro lets you shoot 4K video at 30 fps. The quality is splendid, but 4K video is a memory hog that claims roughly 350MB for just one minute of video. The first-generation 12.9-inch iPad Pro supports 1080p video recording at 30 fps.

You can shoot video with the front-facing FaceTime camera as well, which includes a sensor that permits *HDR*, or *high dynamic range*, video. (Read Chapter 9 for more on HDR.)

Now that we've dispensed with that little piece of business, here's how to shoot video on the iPad:

1. **On the Home screen, tap the Camera icon.**

2. **Drag along the right edge of the screen until Video mode is selected.**

   The word *Video* is highlighted in yellow. On some models you can also choose Time Lapse or Slo-Mo. If either of your other options, Photo or Square, is selected, it will appear in yellow instead. (Read Chapter 9 for more on these options.)

TIP

   You can't switch from the front to the rear camera (or vice versa) while you're capturing a scene. So before shooting anything, think about which camera you want to use, and then tap the front/rear camera icon in the top-right corner of the screen when you've made your choice.

3. **Tap the red record button (labeled in Figure 8-7) to begin shooting a scene.**

   When you choose a non-video shooting format — Photo or Square — the round shutter button is white. In any case, while you're shooting a scene, the counter will tick off the seconds.

4. **Tap the red record button again to stop recording.**

   Your video is automatically saved to the All Photos album (labeled in Figure 8-7), alongside any other saved videos and digital stills that land in the Photos app.

TIP

   As of this writing, not every iPad model offers a flash. If yours doesn't, you'll need good lighting to capture the best footage.

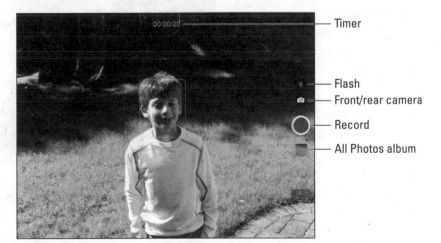

FIGURE 8-7: Lights, camera, action.

Timer

Flash
Front/rear camera
Record
All Photos album

Going slow

If you have the iPad Air 2, iPad mini 4, or iPad Pro, you get another shooting benefit: the capability to capture video in slow motion, which we think is truly nifty. Now you can play back in slow motion your kid's amazing catch in the varsity football game.

When shooting in slow motion on the Air 2, the iSight camera records video at a high rate of 120 frames per second (fps) in 720p high-definition video. You get to select where to play back the video at quarter speed, as we show you in a moment. On the 9.7-inch iPad Pro, 10.5-inch iPad Pro, or second-generation 12.9-inch iPad Pro, you can record in slo-mo at 120 fps in 1080p HD or 240 fps at 720p; on the first-generation 12.9-inch Pro, you can record in slo-mo at 120 fps at 720p.

But first things first: You have to grab the video before you can play it back. To shoot in slow motion, launch the Camera app and select Slo-Mo as your shooting format of choice. Shoot your slow-motion footage the same way you shoot at regular speeds. Note that the white circle surrounding the red shutter icon has teeny-tiny lines around it.

Tap the slow-motion video you want to watch. The video starts playing at normal speed, and then slows at a point determined by the iPad. You can adjust this slow-motion section. Tap Edit and slide the vertical bars just above the frame viewer, as shown in Figure 8-8. (When the vertical lines are close, the video plays at a normal speed; when the lines are spread apart, the video plays slowly.) Note that when you play back a segment in slow motion, any accompanying audio is slowed too. Tap Revert to revert to the point at which the iPad arranged for the video to start going slow.

FIGURE 8-8:
Adjusting your slow motion playback.

Going fast

The Time-Lapse camera feature on your iPad has the opposite effect of Slo-Mo, enabling you to capture a scene and play it back at a warped speed. (Unlike Slo-Mo, the Time-Lapse feature is on all iPad models currently for sale.) Choose Time-Lapse the same way that you select other shooting modes, and then tap the record icon. The app captures photos at dynamically selected intervals. When you're ready to watch the sped-up sequence, tap play as you do with any other video.

Editing what you shot

We assume that you captured some really great footage, but you probably shot some stuff that belongs on the cutting room floor as well. No big whoop — you can perform simple edits right on your iPad. Tap the All Photos album just below the shutter button in the Camera app to find your recordings, or tap the Videos album, Slo-Mo album, or Time-Lapse album, which Apple conveniently set up for you in the Photos app if you've taken those kinds of videos. Then:

1. **If the on-screen controls are not visible, tap a video recording.**

2. **Tap the Edit button.**

3. **Drag the start and end points along the frame viewer at the bottom of the screen to select only the video you want to keep.**

   The lines turn yellow.

4. **Tap Done and then tap either Trim Original or Save as New Clip (as shown in Figure 8-9).**

   If you choose Trim Original, Photos will alter the original file — be careful when choosing this option. Save as New Clip creates a newly trimmed video clip; the original video remains intact. The new clip is stored in the All Photos, Videos, Slo-Mo, or Time-Lapse album.

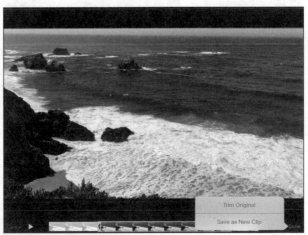

5. **Tap Cancel to start over.**

FIGURE 8-9:
Getting a trim.

This method will let you edit footage captured only on an iOS device, not video from a digital camcorder or camera — even if you sync it to the iPad.

TIP

For more ambitious editing on the iPad, consider iMovie for iPad, a free app closely related to iMovie for Mac computers. Among its tricks: You can produce Hollywood-style movie trailers, just like on a Mac.

WARNING

Any video edited with the iOS version of iMovie must have originated on an iOS device. You can't mix in footage shot with a digital camera or obtained elsewhere.

Sharing video

You can play back what you've just shot in portrait or landscape mode. And if the video is any good, you'll likely want to share it with a wider audience. To do so, open the All Photos album, Videos album, or another album, and tap the thumbnail for the video in question. Tap the share icon, and you can email the video (if the video file isn't too large), send it as a Message (see Chapter 5), or keep a copy in Notes.

And you have many other options: You can save the video to iCloud or share it in numerous other places, including Twitter, Facebook, Flickr, YouTube, Vimeo, and (if a Chinese keyboard was enabled) the Chinese services Youku and Tudou. You can also view your video as part of a slideshow (see Chapter 9) or, if you have an Apple TV box, dispatch it to a big-screen television via AirPlay.

Seeing Is Believing with FaceTime

We bet you can come up with a lengthy list of people you'd love to be able to eyeball in real time from afar. Maybe the list includes your old college roommate, or old college sweetheart, or your grandparents, who've long since retired to a warm climate. That's the beauty of *FaceTime*, the video chat app. FaceTime exploits the two cameras built into the devices, each serving a different purpose. The front FaceTime camera as it's called, lets you talk face to face. The back camera shows what you're seeing to the person you're talking to.

To take advantage of FaceTime, here's what you need:

>> **Access to Wi-Fi or cellular:** The people you're talking to need Internet access, too. On an iOS device, you need Wi-Fi or a cellular connection. If you want to

go with the cell connection, you need at least a third-generation iPad running iOS 6 (okay, so we can't imagine anyone still running software that old). On a Mac, you need an upstream or downstream Internet connection of at least 128 Kbps, quite slow nowadays. You also need at least a 1Mbps upstream and downstream connection for HD-quality video calls.

WARNING

Using FaceTime over a cellular connection can quickly run through your monthly data allotment and prove hazardous to your budget. However, you can do an audio-only FaceTime call, which can cut down significantly on your data usage.

>> **FaceTime on recipient's device:** Of course you can do FaceTime video only with someone capable of receiving a FaceTime video call. That person must have an iPad 2 or later, an Intel-based Mac computer (OS X 10.6.6 or later), a recent-model iPod touch, or an iPhone 4 or later. (FaceTime first appeared on Apple's prized smartphone.)

Getting started with FaceTime

When you use FaceTime for the first time, after you tap the app's icon from the Home screen, you're required to sign in to FaceTime using your Apple ID, which can be your iTunes Store account, iCloud ID, or another Apple account. (You may have previously supplied this info when setting up your iPad.) If you don't have an account, tap Create New Apple ID to set one up in FaceTime. You also must supply an email address or a phone number that callers use to call you from their own FaceTime–capable iPad, Mac, iPhone, or iPod touch.

REMEMBER

If this is the first time you've used a particular email address for FaceTime, Apple sends an email to that address to verify the account. Tap (or click) Verify Now and enter your Apple ID and password to complete the FaceTime setup. If the email address resides in Mail on the iPad, you're already good to go.

If you have multiple email addresses, callers can use any of them for Face-Time. To add an email address after the initial setup in iOS 11, tap Settings ⇨ *yourname* ⇨ Name, Phone, Numbers, Email ⇨ Reachable At, and tap Edit. Add Email or Phone Number appears. Tap that and you can add or delete email addresses or phone numbers. Apple will send confirmation messages to both.

You can turn FaceTime on or off in Settings. However, if you don't turn off Face-Time, you don't have to sign back in when you launch the app.

Making a FaceTime call

Now the real fun begins — making a video call. (We say specifically "video call" because you can also make FaceTime audio calls.) Follow these steps:

1. **Start the FaceTime app from the Home screen or by asking Siri to open the app on your behalf.**

   You can check out what you look like in a window prior to making a FaceTime call. So powder your nose and put on a happy face.

2. **Tap the Video tab.**

   Alternately, tap the Audio tab to make an audio-only FaceTime call.

3. **Choose someone to call:**

   - *Your contacts:* Tap the + icon to choose the name, and then tap the email address or phone number that the contact has associated with FaceTime.

   - *Someone new:* Tap the field in which to enter a name, email address, or number, and then tap the appropriate number in the list that appears. If this is the first time you're entering a number, you'll have the option to create a contact or add the number to an existing contact.

4. **If necessary, move the picture-in-picture window.**

   When a call is underway, you can see what you look like to the other person through a small picture-in-picture window, which you can drag to any corner of the video call window. The small window lets you know if your mug has dropped out of sight.

5. **(Optional) To toggle between the front and rear cameras, tap the camera icon (labeled in Figure 8-10).**

6. **Tap the End Call button when you're ready to hang up.**

How you look to the other person

Whom you're talking to

Switch cameras   Mute

End call

FIGURE 8-10:
Bob can see Ed, and Ed can see Bob (and Zeke the dog) in FaceTime.

While you're on a FaceTime call, the following tips will be handy:

>> **Rotate the iPad to its side to change the orientation.** In landscape mode, you're more likely to see everybody at once.

>> **Silence or mute a call by tapping the microphone icon.** Be aware that you can still be seen even though you're not heard (and you can still see and hear the other person).

TIP

>> **Momentarily check out another iPad app by pressing the Home button and then tapping the icon for the app.** At this juncture, you can still talk over FaceTime, but you can no longer see the person. Tap the green bar at the top of the iPad screen to bring the person and the FaceTime app back in front of you.

Through the Split View feature added to the iPad, you can conduct and view a FaceTime video call while engaged in other activities on the iPad, provided you have an iPad Air 2, iPad mini 4, or iPad Pro.

TIP

Caller ID on FaceTime works just like caller ID on a regular phone call. You can choose the email address or phone number you want to display to someone when you call that person via FaceTime. Just tap the designated number under Caller ID in FaceTime settings.

Receiving a FaceTime call

Of course, you can get FaceTime calls as well as make them. FaceTime doesn't have to be open for you to receive a video call. Here's how incoming calls work:

>> **Hearing the call:** When a call comes in, the caller's name (or email address) is prominently displayed on the iPad's screen, as shown in Figure 8-11, and the iPad rings.

>> **Accepting or declining the call:** Tap the green Accept button to answer the call or Decline if you'd rather not. If your iPad is locked when a FaceTime call comes in, answer by sliding the Slide to Answer button to the right, or decline by doing nothing and waiting for the caller to give up. You can also tap Message to send a canned iMessage *(Sorry, I can't talk right now; I'm on my way; Can I call you later?)* or a custom message. Or you can tap Remind Me to be reminded in one hour that you may want to call the person back.

>> **Silencing the ring:** You can press the sleep/wake button at the top of the iPad to silence the incoming ring. If you know you don't want to be disturbed by FaceTime calls before you even hear the ring, visit Control Center (see Chapter 14) to put your iPad on mute. In Settings (or Control Center), you can also turn on Do Not Disturb to silence incoming FaceTime calls.

>> **Blocking unwanted callers:** If a person who keeps trying to FaceTime you (yep, we're treating it as a verb) becomes bothersome, you can block him or her. Go to Settings ⇨ FaceTime ⇨ Call Blocking & Identification, and choose the person's name from your contacts. In the FaceTime app, you can block a caller who shows up on your caller list by tapping the *i*-in-a-circle next to the caller's name and then tapping Block This Caller.

FIGURE 8-11:
Tap the green button to accept the call.

>> **Removing people from the call list:** If you don't want to block a caller but don't want the person clogging up your call list, tap Edit, tap the circle next to the person's name so that a check mark appears, and then tap Delete.

TIP

You can also receive calls to your iPhone on your iPad, as long as they're on the same Wi-Fi network. Go to Settings ⇨ FaceTime ⇨ Calls from iPhone and change the option so that the button turns to green.

Although we heavily endorse the use of FaceTime, we'd be remiss if we didn't acknowledge other video-calling services that you can easily take advantage of on your iPad. These include Microsoft-owned Skype, Google's Hangout, Facebook Messenger, Whatsapp, LINE, Snapchat, and a host of others.

With that, we hereby silence this chapter. But you can do more with the cameras on your iPad, and we get to that in Chapter 9.

Chapter **9**

Photography on a Larger Scale

Throughout this book, we sing the praises of the iPad's vibrant multitouch display. You'd be hard-pressed to find a more appealing portable screen for watching movies or playing games. As you might imagine, the iPad you have recently purchased (or are lusting after) is also a spectacular photo viewer. Images are crisp and vivid, at least those you shot properly. (C'mon, we know Ansel Adams is a distant cousin.)

What's more, you can shoot some of those pictures directly with your prized tablet. The reasons, of course, are the front and rear cameras built into the device. If you read Chapter 8, you already know you can put those cameras to work capturing video. In this chapter, you get the big picture on shooting still images.

Okay, we need to get a couple of things out of the way: The iPad may never be the most comfortable substitute for a point-and-shoot digital camera, much less a pricey digital SLR. As critics, we can quibble about the fact that some models have no flash and shooting can be awkward.

But we're here, friends, to focus on the positive. And having cameras on your iPad may prove to be a godsend. With the iPad Air 2, iPad mini 3, iPad mini 4, and both iPad Pro models, Apple has jazzed up the cameras to something splendid, and the rear camera on the 9.7-inch iPad is pretty good, too.

In this chapter, we point out other optical enhancements in the most recent iPads. The 10.5-inch iPad Pro and second-generation 12.9-inch iPad Pro have a 12-megapixel camera with backside illumination, an impressive $f/1.8$ aperture, and a six-element lens. The iPad mini 4 and iPad 9.7-inch have an 8-megapixel camera with an $f/2.4$ aperture. All these models have a hybrid infrared filter (like that on an SLR), for more uniform colors. And face detection makes sure the balance and focus are just right for up to ten faces on the screen.

Such features are photographer-speak for potentially snapping darn sweet pictures. And we can think of certain circumstances — selling real estate, say, or shopping for a home — where tablet cameras are quite convenient.

Apple has made finding pictures in your stash an easier task, too, with an organizational structure that arranges photos in the Photos app by collections, moments, and years. And iOS 11 automatically gathers collections that are meant to trigger precious memories.

Meanwhile, you're in for a treat if you're new to *Photo Booth*, a yuk-it-up Mac program that is also on the iPad. Photo Booth may be the most fun use of the cameras yet. We get to Photo Booth at the end of this chapter. Over the next few pages, you discover the best ways to make the digital photos on the iPad come alive, no matter how they arrived on your tablet.

Shooting Pictures

You can start shooting pictures on the iPad in a few ways. So we're going to cut to the chase immediately:

1. **Fire up the camera itself. Choose one of the following:**

   - On the Home screen, tap the Camera app icon.

   - From the lock screen, swipe from right to left.

   - Drag Control Center up from the bottom of the screen and tap the Camera app icon.

   - Ask Siri (read Chapter 14) to open the Camera app for you.

   However you get here, your iPad has turned into the tablet equivalent of a Kodak Instamatic, minus the film, and in a form factor that is obviously much bigger. But you're also effectively peering through one of the largest viewfinders imaginable!

2. **Keep your eyes peeled on the iPad display, and use the viewfinder to frame your image.**

3. **Select a shooting format:**

- *Photo:* Think snapshot.

- *Square:* This gives you a picture formatted to make nice with the popular Instagram photo-sharing app.

- *Pano:* Short for panorama, this shooting mode lets you capture epic vistas.

- *Video, Slo-Mo,* or *Time Lapse:* We kindly refer you to Chapter 8.

   You move from one format to another by swiping up or down along the right edge of the screen so that the format you've chosen is highlighted in yellow.

4. **Snap your image by tapping the white round camera button.**

   The button is at the middle-right edge of the screen whether you're holding the iPad in portrait mode or landscape mode (see Figure 9-1).

   The image you shot lands in the All Photos album, labeled in Figure 9-1. We explain what you can do with the images on the iPad later in this chapter.

Live photos
HDR
Timer
Flash (9.7-inch iPad Pro only)
Front/rear camera

Camera button

All Photos album

Shooting formats

FIGURE 9-1:
Using the iPad
as a camera.

Here are some tips for working with the Camera app:

» **Adjust the focal point.** Tap the portion of the screen in which you see the face or object you want as the image's focal point. A small rectangle surrounds your selection, and the iPad adjusts the exposure and focus for that part of the image. (The rectangle is not visible in Figure 9-1). Your iPad can detect up to ten faces in a picture. Behind the scenes, the camera is balancing the exposure across each face. If you want to lock the focus and exposure settings while taking a picture, press and hold your finger against the screen until the rectangle pulses. AE/AF Lock will appear. Tap the screen again to make AE/AF Lock disappear.

TIP

Next to the focus box is a sun icon. When that sunny exposure icon is visible, drag your finger up or down against the screen to increase or decrease the brightness in a scene. And you can lighten or darken scenes for both still photos and video.

>> **Zoom in or out.** Tap the screen with two fingers and spread (unpinch) to zoom in or pinch to zoom out, or drag the slider up or down on the left side of the screen. The iPad has a 5X digital zoom, which basically crops and resizes an image. Such zooms are lower quality than optical zooms on many digital cameras. Be aware that zooming works only with the rear camera.

>> **See grid lines to help you compose your picture.** Tap Settings ⇨ Camera and tap the Grid switch to turn it on (the switch turns green). Grid lines can help you frame a shot using the photographic principle known as the rule of thirds.

TIP

>> **Toggle between the front and rear cameras.** Tap the front/rear camera icon (see Figure 9-1). The front camera is of lower quality than its rear cousin but is more than adequate for most things, including FaceTime and Photo Booth.

>> **Shoot in HDR.** To exploit *HDR (high dynamic range)* photography, tap the HDR icon. The HDR feature takes three separate exposures (long, normal, short) and blends the best parts of the three shots into a single image. In Settings (under Photos & Camera), you can choose to keep the normal photo along with your HDR result or just hang on to the latter.

>> **Burst out.** In the blink of an eye, burst mode on the iPad can capture a burst of pictures — up to ten continuous images per second. Just keep your finger pressed against the camera button to keep on capturing those images. This feature works with the front FaceTime camera and the rear camera.

>> **Capture panoramas.** If you're traveling to San Francisco, you'll want a picture of the magnificent span that is the Golden Gate Bridge. At a family reunion, you want that epic image of your entire extended clan. We recommend the panorama feature, which lets you shoot up to 240 degrees and stitch together a high-resolution image of up to 43 megapixels.

To get going, drag the screen so that Pano becomes your shooting mode of choice. The word *Pano* will be in yellow. Position the tablet so it's at the starting point and tap the camera button when you're ready. Steadily pan in the direction of the arrow. (Tap the arrow if you prefer panning in the opposite direction.) Try to keep the arrow just above the yellow horizontal line. When the task is complete, you can admire your handiwork.

>> **Geotag your photos.** The iPad is pretty smart when it comes to geography. Turn on Location Services (in Settings ⇨ Privacy) and the specific location settings for the camera appear in Settings. Pictures you take with the iPad cameras are *geotagged,* or identified by where they were shot.

WARNING

Think long and hard before permitting images to be geotagged if you plan on sharing them with people from whom you want to keep your address and other locations private — especially if you plan on sharing the photos online.

>> **Use the self-timer.** Many physical cameras have a self-timer that lets you be part of a picture. The self-timer built into the Camera app adds this functionality to your iPad, whether you're using the front or rear camera.

Tap the timer icon and choose 3 seconds or 10 seconds as the time interval between when you press the camera button and when the picture is captured. You'll see a countdown on the screen leading up to that moment. To turn off the self-timer, tap the Off button.

You can also add pictures to your iPad in several other ways. Alas, one of these methods involves buying an accessory. We zoom in in the following sections.

Syncing pix

We devote an entire chapter (see Chapter 3) to synchronizing data with the iPad, so we don't dwell on it here. But we'd be remiss if we didn't mention it in this chapter. (The assumption in this section is that you already know how to get pictures onto your computer.)

When the iPad is connected to your computer, click the Photos tab on the iPad Device page in iTunes on the Mac or PC. Then select a source from the Sync Photos From pop-up menu.

Connecting a digital camera or memory card

Almost all the digital cameras we're aware of come with a USB cable that you can use to transfer images to a computer. Of course, the iPad isn't a regular computer, isn't equipped with a USB port, and doesn't have a memory card slot. So, you'll need an adapter.

For its part, Apple sells an optional Lightning–to–USB camera adapter ($29), as well as Lightning–to–SD card camera reader cables (also $29) for iPad models with the Lightning connector.

The SD card reader connector accommodates the SD memory cards common to many digital camera models.

The camera connection kit and the Lightning connectors support many common photo formats, including JPEG and RAW. The latter is a format favored by photo enthusiasts.

Saving images from emails and the web

You can save many of the pictures that arrive in emails or you come across on the web: Just tap and hold down on an image, and then tap Save Image when the menu pops up. Pictures are stored in the All Photos album, which we get to shortly. You can also tap Copy to paste said image into another app on your device.

Tracking Down Your Pictures

So where exactly do your pictures live on the iPad? We just gave some of the answer away; the images you snap on the device first land in a photo album appropriately dubbed All Photos or, historically, Camera Roll.

In the Photos or Camera app — you can get to the former by tapping a thumbnail image in the latter — you'll also find pictures you've shared with friends and they've shared with you through the iCloud photo-sharing feature. The photos you imported are readily available, and are grouped in the same albums they were in on the computer.

Moreover, every picture you take with your iPad (and other iOS devices) can be stored in an iCloud photo library. You can access any of these pics if you have a Wi-Fi or cellular connection to the Internet. No more fretting about images hogging too much storage space on your tablet. What's more, the pictures are stored in the cloud at their full resolution in their original formats. (Apple will leave behind versions that are ideally sized for your tablet.)

You can still download to the iPad images that you want available when you're not connected to cyberspace.

In this section, we show you not only where to find these pictures, but also how to display them and share them with others — and how to dispose of the duds that don't measure up to your lofty photographic standards.

Get ready to literally get your fingers on the pics (without having to worry about smudging them). Open the Photos app by tapping its icon on the Home screen or by going through the Camera app. Then take a gander at the buttons at the bottom of the screen: Photos, Memories, Shared, and Albums, as shown in Figure 9-2. We take these on one by one.

Choosing albums

Tapping Albums lists all the albums you have on your iPad, with your All Photos album at the upper left (refer to Figure 9-2). Apple has kindly supplied additional premade albums: Panoramas, for all the panoramic scenes you've captured, Bursts, for your burst pictures, Selfies, Screen-shots, Videos (shooting videos is described in Chapter 8), and Recently Deleted, to give you a chance to recover any images that were accidentally given the heave-ho. Apple also displays the number of days before those pictures are permanently gone.

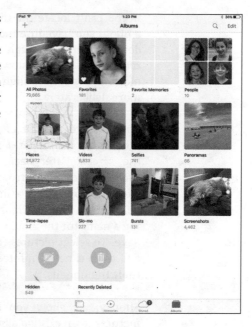

FIGURE 9-2:
All Photos tops your list of albums.

Tap an album listing to open it. You'll see the minimalistic interface shown in Figure 9-3, which reveals the by-now-familiar All Photos album.

Browse the thumbnails until you find the picture or video you want and tap it. We show you all the cool things you can do from there.

REMEMBER

You'll know when a thumbnail represents a video rather than a still image because the thumbnail includes the length of the video.

Meanwhile, you can tell whether a photo is part of a burst binge in a couple ways. The first is exposed here in All Photos. The thumbnail that represents this sequence of shots will appear as though it's sitting on a stack of photos. (You'll see this thumbnail stack also when you come to the collections view in the Photos app; we describe collections shortly.) Tap the thumbnail now. In the second way, the word *Burst* appears in the upper left of an image you've opened, with a numerical count of burst photos in parentheses. You can keep any burst images you've captured. Third, there's the aforementioned premade Bursts album.

If you can't locate the thumbnail for a photo you have in mind, flick up or down to scroll through the pictures rapidly, or use a slower dragging motion to pore through the images more deliberately.

To return to the list of albums, tap Albums at the upper-left corner of the screen. After backing out, you can create an album from the albums view by tapping the + in the upper-left corner (refer to Figure 9-2), typing a name for the album, and tapping Save. To select pictures (or videos) to add to your newly minted album, tap their thumbnails.

Shortly, we show you how to add pictures to an *existing* album.

REMEMBER

Albums you create on the iPad reside only on the iPad. They can't be synced or copied to your PC or Mac, at least without work-arounds through a third-party app such as Dropbox.

Categorizing your pics

Placing pictures into photo albums has been the way of the world forever. But albums *per se* are not the only organizing structure that makes sense. Apple has cooked up a simple, but ingenious, interface for presenting pictures that is essentially a timeline grouped by years, collections, and moments.

Pictures categorized by years are indeed all the pictures taken in a given year. Can't be more straightforward than that.

The collections category is a subset within a year, such as your holiday pictures in Las Vegas. Within that grouping is another subset called moments — the pictures, say, that you took by the dancing fountains at the Bellagio Hotel.

Tap for action items or to add selected images to albums.

Video thumbnail

Return to Albums list   Slideshow

View photo Memories   View by albums

View by years, collections, or moments.

View photos you or others shared.

FIGURE 9-3:
Digging into the All Photos album.

Figure 9-4 shows side-by-side-by-side views of these groupings, which appear as a grid of Lilliputian thumbnails in the case of years — you can barely make out any of the pictures.

FIGURE 9-4:
View your photos by years (left), collections (center), and moments (right).

Tap the years view (Figure 9-4, left), and slightly bigger thumbnails appear as part of the collections view (Figure 9-4, center). Tap again, and the thumbnails get just a little bit bigger in the moments view (Figure 9-4, right).

Through all these views, you'll see location information headings that get more specific as you move from years to collections to moments, assuming your iPad knows where the pictures were taken. (Location Services must be turned on under Privacy Settings for your iPad to know where these images were captured.) If you tap a place location, Apple will fire up a map and show you how many pictures were taken in that location, as shown in Figure 9-5. Maps also show up as part of the Memories collections we get to shortly.

To quickly skim all the pictures in the years view, press and drag your finger across the grid — as you do so, the thumbnails swell in size, one by one. Lift your finger and that last thumbnail takes over a chunk of the screen, ready for you to admire it, edit it, or share it.

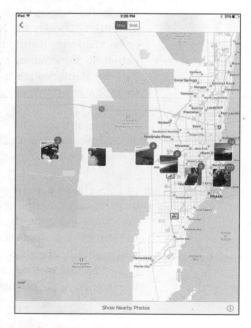

FIGURE 9-5:
Finding pictures on a map.

You can also tap a thumbnail in moments view to see icons for sharing the picture, discarding it, and editing it, as shown in Figure 9-6. Tap again and those picture controls disappear and the picture is bordered on the top and bottom by black bars.

TIP

Your iPad shows all the pictures in your library in all the views. However, you can save some space by choosing compact summarized views in Collections and Years. To do so, go to Settings ⇨ Photos and tap Summarize Photos so that it's green, assuming it isn't already that way.

Making memories

Hidden within everyone's photo collection are the crown jewels, those images that trigger the most precious memories. The Photos app in iOS 11 has a Memories feature that can help gather such memories automatically. Tap the Memories tab to take a photographic trip down memory lane.

Shows people, places, and related photos

Share Delete

Make favorite Edit

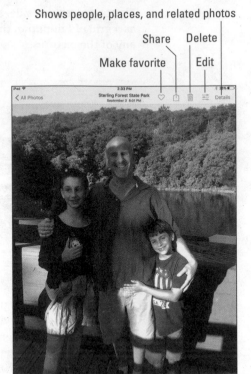

FIGURE 9-6:
You can share, discard, or edit a photo.

How does it work? The Photos app scans your picture library and collects images around vacations, birthday parties, and whatever the app deems are the best pictures you took during a given year or shorter time frame.

In Ed's Photos app, for example, the Memories feature built memories based on beach vacations (trips he and his family took to South Carolina and elsewhere) and even built collections based on what Apple considered the best photos, as shown in Figure 9-7. Within such memories, you can play a Memories movie that the app automatically generates, complete with theme music, titles, and transitions. You can edit those movies too, by changing the title, music, duration, and photos in the movies. Apple promises to deliver up to three new memories daily.

Inside a memory, you can view pictures the app thinks are related, as well as by the people in them or by place (with photos plotted on a map).

In grouping photos into albums and such, Apple exploits advanced computer machine learning using facial, object, and scene recognition along with location data to make intelligent choices.

If you cherish any of the memories that Apple has kindly put together on your behalf, tap Add to Favorite Memories at the bottom so you can easily access it whenever you choose. If you change your mind, tap Remove from Favorite Memories. And if you don't like a memory from the start — perhaps it is too bittersweet — tap Delete Memory to get rid of it, though the individual pictures remain in your collection.

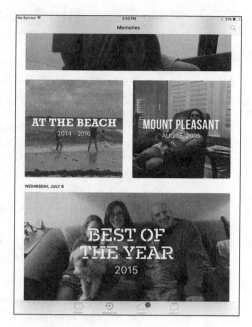

FIGURE 9-7:
Thanks for the Photos memories.

Want to see memories built around holiday events in your home country? Go to Settings ⟳ Photos and tap to enable the Show Holiday Events switch.

TIP

Live Photos

Did you know that photos can come alive? It's true. A Live Photo looks like a normal photo, but if you tap and hold down on one, it turns into a 3-second video. It's practically magic, just like the books about the kid with the lightning bolt scar on his forehead.

Live Photos require an iPad Pro or iPad 9.7-inch model. To put the camera app in Live Photo mode, tap the icon just above HDR (labeled in Figure 9-1). The Live Photos feature is active when the icon is yellow. When you take a photo, your iPad will capture 1.5 seconds before you press the button and 1.5 seconds after you press the button and make your photo live! It's a terrific effect, and we're confident that you'll be delighted and amazed by it. When you want to stop taking Live Photos, just tap that button again.

A moment for HEIF

NEW

iOS 11 brought a big under-the-hood improvement called the High Efficiency Image Format (HEIF) for still images. HEIF's calling card is smaller photos with the same or higher quality as before. Plus, they support editing Live Photo in new and unique ways.

So far, the new file format is used only internally by the Photos app on the Mac and the Camera and Photos apps on the iPad running iOS 11. You can't currently export files in the HEIC format, and iOS 11 intelligently exports more common file formats. In other words, you don't need to worry about HEIF; it's just something Apple is using to make photos take up less space. We expect this to change over time, because HEIF is an industry standard like its predecessor, JPEG.

Searching for pictures

Your iPad has one more feature to help you find a given photo among the thousands or tens of thousands you've shot. You can search your entire photo library in the cloud. From the Photos app, tap the search icon, the one that resembles a magnifying glass.

Apple has kindly grouped some of your pictures into potentially helpful search categories: Nearby, Home, those taken from a specific time period or location, and Favorites, which are so designated each time you tap the heart icon above a chosen image. You can also consult a Recent Searches grouping. Or just type a search term with the on-screen keyboard, perhaps the date or the time a photo was taken or the location where it was shot.

But the big breakthrough comes with the ability to search pictures by what's in them: mountains, beaches, lakes, cats, whatever. The app won't get it right every time, but it gets it right enough that you can't help but be impressed.

TIP

You can also enlist Siri to search for specific photos. For example, tell your obedient voice assistant something like, "Show me all the pictures I took at the baby shower."

Sharing your photos

Apple recognizes you might want to share your best images with friends and family and have those pictures automatically appear on their devices.

An impressive and aptly named solution called Shared Photo Streams arrived on the iPad, iPod touch, and iPhone with iOS 6 (and a bit earlier on Macs running OS X Mountain Lion). It's now referred to as iCloud photo sharing. (Somewhat confusingly, there is also My Photo Stream, a way to send photos to your various iCloud devices.) The feature enables you to create albums of pictures and videos to share with other folks and lets you receive photo streams other people make available to you. Here's how:

1. **On the Home screen, tap Settings.**

2. **Tap Photos & Camera.**

3. **If the iCloud Photo Sharing option isn't on (green), tap it to turn it on.**

4. **Open the Photos app and tap the Shared tab.**

5. **Tap the + at the upper-left corner of the screen, and then type a name for your stream in the iCloud dialog that appears.**

   The name is your call, but we recommend something descriptive, along the lines of *My Trip to Paris* (and you should be so lucky).

6. **Tap Next and choose who will receive your stream.**

   You can type a phone number, a text address, or an email address, or choose one of your contacts by tapping the + in a circle in the To field of the iCloud pop-up window.

7. **Above the To field, tap Create.**

8. **Add photos as follows:**

   a. *Make sure the Shared icon is selected, and then tap the selected stream.*

   b. *Tap the + in a square. The Photos tab at the bottom of the display is selected. Tap each photo you want to include. You can choose from years, collections, or moments.*

   c. *Tap Done.*

9. **(Optional) Enter a comment.**

10. **Tap Post.**

    The recipient will receive an email and can choose to subscribe to your shared album by tapping the button shown.

TIP

We recommend checking out the activity view at the top of the Shared tab. It provides a nice summary of photos you and your pals posted.

You can share photos and videos with pretty much anyone — people don't need to join iCloud. If you want to share your pictures with everyone, you can do so through a public gallery on iCloud.com. To do that, tap the share icon at the bottom of the Photos app, then tap the iCloud pictures in question. This time, tap People near the upper-right corner of the screen, and then flip the Public Website switch on (green).

If the people with whom you're sharing have their own iCloud accounts and have iOS 6 or later or are using a Mac computer running OS X Mountain Lion or later, they can not only glom onto your stream to view your photos, but also leave comments. Don't worry — you have the power to remove snarky remarks.

If the people you're sharing with have iOS 7 or later, they can add their own photos and videos to the stream, provided it's okay with you. If it is, turn on the Subscribers Can Post switch. At your discretion, you can also receive notifications when your subscribers weigh in with a comment or add their own pictures or videos to the shared stream. After tapping the People tab, you can invite more people to view your stream.

If you're ultimately unhappy with the shared stream or the people with whom you're sharing it, you can kill the shared stream or kick those people off the list. To kill the stream, tap Shared, tap the Edit button, and tap the circled dash that appears on the thumbnail image that represents the given stream. To remove a subscriber, tap the stream, tap People, and then tap the name of the person with whom you're sharing the stream. Scroll down to the bottom and tap Remove Subscriber. You'll be asked to tap a Remove button just to make sure or tap Cancel if you have second thoughts. If you do remove a subscriber, you can always reinvite that person later.

Admiring Your Pictures

Photographs are meant to be seen, not buried in the digital equivalent of a shoebox. The iPad affords you some neat ways to manipulate, view, and share your best photos.

Maneuvering and manipulating photos

You've already found out how to find individual pictures in albums, via iCloud, and in years, collections, moments, and memories groupings. You may already know (from previous sections in this chapter) how to display picture controls. But you can do a lot of maneuvering of your pictures without summoning those controls. Here are some options:

>> **Skip ahead or view the preceding picture:** Flick your finger left or right.

>> **Switch from landscape or portrait mode:** When you turn the iPad sideways, the picture automatically reorients itself from portrait to landscape mode. Rotate the device back to portrait mode and the picture readjusts accordingly.

>> **Zoom:** Double-tap to zoom in on an image and make it larger. Do so again to zoom out and make it smaller. Alternatively, on the photo, spread your thumb and index finger apart to zoom in and pinch them to zoom out.

>> **Pan and scroll:** This cool little feature was once practically guaranteed to make you the life of the party. Now it's commonplace, if no less cool. After you zoom in on a picture, drag it around the screen with your finger, bringing the part of the image you most care about front and center. In this way, you can zoom in on Fido's adorable face as opposed to, say, the unflattering picture of the person holding the dog in his lap.

Launching slideshows

Those of us who store a lot of photographs on computers are familiar with running slideshows of those images. It's a breeze to replicate the experience on the iPad:

1. **Choose an album in the albums list.**

    Tap the Photos icon from the Home screen or tap the Recently Added button in the Camera app.

2. **Do one of the following:**

    - *In the Photos app:* Select an album and tap Slideshow in the upper-right corner. You've designated every photo and video in that album to be part of the slideshow.

    To cherry-pick the pictures in the slideshow, tap Select and then tap each image you want to include so that a check mark appears. Under this scenario, tap Add To and then add the chosen images to a new or an existing album. When that album is readily loaded, skip to the next step.

    - *In the Camera app:* Tap the image in the lower-right corner of the screen to display the most recent image you've shot, and find a picture to include in your slideshow. From there, follow the instructions for the Photos app to tap and choose other images for the slideshow or to choose an entire album.

3. **Tap Slideshow to start the slideshow, tap the screen, and then tap Options.**

4. **Choose a theme and the music (if any) that you'd like to accompany the slideshow.**

    You have five theme choices (Origami, Magazine, Dissolve, Ken Burns, and Push). Why not try them all, to see what you like? You can go with Apple's theme music or choose from your iTunes stash.

5. **Choose whether the slideshow should repeat rather than end automatically and determine the length between slides.**

How long each slide plays is determined by how far you drag the slider that shows up in options from all the way to the left (a tortoise icon) to all the way to the right (a hare).

6. **Choose where you get to see the slideshow.**

You can view the slideshow on the iPad itself or have it beamed wirelessly to an Apple TV. Tap the icon in the upper right to make that selection.

7. **Tap the play button to start the slideshow.**

Press Done when you're done watching. That's it! Enjoy the show.

Storing pictures in the (i)Cloud

As mentioned, through the iCloud service, any photo you take with the iPad or with another iOS 8 or later device can be automatically stored in the cloud and pushed to another iPad, or your PC, Mac, iPhone, iPod touch, or Apple TV (third generation or later). Pictures are uploaded when your iCloud devices are connected to Wi-Fi.

WARNING

There's a catch to using the iCloud photo library: You have to pay for storage. You get 5GB of iCloud storage gratis, but shutterbugs will use that up in a flash. So you'll likely spring for one of the following monthly plans: 50GB of storage for 99¢, 200GB for $2.99, 1TB for $2.99, or 2TB for $9.99 a month.

Photos taken on the iPad aren't whisked to iCloud until you leave the Camera app. That way, you get a chance to delete pictures you'd rather not have turn up everywhere. But after you leave the Camera app, all the photos there are saved in the All Photos album (in the list of Albums in the Photos app), including pictures that arrived as email attachments that you saved as well as screen captures taken on the iPad.

You can save pictures in the All Photos album to any other album on the tablet. Start by tapping the Select button at the upper-right corner of the screen. Next, tap each photo you want to move. Tap the Add To button that shows up at the top of the screen and choose the new album destination for your chosen images.

TIP

If for some reason the pictures you snap on the iPad are not uploaded, go to Settings ⇨ Photos, and make sure My Photo Stream is turned on.

Editing and Deleting Photos

The Photos app is never going to serve as an editing substitute for, say, Adobe Photoshop. But you can dramatically (and simply) apply touchups and alter the composition of your pictures right from the Photos app.

To start, choose an image and tap Edit. You'll see the Edit Photo screen, as Figure 9-8 reveals.

The screen sports the following icons, from left to right:

FIGURE 9-8:
Who says you can't improve the quality of the picture?

 » **Auto-enhance:** Tapping the icon to the right of Cancel lets the iPad take a stab at making your image look better. Apple lightens or darkens the picture, tweaks color saturation, and more. Tap Done if you like the result.

 » **Rotate, straighten and crop:** Tapping this icon summons a number of additional icons and controls, as shown in Figure 9-9, top. You can

 • *Rotate the entire image counterclockwise.*

• *Straighten a crooked image or vice versa.* Rotate the numbered dial or wheel and watch the effect on the photo. Click Done when you're satisfied with how the image looks.

 • *Crop the image.* Tap the crop icon, and choose among the various aspect ratio options. Press your finger against the image to drag the photo around a crop grid to get it just as you would like, pinching and unpinching as you see fit to get closer up or farther away. When satisfied, tap Crop and then tap Save.

 » **Add a filter:** As Figure 9-9, center, shows, you can choose a filter: Vivid or Dramatic, with two variations (Warm and Cool) for each. There's also Mono, Silvertone, and Noir. Better yet, you can apply these after the fact. If you're not satisfied after applying a filter, tap Original or Cancel to go back to the original.

» **Adjust light, color, B&W:** Apple provides numerous editing controls to adjust brilliance, exposure, highlights, shadows, brightness, contrast, and black point (light); saturation, contrast, and cast (color); and intensity, neutrals, tone, and grain (B&W). The controls shown in Figure 9-8, bottom, let you play with shadows, among other options.

To get at these, tap the fourth icon at the bottom of the display, which appears with other icons just to the left of the Done button. From there, tap Light, Color or B&W (as shown in Figure 9-9, bottom) to select the editing control you want to mess with. Then drag the slider at the bottom of the screen in either direction until you reach a level you're satisfied with — you see the effect on the image as you drag the slider. To fine-tune this even further, tap the icon with three horizontal lines and choose among your additional options. Tap Done when you're finished or Cancel to start over.

FIGURE 9-9: From straightening to cropping, you can make a good picture better.

>> **Red-eye:** Tap this icon, and then tap each red-eye you want to repair. The red-eye tool is visible only when you're trying to correct a photo with subjects who have a red-eye issue. (That's why you don't see this icon in Figure 9-8.)

>> **Markup and more:** Tap this icon to mark up the image. In addition to Apple's tools for drawing or writing on the image you can use your finger, an Apple Pencil (on iPad Pros), or a third-party stylus. And Apple now allows third-party app makers to make their own filters and editing tools accessible from the Photos app. Tap More to gain access to such apps. (See Chapter 5 for more on the Markup feature.)

TIP

If you aren't satisfied with any of the edits that you've applied to your pictures, you can always tap Cancel followed by Discard Changes to restore the original. If you tap Done instead and apply the changes, you can still change your mind later. Open the image, tap the Edit icon, tap Revert, and then tap Revert to Original, which will remove all edits made to the pic.

Editing Live Photos

NEW

Apple added the ability to edit Live Photos in iOS 11. With some simple controls that look a lot like the editing tools discussed in the preceding section, you can trim the length of a Live Photo, set the keyframe, apply effects, turn off sound, and more.

The biggest difference in editing a Live Photo and a regular photo is setting the *keyframe,* which is the still you see when you're not tapping and holding down on a Live Photo. To change the keyframe, tap your Live Photo, and then tap the Edit button in the upper right of the screen. In addition to the familiar editing and filter options at the bottom of the screen, you'll get a video timeline that will look familiar if you read Chapter 8, which covers video features of the iPad.

One of the frames in that timeline will have a white square around it. Just tap and drag that square along the timeline until you get a frame you like. When you've finished editing, tap Done, and your Live Photo will be represented by its new keyframe.

To mute sound, tap the volume button, as shown on the bottom right of Figure 9-10. To convert your Live Photo to a boring old regular photo, tap the Live button on the bottom left. To trim the length of your Live Photo, grab the handles at either end of the timeline and move them where you want them. Otherwise, the editing tools are the same ones we described previously.

FIGURE 9-10:
Set the keyframe in a Live Photo by sliding the box on the timeline.

Okay, so we told a tiny fib by intimating that photographs are meant to be seen. We should have amended that statement by saying that *some* pictures are meant to be seen. Others, you can't get rid of fast enough. Fortunately, the iPad makes it a cinch to bury the evidence:

1. **Tap the objectionable photograph.**

2. **Tap to display the picture controls, if they're not already displayed.**

3. **Tap the trash icon.**

4. **Tap Delete Photo (or tap anywhere else to cancel, if you change your mind).**

   In an instant, the photo is mercifully disposed of. It's also deleted from the iCloud photo library across all your devices.

More (Not So) Stupid Picture Tricks

You can take advantage of the photos on the iPad in a few more ways. In each case, you tap the picture and make sure the picture controls are displayed. Then tap the share icon (shown in the margin) to display the choices shown in Figure 9-11. (Not all the options are visible in the figure.)

Here's a rundown of each choice:

FIGURE 9-11:
Look at what else I can do!

>> **AirDrop:** AirDrop is a neat wireless method for sharing photos, videos, or other files with folks who happen to be nearby and also have an iOS 7 or later device or a Mac running Yosemite, El Capitan, Sierra, or High Sierra. You turn on the feature in Control Center (see Chapter 2) and choose whether to make your iPad discoverable to everyone or just contacts who are in the vicinity. Tap a photo to select it and then tap the photo or icon representing the person and the device with whom you are trying to share the image (refer to Figure 9-11). That person will receive an invitation to accept the photograph or reject it on his or her device. If the photo is accepted, the picture lands on the person's phone almost immediately.

>> **Message:** Apple and your provider support picture messaging through MMS (Multimedia Messaging Service). Tap the Message option, and the picture is embedded in your outgoing message; you need to enter the phone number, email address, or name of the person to whom you're sending the picture. If that person is using an iOS 5 or later device, the photo will be sent as an iMessage, which doesn't count against your texting allotment. (See Chapter 5 for more on iMessages.)

>> **Mail:** Some photos are so precious that you just have to share them with family members and friends. When you tap Mail, the picture is embedded in the body of an outgoing email message. Use the virtual keyboard to enter the email addresses, subject line, and any comments you want to add — you know, something profound, such as "Isn't this a great-looking photo?" After tapping Send to whisk picture and accompanying message on their way, you have the option to change the image size (small, medium, or large) or keep the actual size. Consider the trade-offs: A smaller-sized image may get through any limits imposed by your or the recipient's Internet service provider or company. But if you can get the largest image through, you'll give the recipient the full picture (forgive the pun) in all its glory. (Check out Chapter 5 for more info on using email.)

>> **Notes:** You can add your chosen image to the Notes app.

>> **iCloud Photo Sharing:** You can post pics to a shared album.

>> **Twitter:** Lots of people send pictures with their tweets these days. The iPad makes it a breeze. Tap Twitter and your picture is embedded in an outgoing tweet. Just add your words, sticking to Twitter's character limit of 140, and tap Post.

>> **Facebook:** Lots (and we mean lots) of people also share photos on the world's largest social network. After your Facebook account is configured, you too can post there from your iPad.

>> **Sina Weibo** and **Tencent Weibo:** If you've enabled a Chinese keyboard, you'll see options for China's own social networks.

>> **Flickr:** The Yahoo!-owned service is another popular photo-sharing destination.

>> **Save PDF to iBooks:** You can turn the image into a PDF that you can stash in the iBooks app.

>> **Copy:** Tap to copy the image and then paste it into an email or elsewhere.

>> **Duplicate:** You may want to duplicate a photo so that you can edit it while also keeping an original.

>> **Slideshow:** We discuss slideshows earlier in this chapter. Here is another starting point for a slideshow, which as you know, can be accompanied by an optional musical soundtrack.

>> **AirPlay:** Own an Apple TV set-top box? You can use AirPlay to stream photos from the tablet to the TV.

>> **Save Image:** If you didn't shoot the image in question on your iPad but want to add it to the device, tap the Save Image option.

>> **Hide:** Don't want the image to be seen (but don't want to delete it either)? Tap Hide and then tap Hide Photo. The selected pic will be hidden from the Moments, Collections, and Years views but still visible in Albums.

>> **Assign to Contact:** If you assign a picture to someone in your contacts list, the picture you assign pops up whenever you receive a FaceTime call or Message from that person. Tap Assign to Contact. Your list of contacts appears on the screen. Scroll through the list to find the person who matches the picture of the moment. As with the Use as Wallpaper option (described next), you can drag and resize the picture to get it just right. Then tap Set Photo.

You can also assign a photo to a contact by starting out in Contacts. To change the picture you assigned to a person, tap his or her name in the contacts list, tap Edit, and then tap the person's thumbnail picture, which also carries the label Edit. From there, you can take another photo with the iPad's digital camera, select another photo from one of your albums, edit the photo you're already using (by resizing and dragging it to a new position), or delete the photo you no longer want.

>> **Use as Wallpaper:** The Apple-supplied background images on the iPad can't measure up to pictures of your spouse, your kids, or your pet. When you tap Use as Wallpaper, you see what the present image looks like as the iPad's background picture. You're given the opportunity to move the picture around and resize it, through the now-familiar action of dragging or pinching against the screen with your fingers. You can even see how the picture looks against the time and date that appear on the lock screen. Another option is to take advantage of the Perspective Zoom setting, which lets you exploit a parallax animation effect in which the picture moves as you move the iPad. Tap the screen to toggle the setting on or off. When you're satisfied with what the wallpaper looks like, tap the Set button. Options appear that let you use the photo as wallpaper for the lock screen, the Home screen, or both, as shown in Figure 9-12. Per usual, you can also tap Cancel. (You find out more about wallpaper in Chapter 15.)

>> **Print:** If you have an AirPrint-capable printer, tap Print to print the photo. You can choose how many copies of the print you want to duplicate.

>> **More:** Tapping here lets you post pictures to other sites with sharing plug-ins or extensions.

Sometimes you want to make decisions about multiple pictures at the same time, whether you're sharing them online, copying or printing them, adding them to a new album, or deleting them in bulk. Here's a convenient way to do so. Launch the Photos app and either tap a specific album in the app or open up to a moments view so that you see thumbnails of your pictures. Next, tap Select at the upper right, and then tap each thumbnail on which you're planning to take action, so that a check mark appears. As you do, the count for each picture you select increases. From here, you can delete them, or you can tap the share icon to share pictures on a social network in bulk, email them, send them via a message, or copy or print them, as discussed previously. The options that appear may vary depending on how many pictures you've selected — for example, the number of photos you can email is limited.

FIGURE 9-12:
Beautifying the iPad with wallpaper.

You won't have to tap the share icon in every case to add pictures to a designated album or to delete them. After making your picture selections, look for Add To and the trash icon at the top of the screen. Tap Add To and then, from the list that appears, tap the album where you want the pictures you've chosen to land. If you tap the trash icon instead, you can dispose of the selected photos.

Entering the Photo Booth

Remember the old-fashioned photo booths at the local Five and Dime? Remember the Five and Dime? Okay, if you don't remember such variety stores, your parents probably do, and if they don't, their parents no doubt do. The point is that photo booths (which do still exist) are fun places to ham it up solo or with a friend as the machine captures and spits out wallet-size pictures.

With the Photo Booth app, Apple has cooked up a modern alternative to a real photo booth. The app is a close cousin to a similar application on the Mac. Here's how Photo Booth works:

1. **Tap the Photo Booth icon.**

   You get the tic-tac-toe-style grid shown in Figure 9-13.

2. **Point the front-facing camera at your face.**

   You see your mug through a prism of eight rather wacky special effects: Thermal Camera, Mirror, X-Ray, Kaleidoscope, Light Tunnel, Squeeze, Twirl, and Stretch. The center square (what is this, *Hollywood Squares?*) is the only one in which you come off looking normal — or, as we like to kid, like you're supposed to look. Some of the effects make you look scary; some, merely goofy.

   You can also use the rear camera in Photo Booth to subject your friends to this form of, um, visual abuse.

3. **Choose one of the special effects (or stick with Normal) by tapping one of the thumbnails.**

   Ed chose Mirror for the example shown in Figure 9-14 because, after all, two Eds are better than one. (Sorry, couldn't resist.) You can pinch or unpinch the image to further doctor the effect.

   TIP If you're not satisfied with the effect you've chosen, tap the icon at the lower-left corner of the app to return to the Photo Booth grid and select another.

FIGURE 9-13:
Photo booths of yesteryear weren't like this.

FIGURE 9-14:
When one coauthor just isn't enough.

4. **When you have your bizarre look just right, tap the camera button on the screen to snap the picture.**

Your pic lands (as do other pictures taken with the iPad cameras) in the All Photos album.

From the All Photos album or from right here in Photo Booth, pictures can be shared in all the usual places or deleted, which you might want to seriously consider, given the distortions you've just applied to your face.

Nah, we're only kidding. Keep the image and take a lot more. Photo Booth may be a blast from the past, but we think it's just a blast.

TIP

Before leaving this photography section, we want to steer you to the App Store, which we explore in greater depth in Chapter 11. Hundreds, probably thousands, of photography-related apps are available there, a whole host of them free. That's too many to mention here, but we know you'll find terrific photo apps just by wandering around the place. Head to the Photo & Video category to get started.

And there you have it. You have just passed Photography 101 on the iPad. We trust that the coursework was, forgive another pun, a snap.

Chapter **10**

Curling Up with a Good iBook

D
on't be surprised if you have to answer this question from an inquisitive child someday: "Is it true, Grandpa, that people once read books on paper?"

That time may still be a ways off, but it somehow doesn't seem far-fetched anymore. Apple is among the tech companies that are major proponents of the electronic-books revolution.

Don't get us wrong; we love physical books as much as anyone and are in no way urging their imminent demise. But we also recognize the real-world benefits behind Apple's digital publishing efforts — and those by companies such as Amazon (which manufactures the market-leading Kindle electronic reader). As you discover in this chapter, the Kindle plays a role on the iPad as well.

For its part, the iPad makes a terrific electronic reader, with color and dazzling special effects, including pages that turn like those in a real book.

We open the page on this chapter to see how to find and purchase books for your iPad, and how to read them after they land on your virtual bookshelf. But first, we look at why you might want to read books and periodicals on your iPad.

Why E-Books?

We've run into plenty of skeptics who ask, "What's so wrong with the paper books that folks have only been reading for centuries that we now have to go digital?" The short answer is that nothing is wrong with physical books — except maybe that paper, over the long term, is fragile, and paper books tend to be bulky, a potential impediment for travelers.

On the other hand, when asked why he prefers paper books, Bob likes to drop one from shoulder height and ask, "Can your iPad (or Kindle) do that?"

Having said that, though, now consider the electronic advantages:

>> **No more weight or bulk constraints:** You can cart a whole bunch of e-books around when you travel, without breaking your back. To the avid bookworm, this potentially changes the dynamic in the way you read. Because you can carry so many books wherever you go, you can read whatever type of book strikes your fancy at the moment, kind of like listening to a song that fits your current mood. You have no obligation to read a book from start to finish before opening a new bestseller just because that happens to be the one book you have in your bag. In other words, weight constraints are out the window.

>> **Feel like reading a trashy novel?** Go for it. Rather immerse yourself in classic literature? Go for that. You might read a textbook, cookbook, or biography. Or gaze in wonder at an illustrated beauty. What's more, you can switch among the various titles and styles of books at will before finishing any single title.

>> **Flexible fonts and type sizes:** With e-books, or what Apple prefers to call *iBooks,* you can change text size and fonts on the fly — quite useful for people with less than 20/20 vision.

>> **Get the meaning of a word on the spot:** No more searching for a physical dictionary. You can look up an unfamiliar word immediately.

>> **Search with ease:** Need to do research on a particular subject? Enter a search term to find every mention of the subject in the book you're reading.

>> **See all the artwork in color:** See your iBook the way it was meant to be seen. For example, the latest iBooks software from Apple lets you experience (within certain limits) the kind of stunning art book once reserved for a coffee table. Or you can display a colorful children's picture book. And the newest multitouch iBooks incorporate embedded videos, animations, 3D elements, narration, and more.

>> **Get updates on books:** At least some e-books you might buy are updated — automatically.

>> **Read in the dark:** The iPad has a high-resolution backlit display, so you can read without a lamp nearby, which is useful in bed when your partner is trying to sleep.

>> **Add multimedia to a book:** Some e-books have audio and video content.

Beginning the iBook Story

To start reading iBooks on your iPad, you have to fetch the iBooks app in the App Store. (For more on the App Store, consult Chapter 11.)

As you might imagine, the app is free, and it comes with access to Apple's iBooks Store, of which we have more to say later in this chapter. For now, just know that the iBooks Store is an inviting place to browse and shop for books 24 hours a day. All the other books you end up purchasing for your iPad library turn up in the cover view shown in Figure 10-1 or in a view that lists your books by title.

The following basics help you navigate the iBooks main screen:

>> **Change the view:** If you prefer to view a list of your book titles rather than use cover view, tap the change

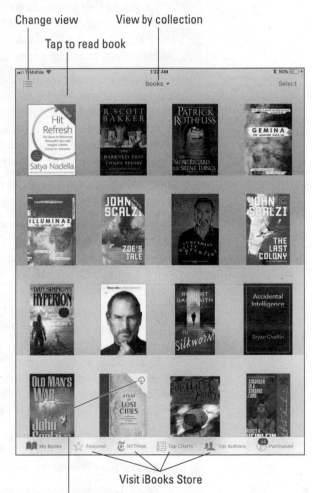

Change view　　View by collection

Tap to read book

Visit iBooks Store

Download from iCloud

FIGURE 10-1:
You can read a book by its cover.

view icon at the upper-left corner of the screen (labeled in Figure 10-1). In cover view, you can sort the list by most recent, titles, authors, or categories, as shown in Figure 10-2.

>> **Remove a book from view:** In cover view, tap Select, and then tap the book covers that you want to remove or tap Select All. Each selected book displays a check mark; tap a cover again to remove its check mark and thus deselect the book. When all the books you want to delete have check marks, tap Delete in the upper-left corner of the display. Apple asks you to tap a Remove Download button.

In list mode, as we like to call it, tap Select as well. This time, blank circles appear next to each title in the list. Tap the circle for each book you want to remove so that a check mark appears, and then tap Delete in the upper left. As before, you must confirm by tapping Remove Download.

TIP

As with other content you purchase from Apple, you can restore (download) any book you've purchased by tapping the Purchased icon at the bottom of the screen in the iBooks Store. The books you purchase from the iBooks Store land in iCloud. You'll know a book is in the cloud (as opposed to being downloaded onto your iPad) when you see the small iCloud icon, as labeled in Figure 10-1. Tap that icon to download the book.

If you prefer, you can hide books that are in iCloud from your iPad. Tap All Books, and then tap the Hide iCloud Books switch.

>> **Organize books by collections:** If you have a vast library of e-books, you might want to organize titles by genre or subject by creating collections of like-minded works. You might have collections of mysteries, classics, biographies, children's books, how-to's, textbooks, even all the *Dummies* books (we hope) you own.

Apple has created four collections on your behalf: books for all titles, audiobooks for the iPad equivalent of books on tape, PDFs for the Adobe PDF files on your iPad, and samples, those short previews of books that you can read before deciding whether to buy. (You can't edit or remove the premade All Books, Audiobooks, PDFs, or Samples collections.) To create, rename, or remove a collection of your own, tap All Books (refer to Figure 10-1) to show off your current list of collections and then choose from the following tasks:

● *Add a collection:* Make sure the My Books tab is selected at the bottom of the screen and then tap All Books at the top (you'll see a drop-down arrow). Tap + New Collection and type a name for the new collection.

● *Delete a collection:* Tap Edit and the red circle, and then tap Delete to finish the job. If the collection contains books, you're asked whether you want to remove the contents of this collection from your iPad. If you choose not to remove them, they're returned to their original collections (Books, PDFs, or any other collection). Remember that you can't delete the premade All Books, Audiobooks, or PDFs collection.

- *Move a book or PDF to a new collection:* Go to the cover or list views, tap Select, tap each work you want to move, and then tap Move. Select the new collection for these titles.

A book can reside in only one collection at a time (aside from the All Books collection).

Here we are telling you how to move or get rid of a book before you've even had a chance to read it. How gauche. The next section helps you start reading.

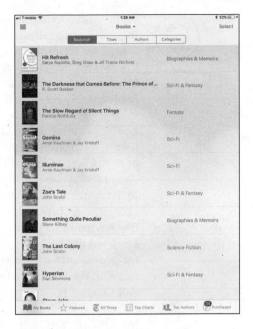

FIGURE 10-2:
Sort a list of your books by most recent, title, author, or category.

Reading a Book

To start reading a book, tap it. The book leaps forward and opens to either the beginning or the place where you left off. (And you may have left off on an iPhone, an iPod touch, another iPad, or a Mac. Through your Apple ID, your virtual place in a book is transported from device to device as long as the devices have an Internet connection.)

Even from the very title page, you can appreciate the color and beauty of Apple's app as well as the navigation tools, as shown in Figure 10-3.

If you rotate the iPad to the side, the one-page book view becomes a two-page view, but the navigational controls remain the same. On newer multitouch books, you may have a scrolling view of a book rather than the typical one-page view.

TIP

While you're lounging around reading, and especially if you're lying down, we recommend that you use the screen orientation lock (see Chapter 1) to stop the iPad from inadvertently rotating the display.

You can take advantage of the iPad's VoiceOver, Speak Selection, or Speak Screen features (Settings ⇨ General ⇨ Accessibility ⇨ Speech) to have the iPad read to you out loud. The feature may not be quite like having Mom or Dad read you to sleep but can be a potential godsend for people with impaired vision. For more on the VoiceOver feature, consult Chapter 15.

REMEMBER

In iOS 11, Siri has dramatically improved, but having her read an entire book to you is cumbersome. Maybe someday it will be seamless and easy. Read Chapter 14 for more on Siri.

Turning pages

You've been turning pages in books your entire life, so you don't want this simple feat to become a complicated ordeal just because you're reading electronically. Fear not; it's not.

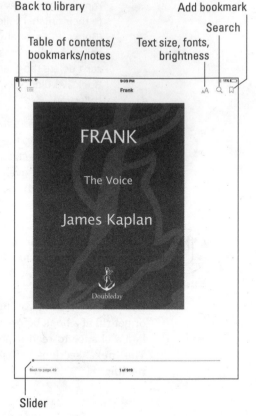

Back to library

Add bookmark

Search

Table of contents/ bookmarks/notes

Text size, fonts, brightness

Slider

FIGURE 10-3:
Books on the iPad offer handy reading and navigation tools.

You have no buttons to press. Instead, to turn to the *next* page of a book, do any of the following:

>> **Tap or flick your finger near the right of the page.** The page turns in a blink.

>> **Drag your finger near the right margin.** The page folds down as it turns, as if you were turning pages in a real book.

>> **Drag down from the upper-right corner of the book.** The page curls from that spot. The effect is so authentic, you can make out the faint type bleeding from the previous page on the next folded-down page.

>> **Drag up from the lower-right corner.** The page curls up from that spot.

>> **Drag from the middle-right margin.** The entire page curls.

REMEMBER

With the spilt multitasking feature (described in Chapter 2), be careful not to drag in from the right margin too close to the edge of the screen. Otherwise, you'll open a second app, rather than turn a page in the book.

To turn to the *previous* page in a book, tap, flick, or drag your finger in a similar fashion, except now do so closer to the left margin. You'll witness the same cool page-turning effects.

TIP

That's what happens by default anyway. Tap Settings ⇨ iBooks ⇨ Both Margins Advance. You have the option to go to the next page instead of the previous page when you tap near the left margin, so tapping either margin would advance you to the next page.

You can also flick to scroll through a book vertically rather than turning pages in portrait view. Tap the font icon (little A and big A), and then flip the Scrolling View switch.

While in Settings, you can also flip switches that turn on (or off) full justification, leading to neat edges on both sides of a book that you're reading. There's also a setting to turn on auto-hyphenation.

Settings for audiobooks let you skip forward or back in the book you're listening to by intervals of 10, 15, 30, 45, or 60 seconds. To skip forward by the selected time interval when you've opened the audiobook, either tap the skip forward icon (which will reveal the time interval you selected) or swipe the book cover from right to left. To retreat by the selected time interval, tap the skip back icon or swipe from left to right.

You'll also note when listening to an audiobook that you can change the playback speed by 0.75x, 1.25x, 1.5x, or 2x. The default speed is 1x.

REMEMBER

The iPad is smart, remembering where you left off. So if you close a book by tapping the Library button in the upper-left corner or by pressing the main Home button, you automatically return to this page when you reopen the book. It isn't necessary to bookmark the page (though you can, as we describe later in this chapter). The one proviso: You need an Internet connection when you close the book, because otherwise the server at Apple doesn't get the new bookmark info to pass on when you open the book on another device. And similarly, you need an Internet connection when you reopen the book to retrieve the information that was passed on.

Jumping to a specific page

When you're reading a book, you often want to go to a specific page. Here's how:

1. **If the page navigator controls aren't visible, summon them by tapping near the center of the page you're reading.**

   The controls are labeled in Figure 10-3.

2. **Drag your finger along the slider at the bottom of the screen until the chapter and page number you want appear.**

3. **Release your finger and — voilà! — that's where you are in the book.**

   Tap Back to Page *xx* at the bottom-left corner of the screen to return to your furthest point. Or tap Go to Page *xx* at the bottom right to return to a previous page you've read.

Going to the table of contents

Most books you read — on your iPad and elsewhere — have a table of contents. Here's how you use a table of contents on your iPad:

1. **With a book open on your iPad, tap the table of contents/list icon near the top of the screen (labeled in Figure 10-3).**

   The Table of Contents screen, as shown in Figure 10-4, appears.

2. **Tap the chapter, title page, or another entry to jump to that page.**

   Alternatively, tap the Resume button that appears at the upper-left corner of the screen to return to the previous location in the book.

Adding bookmarks

Moving around to a particular location on the iPad is almost as simple as moving around a real book, and as we explain in the earlier section

FIGURE 10-4:
Perusing a table of contents.

"Turning pages," Apple kindly returns you to the last page you were reading when you closed a book.

Still, occasionally you want to bookmark a page so that you can easily return to it. To insert a bookmark somewhere, merely tap the bookmarks icon near the upper-right reaches of the screen. The bookmarks icon turns red, signifying that a bookmark is in place. Tap the ribbon if you want to remove the bookmark. Simple as that.

After you set a bookmark, here's how to find it later:

1. **Tap the table of contents/list icon (labeled in Figure 10-3).**

2. **Tap Bookmarks (if it's not already selected).**

   Your bookmark is listed along with the chapter and page citations, the date you bookmarked the page, and a phrase or two of surrounding text, as the example in Figure 10-5 shows.

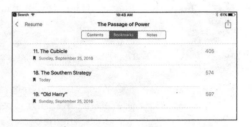

3. **Tap your desired bookmark to return to that page in the book.**

FIGURE 10-5: Finding the pages you bookmarked.

You can remove a bookmark from the bookmarks list by swiping your finger to the left along the bookmark and then tapping the red Delete button that appears.

Adding highlights and notes

In addition to setting bookmarks to jump to pages you want to read again, you can highlight words or passages on a page as well as add annotations or comments, which is handy for school assignments. Pardon the pun, but Apple is on the same page. Here's how to do both:

1. **Press and hold down against the text and drag the grab points to select text. Then lift your finger.**

2. **Tap the selected text.**

   You see a toolbar of buttons: Copy, Highlight, Note, Search, and Share.

3. **Tap one of the following to add a highlight or note:**

   - *Copy:* The word or passage you select can be pasted someplace else.

   - *Highlight:* The word or passage you selected is highlighted in color. You can read the highlight later by returning to the table of contents page in the same way that you find a bookmark. (See the preceding section and refer to Figure 10-5.)

- *Note:* A Post-it–like note appears on the screen. Using the virtual keyboard, type your note.

THE iPAD GOES TO SCHOOL

Apple has been pushing iPads in K-12 and higher education. As part of its vision for the iPad, the company is throwing its considerable weight behind digital textbooks, works that include interactive captions, quizzes, 3D objects, and video. Apple even unveiled free software for the Mac called iBooks Author to encourage teachers and others to produce their own interactive books for learning.

In the meantime, among the early high school textbooks produced for the iPad are titles that cover algebra, environmental sciences, physics, and other subjects.

E. O. Wilson's *Life on Earth* is an especially rich interactive digital biology textbook like none you've seen, from 3D models of DNA to animated maps of global photosynthesis. The introduction to the book was made available for free, after which you were able to purchase additional chapters as they were released, at $1.99 apiece. Eventually, everything became free. (In general, publishers will have to work out pricing on most emerging textbooks.) Wilson's book could be viewed only by using iBooks 3.0 or later on an iPad running iOS 5.1 or later. (iBooks was up to iBooks 4.13 in iOS 11 at the time of this writing.)

Meanwhile, if a book supports it, you can turn your notes into study cards — a great way for students to learn vocabulary or prepare for exams. (If the option is available, you'll see an icon that looks like a notepad just to the right of the Table of Contents button.) You can swipe the cards to move from one to another, or tap a card to see one side with glossary terms or material you've highlighted and the other with any notes you've supplied. You'll see an icon that looks like a small gear with a peace symbol inside it. Apple has the backing of such prominent textbook publishers as Houghton Mifflin Harcourt, McGraw-Hill, and Pearson. What's more, some third-party publishers such as Kno and Inkling are producing some interesting interactive textbooks.

According to Apple, hundreds of thousands of books in the iBooks Store can be used in school curriculums, including novels for English or social studies. A world of educational content is accessible also via the iTunes U app.

We should point out that although educational materials are a main impetus behind iBooks, other books rich in audio, video, and other interactive materials take full advantage of Apple's latest software.

TIP

After you add a highlight or note, the following tips are handy to know:

>> **Remove a highlight or note.** Tap the highlighted text or note, and then tap the trash icon on the toolbar that appears. Alternatively, from the Notes section in the table of contents page, swipe your finger from right to left along an entry and then tap the red Delete button that appears.

>> **Change the color of a highlight or note.** You can change the color from the default yellow to green, blue, pink, or purple. Touch the highlighted selection for a moment and then lift your finger. From the toolbar, tap the icon with the color that you prefer. You can underline a passage instead by tapping the icon with an underlined letter A. This icon is adjacent to the icons representing your color choices.

>> **Share or print notes.** On the table of contents page, tap the share icon (shown in the margin) in the upper-right corner. Tap Mail to email your notes, or tap Print to print them (provided you have a compatible printer; see Chapter 2 for details about printing). You also have options to share via Message, or to post on Twitter, Facebook, or Sina Weibo, the Chinese social network (if a Chinese keyboard is enabled). We don't know how that will play politically in China. A third-party app sharing option may also present itself. Oh, and you can share notes in the iPad's own Notes app. It's so meta. Meanwhile, to see other possibilities for notes and iBooks generally, read the nearby sidebar "The iPad goes to school."

TIP

With iBooks, you can sync bookmarks and notes, as well as your collections across all your devices (Macs, iPhones, iPod touches, and of course your iPad). But if you don't want to do so, head to Settings and flip the switches to turn off these options. You also have the option to flip a switch that lets you allow books to access a publisher's content from the Internet.

Changing the type size, font, and page color

If you want to change the way a page looks, begin by tapping the Aa icon at the top right of the screen. You can then change the following:

>> **Typeface size:** Tap the uppercase *A* or the lowercase *a* to make the text larger or smaller, respectively.

>> **Font:** Tap Fonts, and then tap the font style you want to switch to. Your choices at this time are Athelas, Charter, Georgia, Iowan, Palatino, San Francisco, Seravek, and Times New Roman. We don't necessarily expect you to know what these look like just by the font names — fortunately, you can examine the change right before your eyes. A check mark indicates the currently selected font style.

- » **Scrolling:** If you prefer to scroll up or down to move from page to page, flip the Scrolling View switch.

- » **Page color:** Tap White (the default), Sepia, Gray, or Night. You can also flip an Auto-Night Theme switch to have the iPad automatically choose the Night theme when you're reading in the wee hours without the lights on.

- » **Brightness:** And speaking of light, you can raise or lower the brightness of the screen as you read by dragging the slider.

Searching inside and outside a book

If you want to find a passage in a book but can't remember where it is, try searching for it. Here's how:

1. **Tap the search (magnifying glass) icon.**

2. **Type your search term or page number on the virtual keyboard that slides up from the bottom.**

   All the occurrences in the book turn up in a window under the search icon, complete with a few lines of text and a page citation.

3. **Tap one of the items to jump to that portion of the book.**

   The words you were searching for are highlighted on that page.

You can also search the web (via Google or your chosen search engine) or Wikipedia, the online encyclopedia, by using the corresponding buttons at the bottom of the search results. If you do so, the iBooks app closes, and the Safari browser fires up Google or Wikipedia, with your search term already entered.

REMEMBER

If you search Google or Wikipedia in this fashion, you are, for the moment, closing the iBooks app and opening Safari. To return to the book you're reading, you must reopen the app. Fortunately, you're brought back to where you left off in the book. And Google is still the search choice through iBooks, even if you selected another search engine in Safari.

Shopping for E-Books

We love browsing in a physical bookstore, and the experience of browsing Apple's iBooks Store is equally pleasurable. Apple makes it a cinch to search for books you want to read, and even lets you peruse a sample before parting with your hard-earned dollars. To enter the store from either the cover or library list view, tap one of the buttons at the bottom of the display: Featured, Top Charts, Top Authors, or Purchased. Of course the other My Books tab at the bottom of the screen brings you back to the library of books you already own. We explore these further shortly.

Meanwhile, a few things to keep in mind: The iBooks Store operates in 51 countries, but free iBooks are available in at least 155 countries as of this writing. More than one billion books have been downloaded. Not all books are available in all markets, of course. Some works — Jay-Z's memoir *Decoded,* to take a single example — are enhanced with video. Meanwhile, the store includes titles from major trade publishers: Hachette Book Group, HarperCollins, Macmillan, Penguin Group, Simon & Schuster, and Random House, as well as several independents. John Wiley & Sons, Inc., is also represented, of course.

Publishers, not Apple, set the prices. Many bestsellers in the joint cost $12.99, though some fetch $9.99 or less. Apple runs specials from time to time. Anne Hillerman's *Spider Woman's Daughter,* which once cost $15.99, was $6.99 at the time of this writing. Stephen King's *Mile 81* is $3.99. Free selections are also available. Prices change all the time, so poke around for something you'll find pleasurable to read and then decide whether the book is worth buying for the price.

Just browsing the iBooks Store

You have several ways to browse for books in the iBooks Store. The top portion of the screen shows ever-changing ads for books that fit a chosen category (Mysteries & Thrillers in the example shown in Figure 10-6). But you can also browse Release Date in the particular category you have in mind. You can scroll to the left or right for more releases to peek at. Or tap See All for many more selections.

Look at the bottom of the screen. You see the following icons:

>> **Featured:** This tab is where you've been hanging out so far in this chapter. Featured works are books being promoted in the store and may include popular titles or an author spotlight from the likes of

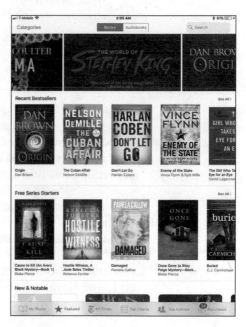

FIGURE 10-6:
The featured page for Mysteries & Thrillers.

The Hunger Games writer Suzanne Collins. You choose a given category to view (such as Fiction & Literature, Biographies & Memoirs, or Kids). In this Mysteries & Thrillers example, you'll see recent bestsellers, as well as authors whose names are in the spotlight. Swipe the featured books at the top of the screen for more choices. Do the same, if you want, for the Coming Soon sections, as well as sections not visible in the image. Or tap See All for more selections. Scroll all the way to the bottom of the screen for links to check out your iTunes account information and redeem iTunes gift cards and gift certificates. You'll also find quick links, including iBooks on Instagram, Books Made into Movies, and Sneak Peeks. Are you a budding author? There's even a link to submit and sell your own books.

>> **NY Times:** Apple offers *The New York Times* Bestsellers lists for fiction and non-fiction, showing the top 14 titles in each. It's a great way to see what's popular.

>> **Top Charts:** Here Apple shows you the most popular books in the iBooks Store. You find lists for Paid Books and Free Books both for print and audio-books. Scroll down to see more of the top books in each category.

>> **Top Authors:** Tapping the Top Authors icon lets you find books by poring through a list of popular authors, shown in a scrollable pane on the left half of the screen. Flick your finger up or down to scroll the list, or tap one of the letters in the margin to jump to authors whose name begins with that letter. When you tap an author's name, a list of his or her available titles appears in a scrollable pane on the right.

>> **Purchased:** Tapping here shows you the books you've already bought, which you can download onto your iPad.

Searching the iBooks Store

In the upper-right corner of the iBooks Store is a search field, similar to the search field in iTunes. Tap the search field, and then use the virtual keyboard to type an author name or title to find the book you seek.

TIP

If you like freebies, search for *free* in the iBooks Store. You'll find tons of (mostly classic) books that cost nothing, and you won't even have to import them. See the section "Finding free books outside the iBooks Store," later in this chapter, for more places to find free books. By Apple's count, free content is distributed in 155 countries. Off the top of our heads, we can't remember how many countries are on Planet Earth, but it's fair to say that when it comes to digital books, Apple has most of them covered.

Deciding whether a book is worth it

To find out more about a book that you come across, you can check out the details page and other readers' reviews or read a sample of the book:

>> **Find the book's details.** Tap its cover. An information screen appears with Details highlighted by default. You can see when the book was published, read a description, see the number of pages, and more.

>> **Find ratings and reviews.** Tap Reviews to see the grades other readers bestowed on the book. If you've already read the book, throw in your own two cents by tapping Write a Review.

>> **Find other books by the same author.** Tap Related to see the covers of other books written by the author. You can also check out other books that customers who bought this book also bought.

>> **Share your interest in a book.** Tap the share icon in the upper-right corner of the information screen. You can then sing the praises of a book by tapping icons for Message, Mail, Notes, Twitter, and Facebook, as well as Chinese social networks Sina Weibo and Tencent Weibo (assuming you enabled a Chinese keyboard). You can also add the book to your Reminders app or tap Copy Link or Gift (if you're feeling generous).

The best thing you can do to determine whether a book is worth buying is to read a sample. Tap Sample, and the book cover almost immediately lands on your bookshelf. You can read it like any book, up until the point where your free sample ends. Apple has placed a Buy button inside the pages of the book to make it easy to purchase it if you're hooked. The word *Sample* is plastered on the cover on the bookshelf to remind you that this book isn't yours — yet. And as we pointed out, there's also a premade collection for your samples.

Buying a book from the iBooks Store

When a book meets or exceeds your lofty standards and you're ready to purchase it, simply do the following:

1. **Tap the price shown in the button on the book's information page.**

   The dollar amount disappears, and the button carries a green Buy Book label. If you tap a free book instead, the button is labeled Get Book.

2. **Tap the Buy Book or Get Book button.**

3. **Enter your iTunes password (if you're prompted).**

The book appears on your bookshelf in an instant, ready for you to tap it and start reading. You get an email receipt acknowledging your purchase via the same mail account in which you receive other receipts from iTunes for music, movies, and apps.

On the iPad Air 2, iPad mini 3, iPad mini 4, iPad 9.7-inch, and iPad Pros with the Touch ID fingerprint scanner, you can authorize the purchase of a book by pressing your finger against the Touch ID scanner when prompted.

Buying books beyond Apple

The business world is full of examples in which one company competes with another on some level, only to work with it as a partner on another level. When the iPad first burst onto the scene in early April 2010, pundits immediately compared it to Amazon's Kindle, the market-leading electronic reader. Sure, the iPad had the larger screen and color, but the Kindle had a few bragging points too, including a longer battery life (up to about a month on the latest Kindle, versus about 10 hours for the iPad), a lighter weight, and a larger selection of books in its online bookstore.

But Amazon has long said that it wants Kindle books to be available for all sorts of electronic platforms, and the iPad, like the iPhone and iPod touch before it, is no exception. So we recommend taking a look at the free Kindle app for the iPad, especially if you've already purchased a number of books in Amazon's Kindle Store and want access to that wider selection of titles. On the iPad, you must purchase new Kindle books through a web browser, not through the Kindle app.

The Barnes & Noble Nook app is also worth a look. You can find several other e-book–type apps for the iPad in the App Store. To name a few:

» CloudReaders from Cloud Readers (free)

» Kobo Reading App – Read Books and Magazines by Kobo

» Bluefire Reader from Bluefire Productions

See Chapter 11 for details about finding and downloading apps.

Finding free books outside the iBooks Store

TIP

Apple supports a technical standard called *ePub*, which is the underlying technology behind thousands of free public-domain books. You can import these to the iPad without shopping in the iBooks Store. Such titles must be *DRM-free*, which means that they're free of digital rights management restrictions.

To import ePub titles, you can download them to your Mac or PC, and then sync them to the iPad through iTunes. There are other methods. If you have Dropbox, for example, you can bring an ePub into your account, and from Dropbox you can share the title with iBooks. You can also email an ePub as an attachment.

You can find ePub titles at numerous cyberspace destinations, among them

- » **Baen:** www.baen.com
- » **Feedbooks:** www.feedbooks.com
- » **Google Play:** http://play.google.com/store/books
- » **Project Gutenberg:** www.gutenberg.org
- » **Smashwords:** www.smashwords.com

(Note that most books at Google Play are free, and Google has a downloadable app.) Also, check out the free titles that you can find through the apps mentioned in the preceding section.

Reading Newspapers and Magazines

People in the newspaper business know that it's been tough sledding in recent years. The Internet has proved to be a disruptive force in media, as it has in so many areas. It remains to be seen what role Apple generally, and the iPad specifically, will play in the future of electronic periodicals or in helping to turn around sagging media enterprises. It's also uncertain which pricing models will make the most sense from a business perspective.

What we can tell you is that reading newspapers and magazines on the iPad is not like reading newspapers and magazines in any other electronic form. The experience is slick, but only you can decide whether it's worth paying the tab (in the cases where you do have to pay).

You can subscribe to or read a single issue of a newspaper or magazine on the iPad. There are several fine publishing apps worth checking out, including *USA TODAY* (where Ed works), *The Wall Street Journal*, *TIME* magazine, *The New York Times*, *The New Yorker*, *Reuters News Pro*, *BBC News*, *Vanity Fair*, and *Popular Science*. Sometimes you can read for free; sometimes you must play for your subscription. We also highly recommend fetching the free Zinio app, which offers more than 6,000 digital publications, including *Rolling Stone*, *The Economist*, *Consumer Reports*, *Forbes*, *Macworld*, *Car and Driver*, *Maxim*, *National Geographic Interactive*, *Spin*, and *Bloomberg Businessweek*. You can buy single issues of a magazine or subscribe, and you can sample and share some articles without a subscription.

In some cases, you have to pay handsomely or subscribe to some of these newspapers and magazines, which you find not in the iBooks Store but in the regular App Store, which we cover in Chapter 11. You also see ads (somebody has to pay the freight).

TIP

Some libraries have their own lending apps for e-books, magazines, and other media. Check out your local library to see what they offer.

Meantime, if you like to read stuff from particular blogs or sites, consider the free Feedly news-gathering app, which you can fetch from the App Store.

The freshest path to reading publications on your iPad is through the News app. It sports content from a gaggle of online and offline content producers, including some of the big name publishers visible in Figure 10-7. When you get started with the News app, you can choose the news sources and topics that you'd like to follow. Apple says you can choose from more than 1 million topics.

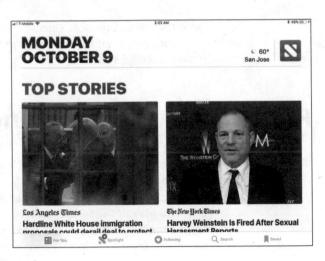

FIGURE 10-7:
Many of the world's leading informational sources contribute to News.

After making your initial content selections, you'll receive a smorgasbord of news stories that are presumably of interest, all delivered in a handsome layout that loosely reminds us of one of our favorite third-party apps, Flipboard. You can sign up for notifications and have news delivered to your inbox.

Apple promises to refine the content it is sending your way as it gets to know your reading preferences over time.

In the meantime, you can search for content as well as share stuff you read, by tapping the now familiar share icon and choosing among a variety of sharing options.

However you choose to read on your iPad — through iBooks, electronic periodicals, or the News app — your experience is likely to be rich, informative, and pleasurable.

4

The iPad at Work

Learn how to shop 'til you drop in the App Store, an emporium replete with a gaggle of neat little programs and applications. Best of all, unlike most of the stores you frequent, a good number of the items can be had for free.

Get down to business and explore staying on top of your appointments and people with Calendar and Contacts.

Discover time- and effort-saving utilities such as Reminders, Notes, and Clock.

Take control of your iPad with Notifications and Control Center.

Get to know Siri, your (mostly) intelligent assistant. She responds to your voice and can do some amazing tasks, including sending messages, scheduling appointments and reminders, searching the web, and playing a specific song or artist.

Chapter **11**

App-solutely!

One of the best things about the iPad is that you can download and install apps created by third parties, which is to say not created by Apple (the first party) or you (the second party). At the time of this writing, our best guess is that there are more than 2.2 million apps available and over 100 billion apps downloaded to date. Some apps are free, and other apps cost money; some apps are useful, and other apps are lame; some apps are perfectly well behaved, and other apps quit unexpectedly (or worse). The point is that of the many apps out there, some are better than others.

In this chapter, we take a broad look at apps that you can use with your iPad. You discover how to find apps on your computer or your iPad, and you find some basics for managing your apps. Don't worry: We have plenty to say about specific third-party apps in Chapters 18 and 19.

Tapping the Magic of Apps

Apps enable you to use your iPad as a game console, a streaming Netflix player, a recipe finder, a sketchbook, and much, much more. You can run three categories of apps on your iPad:

>> **Apps made exclusively for the iPad:** This is the rarest kind, so you find fewer of these than the other two types. These apps won't run on an iPhone or iPod touch, so you can't even install them on either device.

>> **Apps made to work properly on an iPad, iPhone, or iPod touch:** These so-called *universal apps* can run on any of the three device types at full resolution. What is the full-screen resolution for each device? Glad you asked. It ranges from 960 x 640 pixels for older iPhones and iPod touches to a whopping 2,732 x 2048 pixels for the 12.9-inch iPad Pro and 2,224 x 1,668 for the 10.5-inch iPad Pro. All other current iPads have 2,048 x 1536 pixels.

>> **Apps made for the iPhone and iPod touch:** These apps run on your iPad but only at iPhone/iPod touch resolution rather than the full resolution of your iPad, as demonstrated in Figure 11-1.

TIP

You can double the size of an iPhone/iPod touch app by tapping the little 2x button in the lower-right corner of the screen; to return it to its native size, tap the 1x button. Figure 11-1 shows you what an iPhone/iPod touch app looks like on an iPad screen.

Frankly, most iPhone/iPod apps look pretty good at 2x size, but we've seen a few that have jagged graphics and don't look as nice. Still, with 2.2 million apps to choose from, we're sure that you can find a few that make you happy.

FIGURE 11-1:
iPhone and iPod touch apps run at a smaller size (left), but can be increased to double size (right).

You can obtain and install apps for your iPad in two ways:

>> The App Store app on your iPad

>> Via automatic download

To switch on automatic downloads on the iPad, tap Settings ⇨ iTunes & App Store. Then tap the Automatic Downloads switch for Apps so that it turns green (on). After you do so, all apps you buy on other iOS devices will automagically appear on your iPad.

TIP

Consider also enabling automatic downloads for Music, Books, and Updates while you have the iTunes & App Store settings on your screen.

TIP

After you've obtained an app from the App Store, you can download it from iCloud to up to ten iOS devices (as long as you log in with the same iCloud account or use Family Sharing).

But before you can use the App Store on your iPad, you first need an iTunes Store account.

REMEMBER

If you don't have an iTunes Store account, you can't download a single cool app — not even the free ones — for your iPad.

So, if you don't have an iTunes Store account, might we suggest that you get one now? Just tap Settings ⇨ iTunes & App Store ⇨ Sign In ⇨ Create New Account and follow the on-screen instructions.

Finding Apps in the App Store

Finding apps with your iPad is easy. The only requirement is that you have an Internet connection of some sort — Wi-Fi or wireless data network — so that you can access the iTunes App Store and browse, search, download, and install apps.

Browsing the App Store

To get started, tap the App Store icon (shown in the margin) on your iPad's Home screen. After you launch the App Store, you see five icons at the bottom of the screen, representing five ways to interact with the store, as shown in Figure 11-2. The first three icons— Today, Games, and Apps— offer three ways to browse the virtual shelves of the App Store. (We get to the fourth and fifth icons, Updates and Search, shortly.)

The Today section, shown in Figure 11-2, highlights curated selections from the App Store, including App of the Day and Game of the Day; themed collections, such as Follow All the MLB Playoff Action! and a handful of baseball-related apps; and staff favorites.

The Games section lets you browse games in categories such as Game-Changing AR, New Games We Love, and Be an Armchair Architect, to name a few. Scroll down and you'll find sections for Top Paid Games, Top Free Games, and Top Game Categories.

The Apps section is like déjà vu all over again if you've already visited the Games section. It also contains categories such as Do More with Drag and Drop, New Apps We Love, and Fall Filter Fun, as shown in Figure 11-3. Scroll down a little farther and you'll find Top Paid Apps, Top Free Apps, Top App Categories, and more.

Most pages in the App Store display more apps than can fit on the screen at once. For example, the New Apps We Love section in Figure 11-3 contains more than the nine apps you can see. A few tools help you navigate the Games, Apps, and other sections of the App Store:

>> **Swipe from right to left** to see more apps in most categories.

>> **Swipe up the screen** to scroll down and see additional categories.

>> **Tap the See All link** at the top right of most sections to (what else?) see all the apps in that section on one screen at the same time.

Updating apps

As we mention earlier in this chapter, every so often the developer of an iPad app releases an update. If an update awaits you, a little number in

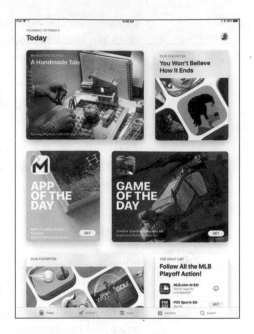

FIGURE 11-2:
The icons across the bottom represent different ways to browse the App Store.

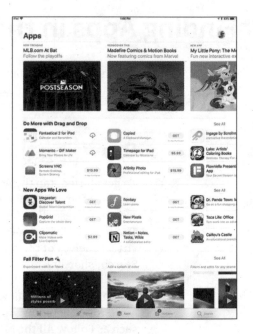

FIGURE 11-3:
The Apps section displays apps organized by themes, such as "Do More with Drag and Drop."

a circle appears on the Updates icon at the bottom of the iPad screen. Follow these steps to update your apps from your iPad:

1. **Tap the Updates icon if any of your apps needs updating.**

   If you tap the Updates icon and see (in the middle of the screen) a message that says *No Updates: All Your Apps Are Up to Date,* none of the apps on your iPad requires an update at this time. If apps need updating, they appear with Update buttons next to them.

2. **Tap the Update button that appears next to any app to update it.**

   If more than one app needs updating, you can update them all at once by tapping the Update All button in the upper-right corner of the screen.

REMEMBER

If you try to update an app purchased from any iTunes Store account except your own, you're prompted for that account's ID and password. If you can't provide them, you can't download the update. This doesn't apply, of course, if you've enabled Family Sharing (see Chapter 15).

WARNING

Sometimes an update is worse than its predecessor. If you have mission-critical apps on your iPad, you probably shouldn't update them without careful consideration and research. And you'll want to disable Automatic Downloads for app updates. To do so, tap Settings ⇨ iTunes & App Store and then tap the Updates switch in the Automatic Downloads section so it's turned off (not green).

One last tip: If you download an app and it doesn't work properly, try deleting and redownloading it from the App Store. Doing so fixes the problem as often as not.

Searching for apps

Finally, the last option at the bottom of the screen is Search, the magnifying glass icon. If you know exactly what you're looking for (or even approximately what you're looking for), just tap Search to bring up the virtual keyboard, and then type a word or phrase. Then tap the Search key to initiate the search.

That's all there is to it.

Finding details about an app

Now that you know how to browse and search for apps in the App Store, the following sections show you how to find out more about a particular app. After tapping an app icon as you browse the store or in a search result, your iPad displays a details screen like the one shown in Figure 11-4.

TIP

Note the blue More link in the lower-right corner of the What's New section in Figure 11-4; click More to see a longer description of the app.

Bear in mind that the app description on this screen was written by the app's developer and may be biased. Never fear, gentle reader: In an upcoming section, we show you how to find app reviews written by people who have used the app (and, unfortunately, sometimes people who haven't).

Understanding the app rating

The Real Racing 3 app is rated for age 4+, as you can see to the far right of the 4.5 user rating (labeled in Figure 11-4). The rating means that the app contains no objectionable material. Here are the other possible ratings:

Download from iCloud   Age rating

User rating   More link

FIGURE 11-4:
Real Racing 3 is a free car racing game with awesome graphics and realistic physics.

>> **9+:** May contain mild or infrequent occurrences of cartoon, fantasy, or realistic violence; or infrequent or mild mature, suggestive, or horror-themed content that may not be suitable for children younger than 9.

>> **12+:** May contain infrequent mildly offensive language; frequent or intense cartoon, fantasy, or realistic violence; mild or infrequent mature or suggestive themes; or simulated gambling that may not be suitable for children younger than 12.

>> **17+:** May contain frequent and intense offensive language; frequent and intense cartoon, fantasy, or realistic violence; mature, frequent, and intense mature, suggestive, or horror-themed content; sexual content; nudity; or depictions of alcohol, tobacco, or drugs that may not be suitable for children younger than 17. You must be at least 17 years old to purchase games with this rating.

Checking requirements and device support for the app

One more thing: Remember the three categories of apps we mention at the beginning of the chapter, in the "Tapping the Magic of Apps" section? Scroll down the page to the Information section (not shown in Figure 11-4), and you'll find that this app *Requires iOS 7.0 or later. Compatible with iPhone, iPad, and iPod touch.*

Reading reviews

The Ratings & Reviews section of the details screen offers reviews written by users of this app. Each review includes a star rating, from zero to five. If an app is rated four stars or higher, you can safely assume that most users are happy with the app.

In Figure 11-4, you can see that this app has a rating of 4.5 stars based on 1.4K user ratings. That means it's probably a pretty good app.

Finally, Tap See All to read more user reviews.

REMEMBER

Don't believe everything you read in reviews. Some people buy an app without reading its description, or they try to use it without following the included instructions. Then, when the app doesn't do what they expected, they give it a low rating. The point is, take the ratings and reviews with a grain of salt. And make sure the review you're reading is for the current version — reviews of older versions may be inaccurate.

To read reviews from your iPad, tap the Reviews tab. If you scroll to the bottom of the page and see a More Reviews button (not visible in Figure 11-4), tap it to see (what else?) more reviews.

Downloading an app

To download an app to your iPad from the App Store, follow these steps:

1. **Tap the blue price button (or the word *Get* or the download from iCloud icon) near the top of the app's details screen.**

    In Figure 11-4, you see the download from iCloud icon instead of a price because we purchased the game previously. For buyers, when tapped the button transforms into a green Buy button.

2. **Tap the blue Purchase button.**

3. **When prompted, type your iTunes Store account password.**

    After you do, the App Store closes, and you see the Home screen where the new app's icon will reside. The new app's icon is slightly dimmed and has the word *Loading* below it, with a pie chart to indicate how much of the app remains to be downloaded (about one third, as shown in the margin).

4. **If the app is rated 17+, click OK on the warning screen that appears after you type your password to confirm that you're 17 or older before the app downloads.**

DOWNLOADING OTHER CONTENT ON YOUR IPAD

You may have noticed that the App Store app on your iPad offers nothing but apps.

To obtain music, movies, and TV shows, you use the iTunes Store app; to read stories from newspapers and magazines, you use either the News app or the Safari app (both are included with your iPad).

But to download books, podcasts, or iTunes U content, you'll need the iBooks, Podcasts, or iTunes U apps, respectively, which may or may not be installed on your iPad.

The good news is that these apps are free in the App Store. So if you want to shop for books, podcasts, and iTunes U content on your iPad, you should probably go download all three apps now if they're not on your iPad.

For what it's worth, these apps work pretty much the same as the App Store. So, now that you understand how to navigate the App Store app, you also know how to use these other Store apps.

The app is now on your iPad. If your iPad suddenly loses its memory (unlikely) or you delete the app from your iPad, you can download it again from the App Store at no charge.

Working with Apps

Most of what you need to know about apps involves simply installing third-party apps on your iPad. However, you might find it helpful to know how to delete and review an app.

Deleting an app

Many of the preinstalled apps that came on your iPad — Photos, Camera, Contacts, Clock, Settings, and Messages, to name a few — can't be removed. But, you have two ways to delete any other app: in iTunes on your computer or directly from your iPad.

TIP

You can, however, hide certain preinstalled apps by choosing Settings ⇨ General ⇨ Restrictions.

To delete an app in iTunes (that is, from your computer), choose Apps in the drop-down menu, click the Library tab, and then do one of the following:

>> Click the app to select it and press the Delete or Backspace key on the keyboard.

>> Click the app to select it and then choose Edit ⇨ Delete.

>> Right-click the app and choose Delete.

After taking any of the actions in this list, you see a dialog that asks whether you're sure that you want to remove the selected app. If you click the Remove button, the app is removed from your iTunes library as well as from any iPad that syncs with your iTunes library.

Here's how to delete an app on your iPad:

1. **Press and hold any icon until all the icons begin to wiggle.**

2. **Tap the little *x* in the upper-left corner of the app that you want to delete.**

   A dialog appears, informing you that deleting this app also deletes all its data, as shown in Figure 11-5.

FIGURE 11-5:
Tap an app's little *x* and then tap Delete to remove the app from your iPad.

3. **Tap the Delete button.**

   You can't delete any of the bundled apps that came with your iPad.

REMEMBER

4. **To stop the icons from wiggling, press the Home or sleep/wake button.**

TIP

You also make icons wiggle to move them around on the screen or move them from page to page. To rearrange wiggling icons, press and drag them one at a time. If you drag an icon to the left or right edge of the screen, it moves to the next or previous Home screen. You can also drag additional icons to the dock (where Safari, Mail, Photos, and Music live) and have a total of anywhere from 11 apps (iPad mini) to 15 apps (12.9-inch iPad Pro) — plus 3 recent items if Recent Items is enabled — available on every Home screen.

Friendly reminder: Rearranging your icons in iTunes is faster and easier than making them wiggle and move on the iPad. See Chapter 3 to find out how.

Writing an app review

Sometimes you love or hate an app so much that you want to tell the world about it. In that case, you should write a review. You can do this in two ways: in iTunes on your computer or directly from your iPad.

To write a review using iTunes on your computer, follow these steps:

1. **Navigate to the details page for the app in the iTunes App Store.**

2. **Click the Ratings and Reviews tab and then click the Write a Review button.**

   You may or may not have to type your iTunes Store password.

3. **Click the button for the star rating (1 to 5) you want to give the app.**

4. **In the Title field, type a title for your review, and in the Review field, type your review.**

5. **Click the Submit button when you're finished.**

   The Preview screen appears. If the review looks good to you, you're done. If you want to change something, click the Edit button.

To write a review from your iPad, follow these steps:

1. **Tap the App Store icon to launch the App Store.**

2. **Navigate to the details screen for the app.**

3. **Tap the Reviews tab and then tap the Write a Review link.**

   You probably have to type your iTunes Store password.

4. **Tap one to five of the stars at the top of the Write a Review screen to rate the app.**

5. **In the Title field, type a title for your review, and in the Review field, type your review.**

6. **Tap the Submit button in the upper-right corner of the screen.**

   Whichever way you submit your review, Apple reviews your submission. As long as the review doesn't violate the (unpublished) rules of conduct for app reviews, it appears in a day or two in the App Store, in the Reviews section for the particular app.

TIP

You can configure the behavior of many apps in the Settings app. Scroll all the way down the list of settings and you'll find an alphabetical list of apps that have settings; tap an app in the list to see its settings.

NEW

One last thing: iOS 11 no longer supports older 32-bit apps. If you try to launch one, you'll see an alert telling you that the app needs to be updated by its developer to work with iOS 11. To see a list of 32-bit apps currently installed on your iPad, tap Settings ➪ General ➪ About ➪ Applications.

Chapter **12**

People, Places, and Appointments

We hate to break the news to you, but your iPad isn't only for fun and games; it has a serious side. The iPad can remind you of appointments and help you keep all your contacts straight.

Working with the Calendar

The Calendar program lets you keep on top of your appointments and events (birthdays, anniversaries, and the like). You open it by tapping the Calendar icon on the Home screen. The icon is smart in its own right because it changes daily, displaying the day of the week and the date.

You can display five calendar views: by year, by month, by day, by week, and by a searchable list view that shows current and future appointments.

Tap one of the four tabs at the top of the screen — Day, Week, Month, or Year — to choose a view. There's a Today button in the lower-left corner of the screen, which returns you to the current date in any view. (Also at the bottom of the screen are the Calendars button and Inbox button, which we get to shortly.)

To get to list view, tap the search icon — a little magnifying glass — in the upper-right corner of the screen.

We take a closer look at these views in the following sections.

Year view

There's not much to the yearly view, but it does let you see the current calendar year with today's date circled in red. You can scroll up or down to see prior or future years, but that's about it; unfortunately, you still can't tell on which days you have appointments in year view. Boo. Hiss.

Month view

Tap any of the months visible in the yearly view to jump to that specific month, as shown in Figure 12-1. When your iPad is in month view, you can see which days have appointments or scheduled events. Tap a day to see the list of activities on the agenda for that day, which leads nicely into the next section.

Day view

As we just mentioned, you have to tap a date to see what you have going on in a 24-hour period — though to see an entire day's worth of entries, you'll have to scroll up or down. You can swipe to the left to advance to the next day of the week and beyond; swipe to the right to retreat one or more days; or tap a day near the top of the screen to jump to it.

FIGURE 12-1:
Month view.

In this day view, all-day events, birthdays, and events pulled from your Facebook account (if you provide your Facebook credentials) appear in a narrow strip above the timeline for the day, as shown for the all-day event *Chicago MUG* in Figure 12-2.

Your daily appointments span the entire time in which they've been scheduled on your calendar. For example, if an appointment runs from 3:00 p.m. to 4:00 p.m., that hour will be blocked off on the calendar like the *MacObserver Dr. Mac's Rants & Raves Column deadline* item shown in Figure 12-2.

You find out how to create calendar entries in a moment, but for now know that you can press on an event and drag it to a new time slot should your plans change. If you have over-lapping appointments, you'll see more than a single entry claim a given time slot, like the 5:30 and 6:00 p.m. entries in Figure 12-2.

Finally, calendars are color-coded according to the calendar in which you scheduled the appointment to help you distinguish an appointment you made on your travel calendar versus, say, a work, family, or Facebook calendar.

Week view

In week view, shown in Figure 12-3, you can see an entire week at a glance. The current date is circled in red.

TIP

You can arrange to start your weekly view on any day of the week. Tap Settings ⇨ Calendars ⇨ Start Week On, and then tap the day on which you want to start your week (Sunday is the default in the United States).

FIGURE 12-2:
Day view.

FIGURE 12-3:
Week view.

SYNCING CALENDARS WITH YOUR DESKTOP

The iPad can display the color-coding you assigned in Calendar (formerly iCal) on a Mac. Cool, huh? If you're a Mac user who uses Calendar, you can create multiple calendars and choose which ones to sync with your iPad. What's more, you can choose to display any or all of your calendars on your iPad. Calendar entries you create on your iPad are synchronized with the calendar(s) you specified in the iTunes Info pane. You can also sync calendars with Microsoft Outlook on a Mac or Microsoft Outlook on a PC.

The best solution we've found is to use iCloud to keep calendars updated and in sync across all your iOS devices and computers. On the iPad, tap Settings ➪ *yourname* ➪ iCloud and make sure the Calendars switch is turned on (green). Your name, plus your face in a circle, appear at the top of the list on the left.

One last thing: If you're a Mac user running OS X 10.9 Mavericks or later, iCloud is the *only* way you can sync calendar data, as we mention in Chapter 3.

List view

List view isn't complicated. You can get to this view by tapping the search (magnifying glass) icon in the upper-right corner of the screen. As you would expect, all your calendar appointments are listed chronologically, as shown in Figure 12-4. If you have a lengthy list, drag up or down with your finger or flick to rapidly scroll through your appointments. If you're looking for a specific calendar entry, you can search for appointments by typing the title, invitee names, location, or note in the search box above your list of entries.

Tap any of the listings to get meeting or appointment details for that entry. If you tap a person's birthday, you see his or her contact information. Sorry, but you just ran out of excuses for not sending a card.

FIGURE 12-4:
List view.

Adding Calendar Entries

In Chapter 3, you discover pretty much everything there is to know about syncing your iPad, including syncing calendar entries from your Windows machine (using the likes of Microsoft Outlook) or Mac (using Calendar or Outlook) or Google Calendars. If you're syncing your calendar entries with iCloud, you can also manage your calendars at `www.icloud.com` from any computer or device with a web browser.

In addition, calendar events from Facebook can automatically show up in the Calendar app. Just tap Calendars at the bottom of the Calendar screen and enable the Facebook Events calendar.

In plenty of situations, you enter appointments on the fly. Adding appointments directly to the iPad is easy:

1. **On the Home screen, tap the Calendar icon, and then (optionally) tap the Year, Month, Week, or Day view.**

2. **Tap the + icon in the upper-right corner of the screen.**

   The New Event overlay appears, as shown in Figure 12-5.

3. **Tap the Title and Location fields in turn (second-generation iPads don't have a Location field) and type as much or as little information as you feel is necessary.**

   Tapping displays the virtual keyboard (if it's not already shown).

   TIP

   Don't forget that you can use dictation or Siri to add a calendar entry. See Chapter 14 for more on dictation and Siri.

FIGURE 12-5:
The screen looks like this just before you add an event to your iPad.

4. **To add start and end times:**

   a. *Tap the Starts field.*

   A carousel wheel, like the one shown for the Ends time in Figure 12-6, appears below the field you tapped.

   b. *Choose the time the event starts.*

   Use your finger to roll separate carousel controls for the date, hour, and minute (in 1-minute intervals) and to specify AM or PM. The process is a little like manipulating a combination bicycle lock or an old-fashioned date stamp used with an inkpad.

   c. *Tap the Ends field and choose the time the event ends.*

TIP

To enter an all-day milestone (such as a birthday), tap the All-Day switch to turn it on. (Green will be showing.) Because the time is no longer relevant for an all-day entry, you won't see Starts, Ends, or Time Zone options.

5. **When you're finished, tap Add.**

TIP

We can't think of any easier way to add an entry than to instruct Siri along the lines of "Set a lunch appointment for tomorrow at noon with the Smiths." Siri is pleased to comply.

That's the minimum you have to do to set up an event. But we bet you want to do more. The Calendar app makes it easy:

FIGURE 12-6: Controlling the Starts and Ends fields is like manipulating a bike lock.

>> **Change the time zone.** If the correct location isn't already present, tap the Time Zone field and type the name of the city where the appointment is taking place.

>> **Set up a recurring entry.** Tap the Repeat field. Tap to indicate how often the event in question recurs. This setting is good for everything from a weekly appointment, such as an allergy shot, to a yearly event, such as an anniversary.

The options are Every Day, Every Week, Every 2 Weeks, Every Month, and Every Year. Tap Never if you are planning to never repeat this entry again.

>> **Add travel time to and from events.** Tap the Travel Time field and enable the Travel Time switch. A list of durations appears, ranging from five minutes to two hours. Tap a duration to specify your travel time.

>> **Assign the entry to a particular calendar.** Tap Calendar, and then tap the calendar you have in mind (Home or Work, for example).

>> **Invite people to join you.** Tap Invitees to specify who among your contacts will be attending the event.

>> **Set a reminder or alert for the entry.** Tap Alert and tap a time.

Alerts can be set to arrive at the actual time of an event, or 1 week before, 2 days before, 1 day before, 2 hours before, 1 hour before, 30 minutes before, 15 minutes before, or 5 minutes before the event. If it's an all-day entry, you can request alerts 1 day before (at 9:00 a.m.), 2 days before (at 9:00 a.m.), or 1 week before.

When the appointment time rolls around, you hear a sound and see a message like the one shown in Figure 12-7.

TIP

If you're the kind of person who needs an extra nudge, set another reminder by tapping the Second Alert field (which you'll see only if a first alert is already set).

>> **Indicate whether you're busy or free by tapping Show As.** If you're invited to an event, you can tap Availability and then tap Free (if it's shown on your iPad).

>> **Enter a web address.** Tap the URL field (at the bottom of the New Event screen) and type the web address.

>> **Enter notes about the appointment or event.** Tap the Notes field (at the bottom of the screen) and type your note.

FIGURE 12-7:
Alerts make it hard to forget.

Tap Done after you finish entering everything.

Managing your calendars

When you have the hang of creating calendar entries, you can make the task much easier with these tips:

>> **Choose a default calendar.** Tap Settings ⇨ Calendar, and flick upward on the list on the left until you reach Calendar. Then tap Calendar ⇨ Default Calendar and select the calendar that you want to use as the default for new events.

>> **Make events appear according to whichever time zone you selected for your calendars.** In the Calendar settings, tap Time Zone Override to turn it on, and then tap Time Zone. Type the time zone's location, using the keyboard that appears. If you travel long distances for your job, this setting comes in handy.

When Time Zone Override is turned off, events are displayed according to the time zone of your current location.

REMEMBER

>> **Turn off calendar alert sounds.** Tap Settings ⇨ Sounds, and then make sure that the selected alert tone is set to None. (You see only the last calendar alert sound that you selected. To see your other choices, tap Calendar Alerts.) You can also set default alert times for birthdays, all-day events, or certain other events. Tap Settings ⇨ Calendar, and scroll down to Default Alert Times. For birthdays or other all-day events, you can choose to be alerted at 9:00 a.m. on the day of the event, at 9:00 a.m. one day before, at 9:00 a.m. two days before, or a week before. For other alerts, you can choose a default alert time at the time of event, 5 minutes before, 15 minutes before, 30 minutes before, 1 hour before, 2 hours before, 1 day before, 2 days before, or 1 week before the event.

>> **Modify an existing calendar entry.** Tap the entry, tap Edit, and then make whichever changes need to be made.

>> **Wipe out a calendar entry.** Scroll down to the bottom of the event (if necessary) and then tap Edit⇨Delete Event. You have a chance to confirm your choice by tapping either Delete Event (again) or Cancel.

Letting your calendar push you around

If you work for a company that uses Microsoft Exchange ActiveSync, calendar entries and meeting invitations from coworkers can be *pushed* to your device so that they show up on the screen moments after they're entered, even if they're entered on computers at work. Setting up an account to facilitate this pushing of calendar entries to your iPad is a breeze, although you should check with your company's tech or IT department to make sure that your employer allows it. Then follow these steps:

1. Tap Settings⇨Accounts & Passwords⇨Add Account.

2. From the Add Account list, tap Microsoft Exchange.

3. Fill in the email address, username, password, and description fields, and then tap Next.

4. If required, enter your server address on the next screen that appears.

   The iPad supports something called the Microsoft Autodiscovery service, which uses your name and password to automatically determine the address of the Exchange server. The rest of the fields should be filled in with the email address, username, password, and description you just entered.

5. Tap Next.

6. Tap the switch to turn on each information type that you want to synchronize using Microsoft Exchange.

   The options are Mail, Contacts, Calendars, and Reminders. You should be good to go now, although some employers may require you to add passcodes to safeguard company secrets.

REMEMBER

If you have a business-issued iPad and it is lost or stolen — or it turns out that you're a double agent working for a rival company — your employer's IT administrators can remotely wipe your device clean.

One more thing: If you sync via iCloud, Google, or Microsoft Exchange, your calendar entries are automatically pushed to your iPad by the server when received.

Displaying multiple calendars

By tapping the Calendars button at the bottom of the yearly, monthly, weekly, or daily view, you can choose the calendar or calendars to display on your iPad. Merely tap each calendar that you want to include so that a check mark appears next to it, as shown in Figure 12-8. To remove the check mark, tap again.

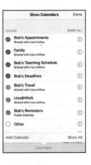

You can tap the Show All button (upper right) when you want your entire schedule to be an open book. You can also turn on Facebook events (in Settings) to display those in your calendar, as well as display birthdays, including those of the people you've friended on the social network.

FIGURE 12-8: Choosing the calendars to display.

From the Calendars list, tap the *i*-in-a-circle for even more tricks. You can assign a color to your calendar, share the calendar with a given individual (tap Add Person to do so), make a calendar public (by flipping a switch), or delete the calendar.

Responding to meeting invitations

The iPad has one more important button in the Calendar app. It's the Inbox button, located at the bottom-right corner of the yearly, monthly, weekly, and daily views. If you partake in iCloud, have a Microsoft Exchange account, or have a calendar that adheres to the CalDAV Internet standard, you can send and receive a meeting invitation, though you also need a compatible email app that understands CalDAV and lets you not only receive but also respond to the invitation.

If you have any pending invitations, you'll see them when you tap the Inbox, which is separated into new invitations and invitations to which you've already replied. You can tap any of the items in the list to see more details about the event to which you've been invited. (Note that the Calendar's Inbox is not the same as your email inbox.)

Suppose that a meeting invitation arrives from your boss. You can see who else is attending the shindig, check scheduling conflicts, and more. Tap Accept to let the meeting organizer know you're attending, tap Decline if you have something better to do (and aren't worried about upsetting the person who signs your paycheck), or tap Maybe if you're waiting for a better offer.

And as we point out previously, you can also invite other folks to attend an event that you yourself are putting together.

Meantime, if you run into a conflict, why not ask Siri to change your schedule? For that matter, you can also call upon Siri to remind you when you have your next appointment. Visit Chapter 14 for more on this clever feature.

TIP

You can choose to receive an alert every time someone sends you an invitation. In the Calendar settings, tap New Invitation Alerts so that the switch is turned on.

As mentioned, if you take advantage of iCloud, Google, or Microsoft Exchange, you can keep calendar entries synchronized between your iPhone, iPad, iPod touch, and Mac or PC. When you make a scheduling change on your iPad, it's automatically updated on your computer and other devices, and vice versa.

Subscribing to calendars

You can subscribe to calendars that adhere to the CalDAV and iCalendar (.ics) standards, which are supported by the popular Google and Yahoo! calendars and by the Mac's Calendar app. Although you can read entries on the iPad from the calendars you subscribe to, you can't create entries from the iPad or edit the entries that are already present.

To subscribe to one of these calendars, tap Settings ⇨ Accounts & Passwords. Tap Other and then choose Add CalDAV Account, Add Subscribed Calendar, or Add macOS Server Account. Next, enter the server where the iPad can find the calendar you have in mind, and if need be, a username, a password, and an optional description.

Finally, some apps, websites, and email messages will offer to add calendar events and subscriptions.

Sifting through Contacts

If you read the chapter on syncing (see Chapter 3), you know how to get the snail-mail addresses, email addresses, and phone numbers that reside on your Mac or PC into the iPad. Assuming that you went through that drill already, all those addresses and phone numbers are hanging out in one place. Their not-so-secret hiding place is revealed when you tap the Contacts icon on the Home screen. The following sections guide you from the main screen to whatever you want to do with your contacts' information.

Adding and viewing contacts

To add contacts from the Contacts app, tap the + icon at the top of the screen and type as much or as little profile information as you have for the person. Tap Add Photo to add a picture from your photo albums or collections (or to take a snapshot with your iPad camera). You can edit the information later by tapping the Edit button when a contact's name is highlighted.

A list of your contacts appears on the left panel of the screen, with the one you're currently viewing shown in gray; see Figure 12-9. At the top on the right, you can see a mug shot of your contact with his or her address. Below that you'll see the contact's phone number, email address, home and another address, and birthday (all blurred in Figure 12-9 to protect Jacob's privacy). You also find an area to scribble notes about a contact.

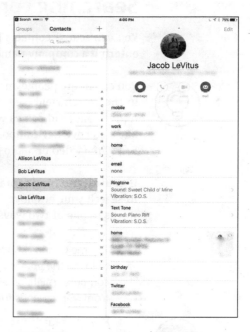

FIGURE 12-9:
A view of all contacts.

TIP

You have three ways to land on a specific contact:

>> **Flick your finger so that the list of contacts on the left side scrolls rapidly up or down,** loosely reminiscent of the spinning Lucky 7s and other pictures on a Las Vegas slot machine. Think of the payout you'd get with that kind of power on a one-armed bandit.

>> **Slide your thumb or another finger along the alphabet on the right edge of the contacts list** or tap one of the teeny-tiny letters to jump to names that begin with that letter.

>> **Start to type the name of a contact in the search field near the top of the contacts list.** Or type the name of the place where your contact works. When you're at or near the appropriate contact name, stop the scrolling by tapping the screen.

TIP

When you tap to stop the scrolling, that tap doesn't select an item in the list. This may seem counterintuitive the first few times you try it, but we got used to it and now we really like it this way. Just think of that first tap as applying the brakes to the scrolling list.

You can change the way your contacts are displayed. Tap Settings ⇨ Mail, Contacts, Calendars. Then scroll down to Contacts settings on the right side of the screen, if it's not already visible. Tap Sort Order or Display Order, and for each one, choose the First, Last option or Last, First option to indicate whether you want to sort or display entries by a contact's first or last name.

Searching contacts

You can search contacts by entering a first or last name in the search field or by entering a company name.

TIP

You can locate people on your iPad without opening the Contacts app. Type a name in the Search field (see Chapter 2), and then tap the name in the search results. And if your iPad comes with Siri, you can not only ask her to find people for you but also have her compose and send them an email or iMessage, or call them via FaceTime video or audio chat.

If you're searching contacts with a Microsoft Exchange account, you may be able to search your employer's *global address list* (GAL for short). This search typically works in one of two ways:

>> Tap the Groups button in the upper-left corner of the All Contacts screen and then tap the appropriate Exchange server name to find folks. Groups on your computer might reflect, say, different departments in your company, friends from work, friends from school, and so on.

TECHNICAL STUFF

>> You can search an LDAP *(Lightweight Directory Access Protocol)* server. It strikes us that nothing is "lightweight" about something called an LDAP server, but we digress. Similarly, if you have a CardDAV account, you can search for any contacts that have been synced to the iPad.

Contacting and sharing your contacts

You can initiate an email from Contacts by tapping an email address under a contact's listings. Doing so fires up the Mail program on the iPad, with the person's name already in the To field. For more on the Mail app, we direct you to Chapter 5.

You can also share a contact's profile with another person. Tap the Share Contact button (you may have to scroll down to see it), and use the Mail or Messages app to send the contact's vCard, which is embedded in the body of a new Mail or Messages message. Just add an address and send it on its merry way. A *vCard*, in case you were wondering, is kind of like an electronic business card. You can identify it by its .vcf file format.

NEW

You can also share a contact's vCard with iOS 11's new drag-and-drop feature. Just press and hold down on a contact in the list, and then drag it to another app (such as Messages or Mail).

Finally, you can tap a contact's snail-mail address to launch the Maps app and see it pinned to a map.

Linking contacts

The people you know most likely have contact entries in more than one account, meaning that you might end up with redundant entries for the same person. The iPad solution is to *link* contacts. Find the contact in question, tap Edit, scroll to the bottom of the Edit screen, and tap Link Contact. Choose the related contact entry and then tap Link. It's worth noting that the linked contacts in each account remain separate and aren't merged.

Removing a contact

Hey, it happens. A person falls out of favor. Maybe he's a jilted lover. Or maybe you just moved cross country and no longer will call on the services of your old gardener.

Removing a contact is easy, if unfortunate. Tap a contact and then tap Edit. Scroll to the bottom of the Edit screen and tap Delete Contact. You get one more chance to change your mind.

One last thing: You can't remove contacts provided by Facebook or other apps. However, you can disable the Facebook (or other) calendar if you don't care to see Facebook contacts in your iOS Contacts app.

And that, gentle reader, should be pretty much all you need to work with Contacts. Onward!

Chapter **13**

Indispensable iPad Utilities

W e'd venture to say that no one bought an iPad because of Notes, Clock, Reminders, or Game Center. Still, these apps help make the iPad indispensable on a daily basis.

In addition to the indispensable apps described in this chapter, we also demonstrate how to create a Wi-Fi hotspot no matter where you are (all iPads with 4G features except the second generation) and how to share with AirDrop.

Taking Note of Notes

Notes creates notes that you can save or send through email. Over the years, it's gained many useful features, including "sketch with your finger" mode, checklists, and enclosures. In addition, many apps now allow you to save data directly to the Notes app (after tapping the share icon). Finally, all your notes can be synced across all your enabled Apple devices via iCloud.

To create a note, follow these steps:

1. **On the Home screen, tap the Notes icon.**

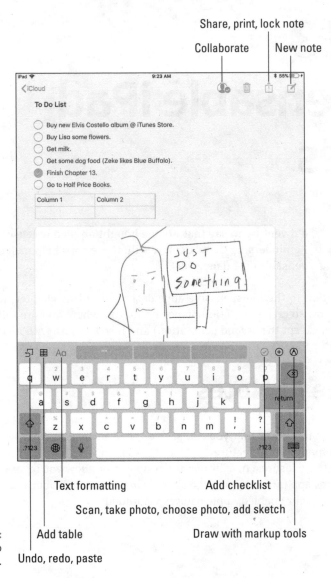

2. **Tap the new note icon (shown in the margin) in the upper-right corner to start a new note.**

   The virtual keyboard appears.

3. **Type a note, such as the one shown in Figure 13-1.**

FIGURE 13-1:
The Notes app
revealed.

Share, print, lock note

Collaborate

New note

Text formatting

Add checklist

Scan, take photo, choose photo, add sketch

Add table

Draw with markup tools

Undo, redo, paste

Figure 13-1 shows off a few of the features in Notes: The list is formatted as a checklist, followed by a table with two columns and two rows, and then a crudely drawn sketch at the bottom.

Other things you can do before you quit the Notes app include the following:

>> Tap the back button in the upper-left corner of the screen (which says iCloud in Figure 13-1) to see either a list of all your notes or — if you sync Notes with more than one account, such as iCloud, Google, or Yahoo! — folders for each service you sync with.

>> When a list of notes is on-screen, tap a folder to see its contents, or tap a note to open and view, edit, or modify it. (*Hint:* The list is always visible when you hold your iPad in landscape mode with the longer edges parallel to the ground.)

>> Tap the share icon at the top-right corner (and shown in the margin) to send the note using the Mail or Messages app (see Chapter 5 for more on Mail and iMessage), copy the note to the Clipboard (see Chapter 2 for the scoop on copy and paste), post it to social media, assign it to a contact, lock it, or print it (see Chapter 2 for more about printing).

>> Collaborate with others by tapping the collaborate icon near the top-right corner (and shown in the margin) and sending them an invitation to collaborate.

>> Tap the trash icon near the top-right corner to delete the note.

When the keyboard is displayed, you can

>> Tap the check mark icon above the top row of keys to create a checklist; select text before you tap it to change existing text into a checklist.

>> Tap the Aa icon above the top row of keys to format text as Title, Heading, Body, Bulleted List, Dashed List, or Numbered List. Select the text before you tap it to change its format.

>> Tap the + icon above the top row of keys to take a picture with the camera, select a picture from your Photos library, create a new finger sketch, or scan a document to add to this note.

New in iOS 11, the Document Scanner automatically senses and scans a document into the Notes app, crops its edges, and removes any skewing or glare. If you have iPad Pro and Apple Pencil, you can then use Apple Pencil to fill in the blanks or sign the document.

>> Tap the squiggly line icon above the top row of keys to sketch with your finger.

TIP

If you're using any iPad except the second-generation model, you can also use Siri to set up and dictate your note by speaking. (You hear more about Siri in Chapter 14.)

As with most iPad apps, your notes are saved automatically while you type them so that you can quit Notes at any time without losing a single character.

We'd be remiss if we didn't remind you one last time that you can sync Notes with your Mac and other devices via iCloud. We'd be remiss also if we didn't mention that unlike other sync functions, you don't enable Notes syncing in iTunes. Instead, you enable it in Settings ➪ iCloud on your iPad and System Preferences ➪ iCloud on your Mac.

TIP

Enable the Notes widget to access your Notes from today view, as described in Chapter 15.

NEW

Finally, one of our favorite new iOS 11 features for those with an Apple Pencil and an iPad Pro is the ability to tap the lock screen with your Apple Pencil to launch Notes to a blank page so you can begin taking notes instantly. If this doesn't work for you, tap Settings ➪ Notes and enable Access Notes from Lock Screen.

And that's all she wrote. You now know what you need to know about creating and managing notes with Notes.

Remembering with Reminders

You can find lots of good to-do list apps in the App Store; if you don't believe us, search for *to-do list*. You'll find more than 100 offerings for the iPad. Many are free, but others sell (and sell briskly, we might add) at prices up to $30 or $40. Most of these third-party reminder apps have nothing to worry about from the Reminders app, although some people love it.

What you get for free is Reminders, a simple to-do list app for making and organizing lists, with optional reminders available for items in your lists.

Tap the Reminders icon on your Home screen, and you'll see something that looks like Figure 13-2.

Reminders on the right side of the screen in Figure 13-2 belong to a list called *To Do - BLTV Show*, as indicated by the list name highlighted on the left side of the screen and appearing at the top of the list.

Working with lists

To create a new list, tap Add List in the lower-left corner of the screen, type a name for the list on the virtual keyboard, and then tap Done. You can have as many or as few lists as you like.

To manage the lists you create, tap the Edit button at the bottom of the screen, shown in Figure 13-2. When you do, the left side of the screen goes into what we like to think of as edit mode, as shown in Figure 13-3.

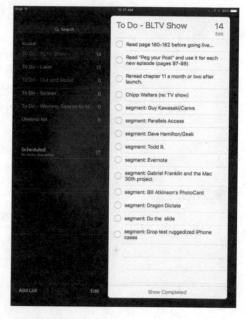

FIGURE 13-2:
The Reminders app.

From this screen, you can

TIP

>> **Delete a list:** Tap the red minus sign for the list. The list's name slides to the left and reveals a red Delete button (see Useless list in Figure 13-3).

You can also delete a list without first tapping the Edit button by swiping the list's name from right to left. The red Delete button appears on the right; tap it to delete the list or tap anywhere else to cancel.

>> **Reorder (move up or down) lists:** Press and hold your finger on the three horizontal lines (shown in the margin) to the right of a list's name in edit mode, and then drag the name up or down. When the list's name is where you want it, lift your finger. Note that the number of items in the list appears to the left of the three horizontal lines.

FIGURE 13-3:
Tap the Edit button to create, delete, or reorder your lists.

Setting up reminders

Reminders is a simple app, and the steps for managing reminders are equally simple. Here's how to remind yourself of something:

1. **On the Home screen, tap the Reminders app.**

2. **On the left side of the screen, tap the list to which you want to attach the reminder.**

   If you haven't created your own lists, you'll see the two default lists: Reminders and Scheduled. Otherwise, you'll see a list of all the reminder lists you've created.

   The virtual keyboard appears.

3. **Tap the + at the bottom of the list to start a new reminder.**

4. **Type a title for the new reminder.**

   Or just ask Siri to remind you. (See Chapter 14 for more about Siri.)

   The item appears in the current reminders list. At this point, your reminder is bare-bones; its date, repeat, and priority options have not been activated. To use those features, continue.

5. **Tap the reminder and then tap the little *i*-in-a-circle to set the following options in the details overlay, as shown in Figure 13-4:**

   - *Remind Me on a Day:* Tap to specify a day and time for this reminder.

   - *Alarm:* Tap to specify a day and time for this reminder.

   - *Repeat:* After you specify a day and time for a reminder, you'll notice that a Repeat button appears. Tap it if you want to set a second reminder for a different day or time.

   - *Remind Me at a Location:* Tap to set a location-based reminder. Just enable the At a Location switch (which is not enabled in Figure 13-4), specify the location, and then choose When I Arrive or When I Leave.

     Location-based reminders can suck your iPad battery dry faster than almost anything else. So, remember to mark location-based reminders as completed by tapping their check boxes when you finish them.

     Bear in mind that the locations are approximate, so you may not receive your alert the precise moment that you arrive or depart, and that this feature is all but useless on Wi-Fi–only iPads.

   - *Priority:* Tap to specify a priority for this reminder. You can select None, Low, Medium, or High.

WARNING

FIGURE 13-4:
Details for Our Shiny New Reminder.

- *List:* Tap if you want this reminder to appear in a different list. Then tap the list to which you want to move this reminder.

- *Notes:* If you have anything else to add, tap the Notes field and type away.

6. **After you've set your options, tap the Done button in the upper-right corner of the details overlay.**

TIP

Choose the list you want your new reminder to appear on *before* you create it.

Viewing and checking off reminders

After you create reminders, the app helps you see what you have and haven't done and enables you to do the following tasks:

>> **Check off reminders.** You probably noticed that every reminder you create includes a hollow circle to its left. Tap the circle to indicate that a task has been completed. When you do, the words Hide (or Show) Completed appear at the bottom of the list. Tap these words to hide or show tasks you've completed in this list.

>> **Search reminders.** To search for a word or phrase in all your reminders, completed or not, tap the search field at the upper left, type your word or phrase, and then tap the search icon (magnifying glass). Or swipe down from the middle of any Home screen to search for it with Search.

>> **Keep reminders on your Mac or PC.** You can create reminders on your Mac or PC with To Do items in iCal (Lion), Reminders (Mountain Lion or Mavericks), or Tasks in Outlook. And if you're using iCloud, your reminders will always be up to date on all your devices.

That's about it. The Reminders app isn't a bad effort. If it lacks a feature or two that you desire, check out the myriad third-party to-do list apps in the App Store.

Loving the Lock Screen and Navigating Notifications

The lock screen is what you see when you first turn on or wake your iPad. You can quickly access the features and information you need most from the lock screen, even while the iPad is locked.

From the lock screen, you can do the following without unlocking your iPad first:

>> Swipe left to open the camera.

>> Swipe right to see today view (as shown in Figure 13-5).

>> Drag up from the bottom to open Control Center.

>> Swipe up from the center of the screen to see older notifications.

TIP

To fine-tune what you see on your lock screen, tap Settings ⇨ Touch ID & Passcode (on supported models) or Settings ⇨ Passcode (on older models). Here you can change settings for Today View, Recent Notifications, Control Center, and more.

When your iPad is locked, notifications appear on the lock screen (as shown in Figure 13-6); when it's unlocked, they appear at the top of the screen.

Note the two dots and the camera icon at the bottom of Figure 13-6, which indicate that two pages plus the camera are available. The black dot in the middle represents the current page, so swipe right to left to use the camera, or left to right to access today view, which provides useful information from various apps while your iPad is locked (refer to Figure 13-5).

To summon older notifications to the forefront of your iPad screen when it's unlocked, all you need is the magical incantation — that is, a swipe from the top of the screen downward. Go ahead and give it a try. We'll wait.

FIGURE 13-5:
The today view in all its splendor.

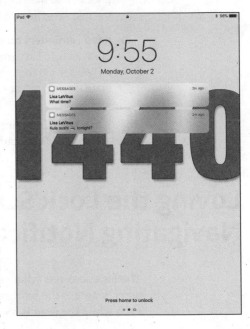

FIGURE 13-6:
Notifications on the lock screen; slide your finger on one to open it.

Here's the rest of what you need to know about navigating notifications:

>> **Open a notification on the lock screen.** Swipe right to open a notification with the appropriate app after authenticating with Touch ID, Face ID, or your passcode.

>> **Open a notification on an unlocked iPad:** Tap the notification to open it in the appropriate program.

>> **Edit or rearrange the widgets on the Today screen.** Tap the Edit button at the bottom of the screen (not shown in Figure 13-5).

>> **Clear a single notification.** Swipe from right to left and then tap the Clear button.

>> **Clear all notifications.** Swipe right to left to get to the Notification screen and then tap the little *x*-in-a-circle to the right of the section heading. The *x* turns into a Clear button; tap the Clear button and all notifications are cleared. If you have notifications from previous days, repeat this procedure for each one.

That's how to summon and use notifications. There's still a bit more to know — including how to change the notification settings for individual apps — but you have to wait until the chapter on settings (which happens to be Chapter 15).

Punching the Clock

Well, yes, most tablets do have a clock. But not every tablet has a *world clock* that lets you display the time in multiple cities on multiple continents. And not every device also has an alarm, a stopwatch, and a timer to boot.

So tap the Clock icon on your Home screen or in Control Center and see what the Clock app is all about.

World clock

Want to know the time in Beijing or Bogota? Tapping World Clock (in the Clock app) lets you display the time in numerous cities around the globe, as shown in Figure 13-7. When the clock face is dark, it's nighttime in the city you chose; if the face is white, it's daytime outside.

To add a city to the world clock, tap the + in the upper-left corner and then use the virtual keyboard to start typing a city name, as shown in Figure 13-8.

The moment you press the first letter, the iPad displays a list of cities or countries that begin with that letter. So, as Figure 13-8 shows, typing *v* brings up Andorra la Vella, Andora; Bantam Village, Cocos (Keeling) Islands; and Boa Vista, Brazil, among myriad other possibilities. You can create clocks for as many cities as you like, though only six cities at a time appear on-screen.

To remove a city from the list, tap Edit and then tap the red circle with the white horizontal line that appears to the left of the city you want to drop. Then tap Delete.

You can also rearrange the order of the cities displaying the time. Tap Edit, and then press your finger against the symbol with three horizontal lines to the right of the city you want to move up or down in the list. Then drag the city to its new spot.

FIGURE 13-7:
What time is it in Tokyo?

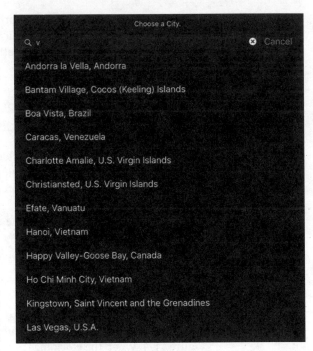

FIGURE 13-8:
Clocking in around the world.

Alarm

Ever try to set the alarm in a hotel room? It's remarkable how complicated setting an alarm can be, on even the most inexpensive clock radio. Like almost everything else, the procedure is dirt-simple on the iPad:

1. **Tap Clock on the Home screen or Control Center to display the Clock app.**

2. **Tap the Alarm icon at the bottom of the screen.**

3. **Tap the + button in the upper-right corner of the screen.**

4. **Choose the time of the alarm by rotating the wheel in the Add Alarm overlay.**

   This step is similar to the action required to set the time that an event starts or ends on your calendar.

5. **Tap Save when the alarm settings are to your liking.**

That's what you can do with a regular alarm clock. What's the big deal, you say? Well, you can do even more with your iPad alarm:

» **Set the alarm to go off on other days.** Tap Repeat and then tell the iPad the days you want the alarm to be repeated, as in Every Monday, Every Tuesday, Every Wednesday, and so on.

» **Choose your own sound.** Tap Sound to choose the tone that will wake you up. You can even use songs from your Music library and any custom tones stored on your iPad.

   Your choice is a matter of personal preference, but we can tell you that the ringtone for the appropriately named Alarm managed to wake Ed from a deep sleep.

» **Set the snooze to sleep in.** Tap Snooze on (showing green) to display a Snooze button along with the alarm. Tap the Snooze button to shut down the alarm for nine minutes.

» **Name your alarm.** If you want to call the alarm something other than, um, Alarm, tap the Label field and use the virtual keyboard to type another descriptor.

TIP

Simple stuff, really. But if you want really simple and have anything except a second-generation iPad, you can ask Siri to set the alarm for you. See Chapter 14 for how to use Siri.

You know that an alarm has been set and activated because of the tiny status icon (surprise, surprise — it looks like a clock) that appears on the status bar in the upper-right corner of the screen.

An alarm takes precedence over any tracks you're listening to on your iPad. Songs momentarily pause when an alarm goes off and resume when you turn off the alarm (or press the Snooze button).

WARNING

When your ring/silent switch is set to Silent, *your iPad still plays alarms from the Clock app.* It stays silent for FaceTime calls, alert sounds, or audio from apps. But it *will* play alarms from the Clock app.

Although it seems obvious, if you want to actually *hear* an alarm, you have to make sure that the iPad volume is turned up loud enough for you to hear.

Bedtime

The aptly named Bedtime feature in the Clock app is all about you getting a healthy and consistent night's sleep. To get started, you're asked a few simple questions, such as what time you would like to wake up, which days of the week the alarm should go off (the default is every day), and how many hours of sleep you need each night. You get to choose when to receive a bedtime reminder and which tone to hear when you wake up.

You can also get a good grasp on your sleep history by displaying data from your wakeup alarm, sleep trackers, and any other sleep data accumulated in HealthKit.

Stopwatch

If you're helping a loved one train for a marathon, the iPad Stopwatch function can provide an assist. Open it by tapping Stopwatch in the Clock app.

Just tap Start to begin the count, and then tap Stop when your trainee arrives at the finish line. You can also tap the Lap button to monitor the times of individual laps.

Timer

Cooking a hard-boiled egg or Thanksgiving turkey? Again, the iPad comes to the rescue. Tap Timer (in the Clock app) and then rotate the hour and minute wheels until the length of time you desire is highlighted.

Tap the sounds icon (shown in the margin) near the bottom of the screen to choose the ringtone that will signify time's up.

After you set the length of the timer, tap Start when you're ready to begin. You can watch the minutes and seconds wind down on the screen, if you have nothing better to do. Or tap Pause to pause the countdown temporarily.

If you're doing anything else on the iPad — admiring photos, say — you hear the ringtone and see a *Timer Done* message on the screen at the appropriate moment. Tap OK to silence the ringtone.

Controlling Smart Appliances

The dedicated Home app that comes with iOS 11 is all about managing HomeKit accessories, which fit into a broader tech trend of connecting devices known as the *Internet of Things (IoT)*. HomeKit is Apple's framework for such IoT accessories in and around the house. We're talking door locks, lightbulbs, thermostats, and various other products you might like to control with your iPad.

Just launch the Home app and tap the Add Accessory button to get started.

TIP

If you have an Apple TV, you can use it as the hub for your HomeKit accessories. Without Apple TV, you can only control your accessories when you're at home and connected to the same Wi-Fi network; with Apple TV, you can access and control most devices from anywhere with Internet access.

Socializing with Social Media Apps

At first glance, the iPad appears light on social media support because Game Center is the only sign of social media on a new iPad. Still, iOS 11 is much more friendly to social media than it appears at first glance. Although your iPad doesn't come with official Facebook or Twitter apps, support for the two most popular social networks is baked right into iOS.

TIP

You don't necessarily need an app to participate in social networking. The networks we talk about in this section can be fully utilized using Safari on your iPad. And frankly, unlike the iPhone, where the Safari experience is hampered by the tiny screen and keyboard, the websites are eminently usable on your iPad. So, if you want to check them out and don't feel like downloading their apps, here are their URLs:

» **Facebook:** `www.facebook.com`

» **Twitter:** `http://twitter.com`

We'd be remiss if we didn't at least point out some of the niceties you get when you access one of these social media networks by using an app instead of a browser, so the following sections offer a few of our insights.

If you use Facebook or Twitter, the first thing to do, regardless of whether you intend to use the apps, is to tap Settings ⇨ Facebook and provide your user-name and password. Then do the same for Twitter, this time tapping Settings ⇨ Twitter. This will let you share photos, maps and directions, videos, URLs, and much more by tapping the share icon and then tapping the icon for Facebook or Twitter.

Facebook

The Facebook iPad app, shown in Figure 13-9, makes it easy to access the most popular Facebook features with a single finger tap.

The biggest difference between the Facebook website and the app is that Safari can't provide push noti-fications for Facebook events such as messages, timeline posts, friend requests and confirmations, photo tags, events, or comments; the iPad app does all that and more.

The bottom line is that there's noth-ing to prevent having the best of both worlds. So if you're a heavy Facebook user, consider using the Facebook iPad app for some things (such as push notifications and status updates) and Safari for others (such as reading your wall or news feeds).

FIGURE 13-9:
Bob's Facebook news feed.

Twitter

Twitter puts a slightly different spin on social networking. Unlike Facebook, it doesn't try to be all encompassing or offer dozens of features, hoping that some of them will appeal to you. Instead, Twitter does one thing and does it well. That thing is letting its users post short messages, or *tweets,* quickly and easily from a variety of platforms, including web browsers, mobile phones, smartphones, and other devices.

Twitter users then have the option of following any other Twitter user's tweets. The result is a stream of short messages like the ones shown in Figure 13-10.

TIP

A tweet is 140 characters or fewer (including spaces). This tip, for example, is precisely 140 characters. Bottom line: Omit needless words.

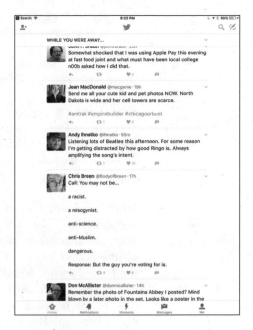

FIGURE 13-10:
The official Twitter iPad app through the eyes of Bob (@LeVitus).

Sharing Your Connection (Personal Hotspot)

If you have a newer iPad (anything newer than a second-generation iPad), the personal hotspot is a feature that lets your iPad with Wi-Fi + 4G share its cellular high-speed data connection with other devices, including computers, iPod touches, and other iPads.

REMEMBER

If your iPad is Wi-Fi only, feel free to skip this section — the Personal Hotspot option is available only on cellular iPads.

To enable your personal hotspot and share your cellular data connection with others, do the following:

1. **On the Home screen, tap Settings.**

2. **Tap Cellular Data, and then tap Personal Hotspot.**

3. **Tap the Personal Hotspot switch to enable it (it will turn green).**

4. **Tap Wi-Fi Password and create or change the password for the Wi-Fi network you create.**

Now Wi-Fi, Bluetooth, or USB-enabled devices can join your hotspot network and share your iPad's cellular data connection.

REMEMBER

Your personal hotspot network adopts your iPad's name, which is *Bob L's iPad Air 2* in Figure 13-11.

Most carriers offer support for personal hotspots in some or all of their data plans in the United States. Some don't, so check with your carrier if you don't see a Personal Hotspot option in the Settings app (and, of course, if your iPad has 4G).

FIGURE 13-11:
Devices can join this network via Wi-Fi, Bluetooth, or USB by following the appropriate connection instructions.

WARNING

Most carriers don't charge extra for this feature, but the data used by connected devices counts against your monthly data plan allotment.

To see how much cellular data you're using, tap Settings ⇨ Cellular Data and scroll down until you see Cellular Data Usage, which displays your cellular usage for the current period as well as data used while roaming.

Dropping In on AirDrop

At various points when you're using your iPad, you encounter AirDrop, a fast, safe, and secure (through encryption) wireless method of sharing photos, videos, contacts, documents, and more with people you are close to physically.

You just tap the share icon (shown in the margin) in any app that offers one. Air-Drop exploits both Wi-Fi and Bluetooth. No advanced setup is required.

To be part of an AirDrop exchange, you and the recipient must be using iOS 7 or later and have an iPhone 5 or later, a fourth-generation iPad or later, an iPad mini, a fifth-generation iPod touch, or a Mac running Yosemite or later.

Taking advantage of this clever feature involves three simple steps:

1. **Turn on the AirDrop feature (if it's not on already) in Control Center.**

You have the option to make your device visible to Everyone (within the vicinity) or just to your contacts.

2. **Tap the share icon when it presents itself in an app and choose the file or files that you want to share.**

3. **Choose the recipients of those items by tapping the circle for the person, as shown in Figure 13-12.**

FIGURE 13-12:
Tap one of the Robert-in-a-circle buttons to send the items to his MacBook Pro or iPad.

Yes, you can choose more than one person. People in range who are eligible to receive the file are represented on your iPad by a circle. (The circles may even contain their pictures as in Figure 13-12.)

The AirDrop process hath begun. The people on the receiving end will get a prompt asking them to accept the picture, video, or what-ever it is you're offering them, as shown in Figure 13-13.

Assuming they take kindly to your offer and grant permission (by tapping Accept rather than Decline), the file lands on their devices in short order, where it is routed to its proper location. That is, a picture or video ends up in the Photos app, a contact in the Contacts app, and the Passbook pass in the Passbook app.

FIGURE 13-13:
Bob is about to receive a note via AirDrop.

Chapter **14**

Taking iPad Controls Siri-ously

How could you not love Siri? The intelligent, voice-activated virtual personal assistant living like a genie inside iPad minis and iPads since the third generation not only *hears* what you have to say but also attempts to figure out the intent of your words. Siri then does her darnedest to respond to your wishes. She — yes, it's a female voice (at least until you change it) — can help you dictate and send a message, get directions, call a friend, discover who won the ballgame, tell you when a movie is playing, ID the song playing in the background, arrange a wake-up call, search the web, find a decent place to eat, help you pay money to a friend, and lots more. Siri talks back, too, sometimes with humor and other times with attitude. When Ed told Siri he was tired, she responded with, "That's fine. I just hope you're not doing anything dangerous."

Siri isn't perfect. Sometimes Siri mishears us, occasionally more often than we'd like, and other times she doesn't quite know what we have in mind. But blemishes and all, we think she's pretty special — and she's become smarter along the way.

Come to think of it, we should probably stop referring to Siri as *she,* even though she, um, started that way. You can now choose a male or female voice to represent Siri. We'll resist saying much more about Siri until later in this chapter because we want to get to one of the most helpful features on your iPad, Control Center, which Apple correctly points out is merely a swipe away.

Controlling Control Center

As its name suggests, Control Center is a repository for the controls, tools, and settings frequently called upon. Indeed, you will almost certainly spend a lot more time in Control Center than in Settings. To access Control Center, swipe up from the bottom of the screen — any screen, even the lock screen.

Unless — and we bet you were waiting for some kind of *but* — an app disallows access to Control Center. If that's the case, you'll have to close that app by pressing the Home button, and then swipe up from your Home screen. Alternately, you can double-tap the Home button.

Apple revamped Control Center in iOS 11, and it's different on the iPad and iPhone. The first major change from the previous version is that the multi-panel Control Center is gone. In its place, you get everything on one screen, along with the application switcher and the dock, as shown in Figure 14-1. You can also customize some of the controls in Control Center, too. That's a big change, so let's take a closer look.

FIGURE 14-1:
Control Center is merely a swipe away.

TIP

If you access Control Center from the lock screen, you won't get the app switcher or the dock.

On the right side of the screen is the new Control Center. It's simplified, sleeker, and semi-customizable.

Five groupings of buttons appear. The first is for the iPad's radios: Airplane Mode, Cellular Data (if your iPad is a Wi-Fi + Cellular model), Wi-Fi, and Bluetooth. If you press and hold down on that group, you'll get expanded controls that add AirDrop and Personal Hotspot, as shown in Figure 14-2. Now that's different than in previous versions, so you might want to consider taking some time to play around with it and become familiar.

NEW

Tapping the Wi-Fi or Bluetooth button in iOS 11's Control Center no longer turns off those radios on your iPad. Instead, it disconnects your iPad from any connected Wi-Fi network or Bluetooth devices, respectively. To truly turn off those radios— say, to save battery life — you need to go to Settings.

FIGURE 14-2:
Expand Control Center groups and buttons by tapping and holding down.

Below the radio controls are the music controls: previous, play, and next. Tap and hold down, and you get a volume slider and AirPlay options.

Next are brightness and volume sliders that look more like a thermometer metaphor than a slider metaphor. Tap and slide in either control to effect screen brightness and volume, respectively. If you tap and hold down on the volume slider, you'll just get a bigger volume slider. But tapping and holding down on the brightness slider will add buttons for Night Shift and True Tone, which we discuss in more depth in Chapter 15.

Stay with us, because there's more! Below the brightness and volume sliders is the control for screen mirroring, where you can choose an Apple TV or other compatible device to mirror your iPad's screen.

And now we get to the last column of buttons: screen lock, mute, do not disturb, flashlight, timer, and camera. Of those, flashlight, timer, and camera will expand if you tap and hold down. (The others, not so much.) The expanded camera control is particularly useful because there are options for Take Selfie, Record Video, Record Slo-mo, and Take Photo.

And this is where things get customizable. Choose Settings ➪ Control Center ➪ Customize Controls. You'll get a list of controls you can remove or add, including

Accessibility Shortcuts, Alarm, Apple TV Remote, Guided Access, Magnifier, Notes, Screen Recording, Stopwatch, and Text Size. Tap the red circle with a minus sign to remove a control. Tap the green circle with a plus sign to add a control. You can add all of them if you want, but your Control Center will be a mess. Also, you can rearrange the order of these buttons by tapping the three little lines next to any control and dragging it where you want.

TIP

The iPhone has more customizable Control Center buttons than the iPad because of Apple Pay, HomeKit, and other features specific to the iPhone.

TIP

You can permit or deny access to Control Center on the lock screen in Settings. Go to Settings ⇨ Touch ID & Passcode ⇨ Allow Access When Locked, and toggle Control Center on or off.

Summoning Siri

NEW

Starting with iOS 11, Siri comes set up on your iPad out of the box. You can't turn her off, but you can control how you access her in Settings ⇨ Siri & Search. There are toggles for Listen for "Hey Siri," Press Home for Siri, and Allow Siri When Locked. We look at each of these methods in this section.

WARNING

Siri requires Internet access. A lot of factors go into accuracy, including surrounding noises and unfamiliar accents. And you also need to be comfortable with the fact that Apple is recording what you say, though the company says it anonymizes the data through something called Differential Privacy. The short version is that Differential Privacy allows Apple to collect anonymized data and mix it with noise in such a way that it can't be tracked back to individual users.

You can call Siri into action in a few ways. The traditional way is to press and hold down the Home button until you hear a tone. Pretty simple, eh? Siri will then listen for your query, as shown in Figure 14-3. Start talking, and your question appears on-screen.

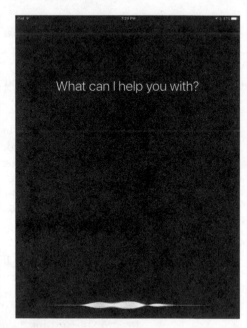

What can I help you with?

FIGURE 14-3:
Siri is eager to respond.

You can also summon Siri by merely saying, "Hey Siri." And yes, this is Apple's answer to the "OK Google" voice command on Android devices. To take advantage of the Hey Siri feature, on iPads prior to iPad Pro, you have to connect your tablet to power. On the iPad Pro, you can use Hey Siri without plugging in your iPad.

Siri also responds when you press and hold down on the call button on most Bluetooth headsets. If you have Apple AirPods, two sharp taps on the outside of either AirPod will activate Siri.

What happens next is up to you. You can ask a wide range of questions or issue voice commands. If you didn't get your words out fast enough or you were misunderstood, tap the microphone icon at the bottom of the screen and try again.

Siri relies on voice recognition and artificial intelligence (hers, not yours). The voice genie responds in a conversational manner, and Siri sounds amazing in iOS 11. But using Siri isn't entirely a hands-free experience. Spoken words are supplemented by information on the iPad screen (as you see in the next section).

Siri seeks answers using sources such as Google, Wikipedia, Yelp, Yahoo!, Open Table, Twitter, and WolframAlpha, making Siri your personal search agent for your iPad's content or outside information. For instance, ask Siri to find all the videos you shot at your kid's graduation party and she'll oblige (at least if you tagged them correctly).

Siri on the iPad can also launch apps — Apple's own as well as third-party apps. Indeed, from your contacts, Siri might be able to determine who your spouse, coworkers, and friends are, as well as knowing where you live. You might ask, "How do I get home from here?" and Siri will fire up Maps to help you on your way. Or you can say, "Find a good Italian restaurant near Barbara's house," and Siri will serve up a list, sorted by Yelp rating. Using Open Table, Siri can even make a restaurant reservation.

Starting in iOS 10, Apple opened up Siri to third-party app producers. For example, you can have Siri arrange a ride through Uber or Lyft, or pay a debt on your behalf through apps such as Venmo or Square Cash.

If you ask about a favorite sports team, Siri will retrieve the score of the team's last game or the game in progress. And if you're rummaging through a longish email that you can't quite get through at the moment, you can have Siri set a reminder for you to follow up later in the evening.

TIP

If you don't want Siri to have access to a particular app, just turn it off. For a list of apps, tap Settings ⇨ Siri & Search. Then tap through to any of your apps and you can turn off Siri support within that app.

Figuring Out What to Ask

The beauty of Siri is that there's no designated protocol you must follow when talking to her. Asking, "Will I need an umbrella tomorrow?" produces the same result as, "What is the weather forecast around here?" Although competing digital assistant platforms such as Amazon Alexa rely on training the user to say exactly the right thing to get a result, Siri has been trained to understand us. She makes her share of mistakes, of course, but Apple's long-view approach is making Siri better and better at understanding the meaning of our words.

Another cool feature is that Siri teams up with Shazam to identify the name and artist of the musical track that's playing. Just ask Siri what song is playing and she'll name that tune (assuming that she indeed knows the song). When the song is properly identified, you even get a chance to buy it.

If you're not sure what to ask, tap the ?-in-a-circle to list sample questions or commands, some shown in Figure 14-4. You can tap any of these examples to see even more samples.

Here are some ways Siri can lend a hand . . . um, we mean a voice:

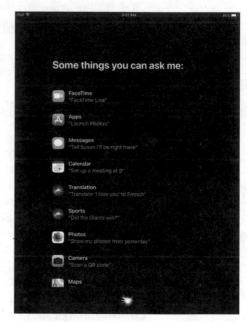

>> **FaceTime:** "FaceTime *phone number* my wife."

>> **Music:** "Play Frank Sinatra" or "Play Apple Music." "What song is this?" "Rate this song three stars."

>> **Messages:** "Send a message to Nancy to reschedule lunch."

>> **Translation:** "Translate 'I miss you so' in French."

>> **Sports:** "Did the Warriors win?"

FIGURE 14-4:
Siri can help out in many ways.

>> **Calendar:** "Set up a meeting for 9 a.m. to discuss funding."

>> **Reminders:** "Remind me to take my medicine at 8 a.m. tomorrow."

>> **Maps:** "Find an ATM near here."

>> **Mail:** "Mail the tenant about the recent rent check."

- » **Photos:** "Show me the photos I took at Samuel's birthday party."

- » **Stocks:** "What's Apple's stock price?"

- » **Web search:** "Who was the 19th president of the United States?"

- » **WolframAlpha:** "How many calories are in a blueberry muffin?"

- » **Clock:** "Wake me up at 8:30 in the morning."

- » **Trivia:** "Who won the Academy Award for Best Actor in 2003?"

- » **Twitter:** "Send tweet, 'Going on vacation,' smiley-face emoticon" or "What is trending on Twitter?"

Correcting Mistakes

As we point out earlier, as good as Siri is, she sometimes needs to be corrected. Fortunately, you can correct her mistakes fairly easily. The simplest way is to tap the microphone icon and try your query again.

You can also tap your question to edit or fix what Siri thinks you said. You can make edits by using the keyboard or by voice. If a word or phrase is underlined, you can use the keyboard to make a correction. Apple will also offer suggestions when you tap the underlined material: "Maybe you meant . . ."

Siri seeks your permission before sending a dictated message. That's a safeguard you might come to appreciate. If you need to modify the message, you can do so by saying such things as, "Change Tuesday to Wednesday" or "Add: I'm excited to see you, exclamation mark" — indeed, *I'm excited to see you* and an *!* will be added.

Using Dictation

All iPads from the third generation on offer a dictation function, so you can speak to your iPad and the words you say are translated into text. It's easy and usually works pretty well. Even if you're a pretty good virtual-keyboard typist or use an accessory keyboard, dictation is often the fastest way to get your words into your iPad.

You can enable dictation without enabling Siri and vice versa.

When you want to use your voice to enter text, tap the microphone key on the virtual keyboard that appears in the app you're using. Begin speaking right away. You'll see the wavy lines as you talk.

The first time you tap the microphone key, a dialog appears asking if you want to enable dictation. Your humble authors are never shy about using our voices, so we happily agree. But why might you choose otherwise? Your voice input, contacts, and location are shared with Apple, which makes some people uncomfortable.

You can always enable or disable dictation later. Go to Settings ⇨ General ⇨ Keyboard and tap to turn the Enable Dictation switch on or off. You won't see the mic key on the keyboard.

REMEMBER

Dictation works only if you're connected to the Internet. If you're not connected, the microphone key will appear dimmed.

Some apps don't display the microphone key on the keyboard. If you don't see a microphone key, the app doesn't accept dictated input.

Tap Done to end the dictation. Older iPads may cogitate for a moment before your words magically appear. On the latest iPad models, words appear more quickly.

TIP

Here are a couple of ways you can improve your dictation experience:

>> You can speak punctuation by saying it. So, remember to say, "period," "question mark," or whatever at the end of your sentences. You can also insert commas, semicolons, dashes, and other punctuation by saying their names.

>> The better your iPad hears you, the better your results will be:

- A wired headset with a microphone is great when you have a lot of ambient noise nearby.

- A Bluetooth headset or Apple's AirPods may be better than the built-in microphone.

- If you use the iPad's built-in mic, make sure the iPad case or your fingers aren't covering it.

WARNING

When dictation is enabled, information is shared with Apple's servers. This hasn't stopped your authors from taking advantage of dictation, but if you have particular privacy concerns, it's helpful to keep this in mind.

Making Siri Smarter

From Settings, you can tell Siri which language you want to converse in. Siri is available in English (Australia, Canada, India, Ireland, New Zealand, Singapore, South Africa, United Kingdom, and the United States), as well as versions of Chinese, Danish, Dutch, Finnish, French, German, Hebrew, Italian, Japanese, Korean, Malay, Norwegian, Portuguese, Russian, Spanish, Swedish, Thai, and Turkish.

You can also request voice feedback from Siri all the time, or just when you're using a hands-free headset. If you want, you can silence the feedback when the mute switch is on. You'll still get voice feedback if using the Hey Siri command.

In the My Info field in Settings, you can tell Siri who you are. When you tap My Info, your contacts list appears. Tap your own name in Contacts.

You can even choose whether Siri has a male or female voice. If you're using English, you can even choose Siri's accent: American, Australian, or British.

WARNING

You can call upon Siri from the lock screen too. (That's the default setting, anyway.) Consider this feature a mixed blessing. Not having to type a passcode to get Siri to do her thing is convenient. On the other hand, if your iPad ends up with the wrong person, he or she would be able to use Siri to send an email or message in your name, post to Facebook, or tweet, bypassing whatever passcode security you thought was in place. If you find this potential scenario scary, tap the Allow Access on Lock Screen setting under Siri settings. Or, tap Settings ➪ Touch ID & Passcode on the iPad Air 2, iPad mini 3, iPad mini 4, and iPad Pros (Settings ➪ Passcode on earlier models). Then enter your passcode and switch the Siri option under Allow Access When Locked from on (green is showing) to off (gray). You'll see the Allow Siri option under Touch ID & Passcode only if Siri is enabled in the first place. For more on Settings, read Chapter 15.

5

The Undiscovered iPad

Explore every single iPad setting that's not discussed in depth elsewhere in the book. By the time you finish reading Chapter 15, you'll know how to customize every part of your iPad that can be customized.

Peruse our comprehensive guide to troubleshooting the iPad, which details what to do when almost anything goes wrong, complete with step-by-step instructions for specific situations.

Gaze longingly at some of the iPad accessories we use and recommend, including physical keyboards, earphones and headphones, and speakers. No, this stuff's not included with your iPad, but we consider most of it essential just the same.

Chapter **15**

Setting You Straight on Settings

D o you consider yourself a control freak? The type of person who has to have it your way? Boy, have you landed in the right chapter.

Settings is kind of the makeover factory for the iPad. You open Settings by tapping its Home screen icon; from there, you can do things such as change the tablet's background or wallpaper and specify your search engine of choice. You can also alter security settings in Safari, tailor email to your liking (among other modifications), and get a handle on how to fetch or push new data.

TIP

The Settings area on the iPad is roughly analogous to System Preferences on a Mac or the Control Panel in Windows, with a hearty serving of app preferences thrown in for good measure.

But you won't have to visit Settings in every case because Control Center (see Chapter 14) grants you immediate access to some settings and controls that used to require a separate visit to the Settings complex. That includes airplane mode and display brightness, which we address in this chapter. But even with Control Center, expect to make some tweaks in Settings from time to time. Because we cover some settings elsewhere in this book, we don't dwell on every setting here. Nor do we describe every setting in the order in which Apple lists them. But you still have plenty to digest to help you make the iPad your own.

Checking Out the Settings Screen

When you first open Settings, you see a display that looks something like Figure 15-1, with a scrollable list on the left side of the screen and a pane on the right that corresponds to whichever setting is highlighted in blue. We say "something like" because Settings on your iPad may differ slightly from what is shown here.

You must scroll down to see the entire list. Also, if you see a greater-than symbol (>) to the right of a listing, the listing has a bunch of options. Throughout this chapter, you tap the > symbol to check out those options.

As you scroll to the bottom of the list on the left, you come to all the settings pertaining to some of the specific third-party apps you've added to the iPad. (See Chapter 11.) These settings aren't visible in Figure 15-1.

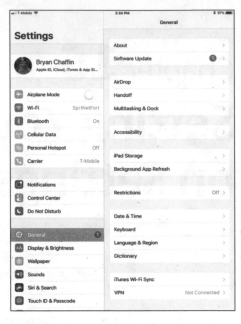

FIGURE 15-1:
Your list of settings.

Everybody has a different collection of apps on his or her iPad, so settings related to those programs will also be different.

The New Apple ID Settings

NEW

If you're familiar with iOS Settings, the first thing you'll notice in the iOS 11 Settings app is the section at the top with your Apple ID info. You'll see your name, the avatar you selected when you set up your device, and an arrow indicating that more settings are a tap away.

Tap through, as shown in Figure 15-2, and you'll find a variety of settings for Apple ID, including some that once resided elsewhere, such as iCloud:

» **Personal Details:** Edit your name, phone numbers, and email addresses associated with your Apple ID.

» **Password & Security:** Turn on or off two-factor authentication (we recommend that you turn it on), as well as trusted phone numbers for your account.

» **iCloud:** See the amount of total and available storage. Tap Manage Storage to, well, manage your iCloud storage, taking note of all your iOS backups. If need be, you can buy more storage. Tap Change Storage Plan to get started.

» **iTunes & App Store:** Use this shortcut to the iTunes & App Store section, described later.

» **Family Sharing:** Manage your iCloud Family Sharing plan or set one up.

» **Devices:** View a handy list of every device associated with your Apple ID. Tap through to any of them and you'll see the device's Find My Mac and Find My iPhone settings, model name, operating system version, and serial number. You can also remove from your account any device except the iPad you're using.

» **Sign Out:** Sign out of your Apple ID and erase data associated with that Apple ID.

Blurred out email address
Apple ID Settings
Personal details
Apple ID Sign Out
Devices attached to this Apple ID

FIGURE 15-2:
Apple ID Settings.

Flying with Sky-High Settings

Your iPad offers settings to keep you on the good side of air-traffic communications systems. No matter which iPad you have — Wi-Fi only or a model with cellular — you have airplane mode.

Using a cellular radio on an airplane is a no-no. Wi-Fi is too, some of the time. But nothing is verboten about using an iPad on a plane to listen to music, watch videos, and peek at pictures. So how do you take advantage of the iPad's built-in music player (among other capabilities) at 30,000 feet, while temporarily turning off your wireless gateway to email and Internet functions? By turning on airplane mode.

To do so, merely tap Airplane Mode on the Settings screen to enable the setting. You'll know it's on rather than off when you see green instead of gray on the switch.

That act disables each of the iPad's wireless radios: Wi-Fi, cellular, and Bluetooth (depending on the model). While your iPad is in airplane mode, you can't surf the web, get a map location, send or receive emails, sync through iCloud, use the iTunes or App Store, or do anything else that requires an Internet connection. If a silver lining exists here, it's that the iPad's long-lasting battery ought to last even longer — good news if the flight you're on is taking you halfway around the planet.

 The appearance of a tiny airplane icon on the status bar at the upper-left corner of the screen reminds you that airplane mode is turned on. Just remember to turn it off when you're back on the ground.

TIP

If in-flight Wi-Fi is available on your flight, which is increasingly the case, you can turn on Wi-Fi independently, leaving the rest of your iPad's wireless radio safely disabled. And it's a breeze to do by toggling the setting in Control Center. Bluetooth, which we get to shortly, can also be enabled independently.

Controlling Wi-Fi Connections

Wi-Fi is typically the fastest wireless network that you can use to surf the web, send email, and perform other Internet tricks on the iPad. You use the Wi-Fi setting to determine which Wi-Fi networks are available to you and which one to exploit based on its signal.

Tap Wi-Fi so that the setting is on, and all Wi-Fi networks in range are displayed, as shown in Figure 15-3.

TIP

Tap the Wi-Fi switch off (gray) whenever you don't have access to a network and don't want to drain the battery. You can easily toggle Wi-Fi on and off in Control Center.

A signal-strength indicator can help you choose the network to connect to if more than one is listed; tap the appropriate Wi-Fi network when you reach a decision. If a network is password-protected, you see a lock icon and need the passcode to access it.

WARNING

When you're in a hotel, at an airport, or at another location, you might still have to enter a password after joining even if the lock link is not present. And make sure you know where a network comes from before joining.

You can also turn the Ask to Join Networks setting on or off. Networks that the iPad is already familiar with are joined automatically, regardless of which one you choose. If the Ask feature is off and no known networks are available, you have to select a new network manually. If the Ask feature is on, your iPad will offer to join new networks as they become available. Either way, you see a list with the same Wi-Fi networks in range.

The iPad can also remember passwords for frequently used networks.

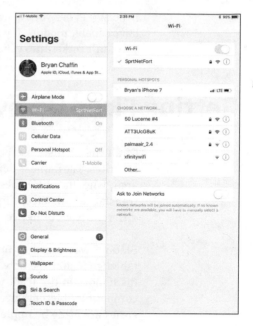

FIGURE 15-3:
Check out your Wi-Fi options.

If you used a particular network automatically in the past but no longer want your iPad to join it, tap the *i*-in-a-circle next to the network in question (in Wi-Fi settings) and then tap Forget This Network. The iPad develops a quick case of selective amnesia.

TECHNICAL STUFF

In some instances, you have to supply other technical information about a network you hope to glom onto. You encounter a bunch of nasty-sounding terms: DHCP, BootP, Static, IP Address, Subnet Mask, Router, DNS, Search Domains, Client ID, and HTTP Proxy. Chances are none of this info is on the tip of your tongue — but that's okay. For one thing, it's a good bet that you'll never need to know this stuff. What's more, even if you *do* have to fill in or adjust these settings, a network administrator or techie friend can probably help you.

Sometimes you may want to connect to a network that's closed and not shown on the Wi-Fi list. If that's the case, tap Other and use the keyboard to enter the network name. Then tap to choose the type of security setting the network is using (if any). Your choices are WEP, WPA, WPA2, WPA Enterprise, and WPA2 Enterprise. Again, the terminology isn't the friendliest, but we figure that someone nearby can lend a hand.

WARNING

Connecting to unfamiliar open networks carries risks. Malicious hackers may be able to get to your personal or business data. Be careful when joining unknown networks, especially open ones.

If no Wi-Fi network is available, you have to rely on a cellular connection if you have capable models. If you don't — or you're out of reach of a cellular network — you can't rocket into cyberspace until you regain access to a network.

Getting Fired Up over Bluetooth

Of all the peculiar terms you may encounter in techdom, *Bluetooth* is one of our favorites. The name is derived from Harald Blåtand, a tenth-century Danish monarch, who, the story goes, helped unite warring factions. And, we're told, *Blåtand* translates to *Bluetooth* in English. (Bluetooth is all about collaboration between different types of devices — get it?)

Blåtand was ahead of his time. Although we can't imagine that he ever used a tablet computer, he now has an entire short-range wireless technology named in his honor. On the iPad, you can use Bluetooth to communicate wirelessly with a compatible Bluetooth headset or to use an optional wireless keyboard. Such accessories are made by Apple and others.

To ensure that your iPad works with a Bluetooth device, it typically has to be wirelessly *paired,* or coupled, with the chosen device. If you're using a third-party accessory, follow the instructions that came with that headset or keyboard so that it becomes *discoverable,* or ready to be paired with your iPad. Then turn on Bluetooth (on the Settings screen) so that the iPad can find such nearby devices and the device can find the iPad.

In Figure 15-4, an Apple wireless keyboard and the iPad are successfully paired when you enter a designated passkey on the keyboard. You won't need a passkey to pair every kind of device, though. You can't, for example, enter a passkey when pairing the iPad with a wireless speaker. Most Bluetooth devices work up to a range of about 30 feet and don't require line of sight.

Bluetooth Pairing Request
Enter the code "6109" on "Edward Baig's Keyboard", followed by the return or enter key.

Cancel

FIGURE 15-4:
Pairing an Apple wireless keyboard with the iPad.

 You know Bluetooth is turned on when the Bluetooth icon (shown in the margin) is on the status bar. If the symbol is white, the iPad is communicating wirelessly with a connected device. If it's gray, Bluetooth is turned on in the iPad, *but* a paired device isn't nearby or isn't turned on. If you don't see a Bluetooth icon, the setting is turned off.

To unpair a device, select it from the device list and tap Forget This Device. We guess breaking up *isn't* hard to do.

The iPad supports stereo Bluetooth headphones, letting you stream stereo audio from the iPad to those devices.

The iPad can tap into Bluetooth in other ways. One is through *peer-to-peer* connectivity, so you can engage in multiplayer games with other nearby iPad, iPhone, or iPod touch users. You can also exchange business cards, share pictures, and send short notes. In addition, you don't even have to pair the devices as you do with a headset or wireless keyboard.

TECHNICAL STUFF

You can't use Bluetooth to exchange files or sync between an iPad and a computer. Nor can you use it to print stuff from the iPad on a Bluetooth printer (although the AirPrint feature handles that chore in some instances). That's because the iPad doesn't support any of the Bluetooth *profiles* (or specifications) required to allow such wireless stunts to take place — at least not as of this writing. We think that's a shame.

You may also see devices that communicate with the iPad through a flavor of Bluetooth called Bluetooth Low Energy (BLE), Bluetooth Smart, or Bluetooth Smart Ready. Apple's iBeacon technology is based on BLE and is a way to tap into your location, another topic for later in this chapter.

You can wirelessly share files also through AirDrop, as noted in Chapter 13 and elsewhere in this book.

Roaming among Cellular Data Options

You see another set of settings only if you have a cellular model iPad. The options appear on the right pane of the Settings screen when you highlight Cellular Data on the left:

>> **Cellular Data:** If you know you don't need the cellular network when you're out and about or are in an area where you don't have access to the network, turn it off. Your battery will thank you later. But even if you have access to a speedy cellular network, be prudent; in a 4G environment where you can easily consume gobs of data, your data allowance may run out all too quickly. And if you haven't set up your cellular data plan yet, you can get started by tapping the carrier of your choice directly in Settings ⇨ Cellular Data. Data rates apply.

>> **Enable LTE:** LTE stands for Long Term Evolution. What it really stands for is speed. Turn Enable LTE on for the fastest possible cellular data connection if you're in range. The biggest disadvantage is that you can eat up data awfully fast.

TIP

REMEMBER

» **Data Roaming:** You may unwittingly rack up lofty roaming fees when exchanging email, surfing with Safari, or engaging in other data-heavy activities while traveling abroad. Turn off Data Roaming to avoid such potential charges.

» **Manage Account:** Tap Manage *your carrier* Account to see or edit your account information or to add more data.

» **Add a SIM PIN:** The tiny *SIM,* or *Subscriber Identity Module,* card inside your iPad with cellular holds important data about your account. To add a PIN or a passcode to lock your SIM card, tap SIM PIN. That way, if someone gets hold of your SIM, he or she can't use it in another iPad without the passcode.

If you assign a PIN to your SIM, you have to enter it to turn the iPad on or off, which some might consider a minor hassle. And be aware that the SIM PIN is different from and may be in addition to any passcode you set for the iPad, as described later in this chapter.

» **Use Cellular Data For:** You can use your cellular connection for iCloud documents, iTunes, a Safari reading list, and certain third-party apps. You can see just how much data you're using on your apps and, if need be, shut down an app that's sucking up way too much. You can also decide whether or not to use cellular connections for FaceTime or for such system services as network-ing and Siri. Use the setting at the bottom of the Cellular Data panel to turn on the Wi-Fi Assist switch, which lets you automatically employ cellular data when your Wi-Fi connection is poor.

» **Cellular Data Usage:** This lists how much cellular data you've consumed for the current period. You also can see whether you're using up data while roaming. Overall, you'll know if you're closing in on your monthly data allowance.

» **Personal Hotspot:** Tap Personal Hotspot to share your iPad's data connection with any other devices you carry: perhaps a computer or smartphone. Just know that extra charges may apply — and even if they don't, you'll rack up that much extra data. You or the owner of the device piggybacking on your Internet connection must enter the designated password generated by the iPad for the Hotspot connection to make nice. You can use the hotspot feature via Wi-Fi or Bluetooth, or by connecting a Lightning-to-USB cable. See Chapter 13 to find out how to use Personal Hotspot.

Managing Notifications

Developers can send you alerts related to the apps you've installed on your iPad. Such alerts are typically in text form but may include sounds as well. The idea is that you'll receive notifications even when the app they apply to isn't running. Notifications may also appear as numbered badges on their corresponding Home screen icon.

The downside to keeping push notifications turned on is that they can curtail battery life (although honestly, we've been pretty satisfied with the iPad's staying power, even when push notifications are active). And you may find notifications distracting at times.

You manage notifications on an app-by-app basis. To do so, tap Notifications on the left side of the Settings screen, and then tap the app you want to manage. All installed apps that can take advantage of notifications (see Chapter 13) appear on the right, as shown in Figure 15-5. Tap an app and choose whether to Allow Notifications by enabling that option. If you choose not to permit notifications for select apps, you'll see the word *Off* in the list next to those app names.

Tap any app to adjust its settings. Figure 15-6 shows notification settings for the Instagram app. Some apps offer other options, including sound alerts, and other apps may offer fewer options.

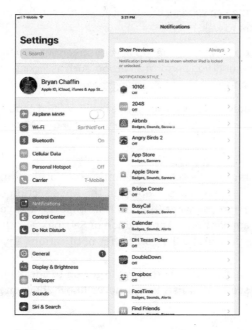

FIGURE 15-5:
Notify the iPad of your notification intentions.

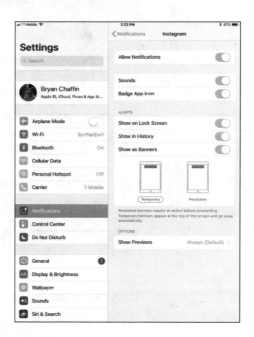

FIGURE 15-6:
Notification settings for Instagram.

To help you get started, here's a rundown of the options shown in Figure 15-6, starting at the top:

>> **Allow Notifications:** Enable or disable notifications for this app. Straightforward enough.

>> **Sounds:** You can choose from a variety of sounds for many Apple Notifications. Apps such as Instagram, however, give you control over only whether or not you hear a sound.

>> **Badge App Icon:** Display the number of pending alerts on the app's icon on your Home screen.

>> **Show on Lock Screen:** See notifications for this app when your iPad screen is locked.

>> **Show in History:** See past notifications when you swipe down from the upper edge of your screen.

>> **Show Banners:** Select the style of alert you want to see:

- *Temporary banners* drop down from the top of your screen, pause for a moment to give you time to read them, and then disappear. You can tap them to be taken to the app sending the notification. You can flick them away if you don't want to wait.

- *Persistent banners* drop down from the top of your screen like temporary banners, but they stay until you perform an action, such as flicking them away or tapping them to go to the app sending the notification.

>> **Show Previews:** See a preview of whatever you're being notified about. In the case of Instagram, the preview would be a thumbnail image of the post you're being alerted about.

Apps that don't take advantage of the settings in Settings ⇨ Notifications can still offer notifications, but you'll have to scroll down to the Apps section on the left side of Settings and tap the app you want to alter. Note that the app you hope to fiddle with doesn't always appear in the Apps section of Settings. For that matter, many of the apps that do appear in the list don't offer notifications anyway.

The broader point we're trying to make is that we urge you to check out the settings for *all* the apps you see in this list. You'll never know about many useful options if you don't.

TIP

If you find you went overboard with notifications at first to the point where they become annoying or distracting, don't fret. You can always go back and redo any notifications you've set up.

Many notifications are interactive, so you can respond to them on the spot. For example, you can reply to an incoming email or message without having to drop by the underlying app.

In the today view, you can make modifications without paying a separate visit to Settings. Open the today view by swiping from left to right on the lock screen, tap Edit at the bottom of the screen, and choose the widgets that should appear in this view. Tap the green circled + to add an available widget or the red circled dash to remove a widget. You can also determine the order in which widgets appear and whether to display them in the right or left column of the today view.

Apple understands that sometimes you don't want to be bothered by notifications or other distractions, no matter how unobtrusive they might be. The result is a feature aptly named Do Not Disturb. Flip the switch so the setting is turned on (green), and a moon icon appears in the status bar. Then you can rest assured that your alerts are silenced until you turn the setting off. Of course, it's even easier to turn this setting on or off in Control Center.

Inside Settings, you can schedule when Do Not Disturb kicks in and when it turns off. You can also tap Allow Calls From to permit incoming FaceTime calls or messages from everyone (or no one). If you enable the Repeated Calls switch, a second incoming FaceTime call from the same person within three minutes will not be silenced; the rationale is if the person is trying to reach you that badly, the call must be really important.

You get to make one more choice here: silence FaceTime calls and notifications always or only when the iPad is locked.

Controlling Control Center

In Chapter 14, we sing the praises of Control Center, the convenient utility that is no farther away than an upward swipe from the bottom of the screen. In Settings, you get to decide whether to make Control Center accessible from the lock screen and whether you can access it within apps. The switches for making these determinations are pretty straightforward.

Location, Location, Location Services

By using the onboard Maps, Camera, or Find Friends app (or any number of third-party apps), the iPad makes good use of knowing where you are. With Location

Services turned on, your iPad has the capability to deliver traffic information and suggest popular destinations in your vicinity. And at your discretion, you can share your location with others.

iPads with cellular use built-in GPS to help determine your location. The Wi-Fi-only iPad can find your general whereabouts by triangulating signals from Wi-Fi base stations.

If such statements creep you out a little, don't fret. To protect your right to privacy, individual apps pop up quick messages (similar to the warning presented by Maps, shown in Figure 15-7) asking whether you want them to use your current location. You can also turn off Location Services in Settings: Tap Privacy and then tap Locations Services to turn off the setting. Not only is your privacy shielded, but you also keep your iPad battery juiced a little longer.

FIGURE 15-7:
Maps wants to know where you are.

Be aware as well that some apps will ask for access when you're in the midst of using them. Consider the request carefully before allowing such access.

While visiting the Privacy setting, you may want to consult the privacy listings for individual apps and functions on your iPad: If any third-party apps request access to these services, they show up here.

Meantime, tap System Settings under Location Services to enable or disable various other location preferences, ranging from compass calibration to location-based Apple ads.

You can also choose to share your location with family members and friends in the Messages and Find My Friends apps, and as part of Family Sharing.

From time to time on the iPad, you can land in the same destination multiple ways. For example, you can access the same privacy settings via the restrictions settings that we address later in this chapter.

Settings for Your Senses

A number of settings control what the iPad looks and sounds like.

Display & Brightness

The brightness slider shown in Figure 15-8 appears when the Display & Brightness setting is highlighted. Who doesn't want a bright, vibrant screen? Alas, the brightest screens exact a trade-off: Before you drag the control to the max, remember that brighter screens sap the life from your battery more quickly.

TIP

That's why we recommend tapping the Auto-Brightness switch so that it's on. But wait, where is it? Before iOS 11, it was right here in the Display & Brightness settings. In iOS 11, it's buried in Settings ⇨ General ⇨ Accessibility ⇨ Display Accommodations. You'll most likely find it switched on. (If it isn't, tap it so that it becomes green.) This setting automatically adjusts the screen according to the lighting environment in which you're using the iPad, saving considerable battery power.

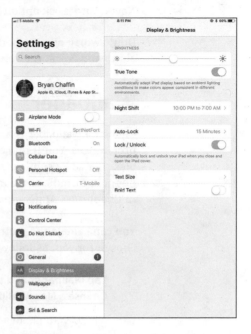

FIGURE 15-8:
Sliding this control adjusts screen brightness.

Another setting you'll find in Display & Brightness (for the iPad Pro) is True Tone. Turn it on and the iPad display can automatically adapt to ambient lighting conditions using special sensors in your iPad Pro.

The Night Shift setting is also found here (as well as in Control Center). As a reminder, it shifts the colors of the display after dark to help you get a good night's sleep, or so the theory goes.

If the app you're spending time in supports dynamic type, you can adjust the type size by dragging a slider. Under Display & Brightness, you'll also find a switch for making text bold. If you choose to apply the Bold Text setting, you'll have to restart your iPad. You'll see similar options in the "Accessibility" section, later in this chapter.

Tap Auto-Lock here under Display & Brightness, and you can how much time elapses before the iPad automatically locks or turns off the display. Your choices are 15 minutes, 10 minutes, 5 minutes, or 2 minutes. Or you can set it so the iPad never locks automatically.

TIP

If you work for a company that insists on a passcode (see the next section), the Never Auto-Lock option isn't in the list that your iPad displays.

Don't worry about whether the iPad is locked. You can still receive notification alerts and adjust the volume.

Wallpaper

Choosing wallpaper is a neat way to dress up the iPad according to your aesthetic preferences. You'll find colorful dynamic animated wallpapers with floating bubbles that add a subtle dizzying effect. But stunning as they are, these images may not hold a candle to the masterpieces in your own photo albums (more about those in Chapter 9). And animations consume more power.

You can sample the pretty patterns and dynamic designs that the iPad has already chosen for you, as follows:

1. Tap Wallpaper and then tap Choose a New Wallpaper.

A list of your photo albums appears, along with Apple's own wallpaper.

2. Tap Dynamic or Stills, or tap one of your own photo albums in the list.

We chose Stills to bring up the thumbnails shown in Figure 15-9.

3. Tap a thumbnail image.

That image fills the screen.

4. When an image is full-screen, choose among the following options, which appear at the bottom of the screen:

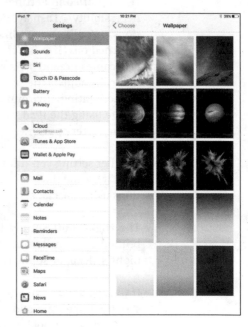

FIGURE 15-9:
Choosing a majestic background.

- *Set Lock Screen:* Your selected image is the wallpaper of choice when the iPad is locked.

- *Set Home Screen:* The wallpaper decorates only your Home screen.

- *Set Both:* Your image is the wallpaper for both the lock screen and the Home screen.

- *Perspective Zoom:* Turn this motion effect on or off.

- *Cancel:* Return to the thumbnail page without changing your Home or lock screen.

Sounds

Consider the Sounds settings area the iPad's soundstage. There, you can turn audio alerts on or off for a variety of functions: ringtones, text tones, new email, sent mail, calendar and reminder alerts, Facebook posts, tweets, and AirDrop. You can also decide whether you want to hear lock sounds and keyboard clicks.

You can alter the ringtone you hear for FaceTime calls and the text tone you hear for iMessages. If you want more, visit the iTunes Store to buy more, typically for $0.99 and $1.29 a pop. You can also create your own ringtones in GarageBand on an iPad. To set a custom tone for individuals in the Contacts app, tap the Edit button and then tap either the Ringtone or the Text Tone option.

To raise the decibel level of alerts, drag the ringer and alerts volume slider to the right. Drag in the opposite direction to bring down the noise. An alternative way to adjust sound levels is to use the physical volume buttons on the side of the iPad, as long as you're not already using the iPad's iMusic or Videos player to listen to music or watch video, respectively.

You can enable and disable the use of physical buttons to alter the volume by using the Change with Buttons switch, below the volume slider.

Siri & Search

We love Siri, the chatty personal digital assistant who can remind you whether to take an umbrella or clue you in on how the Giants are faring in the NFL, and devoted a good chunk of Chapter 14 to learning more about her. Here in Settings, you can change her voice from female to male, choose a default language, let Siri know your name, and decide whether to summon her through the "Hey Siri" command.

You can also tell the iPad which apps you want to search for by flipping the switch for each one. There's also a switch here to turn on Siri Suggestions, a list of apps, people, locations, and such that appear before you even enter a search query. You can also choose whether to enable Suggestions when you're exploiting the iPad's Look Up capabilities, by tapping into the web, iTunes, App Store, locations, and even movie showtimes.

We address Search in Chapter 2 and Siri in Chapter 14. As a reminder, you can initiate a search on the iPad by dragging down from near the top of the screen.

Transactional Settings

You use your iPad to shop and pay for stuff, areas where the following settings apply.

iTunes & App Store

In the iTunes & App Store section, you decide whether your iPad should automatically download music, apps, books, audiobooks, and updates. And if you give the okay, you can choose whether to tap into your cellular network (if applicable) when downloading these items.

Wallet & Apple Pay

If you have a Touch ID-capable iPad and want to take advantage of Apple's mobile payments Apple Pay system, you can add a new credit or debit card in the Wallet & Apple Pay section. Apple Pay lets you make secure online purchases right from your tablet.

Exploring Settings in General

Certain miscellaneous settings are difficult to pigeonhole. Apple wisely lumped these under the General settings moniker. Here's a closer look at your options.

About About

You aren't seeing double. This section, as shown in Figure 15-10, is all about the About setting. And About is full of trivial (and not-so-trivial) information *about* the device. What you find here is straightforward:

>> **Network you use (cellular models only):** AT&T, Sprint, T-Mobile, Verizon in the United States.

>> **Number of songs stored on the device**

>> **Number of videos**

>> **Number of photos**

>> **Number of apps**

>> **Storage capacity used and available:** Because of the way the device is formatted, you always have a little less storage than the advertised amount of flash memory.

>> **Software version:** As this book goes to press, we're up to version 11.0. But as the software is tweaked and updated, your device takes on a new build identifier, indicating that it's just a little bit further along than some previous build. In parentheses next to the version number, a string of numbers and letters, such as 14B55c, tells you more precisely what software version you have. The number/letter string changes whenever the iPad's software is updated and is potentially useful to some tech-support person who might need to know the precise version.

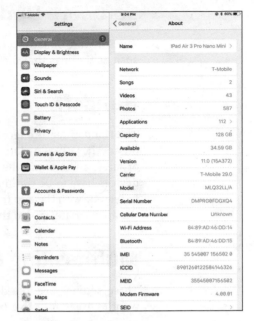

FIGURE 15-10:
You find info about your iPad under About.

>> **Carrier (Wi-Fi + cellular versions only)**

>> **Serial and model numbers**

>> **Cellular Data Number:** For billing purposes only.

>> **Wi-Fi address**

>> **Bluetooth address:** See the earlier section to find out more about this wireless feature.

>> **IMEI, ICCID, MEID, and CSN:** These stand for International Mobile Equipment Identifier, International Circuit Card Identifier, Mobile Equipment Identifier, and Chip Serial Number, respectively. All live up to their geeky acronyms by helping to identify your specific device.

>> **Modern Firmware:** The version of your iPad's firmware, which is a combination of hardware and software that helps your iPad function as an iPad.

>> **SEID:** This is an identifier for the Secure Element used in the Apple Pay mobile payments system.

>> **Legal Notices, License, Warranty, Regulatory RF Exposure, and Trusted Store:** You had to know that the lawyers would get in their two cents somehow. You find all the fine print here.

Software Update

The Software Update section is self-explanatory. When Apple unleashes an update, such as the ones that moved the device from iOS 10 to iOS 11, you can find it here.

Handoff

The Handoff feature lets you start a task (such as typing an email) on your iPad, on another iOS 8 or later device, or on a Mac computer running OS X Yosemite or later, and resume the task on another compatible iOS device, or Mac. All the devices have to be running the same iCloud account. On the tablet, you'll be able to resume with the app from your lock screen or app switcher. On a Mac, you'll see the appropriate app on the dock.

Multitasking & Dock

Three settings are found under Multitasking. Enable the Gestures option if you want to use four or five fingers to

>> Pinch to the Home screen.

>> Swipe up to the app switcher.

>> Swipe left or right to switch among open apps.

TIP

By all means, enable this option if it isn't enabled. These gestures improve the multitasking experience, and we recommend that you give them a try. If you hate them, you know where to turn them off.

You'll also find a Multitasking setting to Allow Multiple Apps. Choose this to swipe from the right edge of the screen to create split view and slide over apps.

Another setting found here, called Persistent Video Overlay, enables you to continue to play a video in an overlay even after you press the Home button.

Accessibility

The Accessibility tools on your iPad are targeted at helping people with certain needs, but there's a lot to dig into and we encourage you to explore the various choices on your own, especially if you or a loved one have a particular area of need.

VoiceOver

The VoiceOver screen reader describes aloud what's on the screen. It can read email messages, web pages, and more. With VoiceOver active, you tap an item on the screen to select it. VoiceOver places a black rectangle around the item and either speaks the name or describes an item. For example, if you tap Display & Brightness, the VoiceOver voice speaks the words "Display and brightness button." VoiceOver even lets you know when you position the iPad in landscape or portrait mode and when your screen is locked or unlocked.

Within the VoiceOver setting, you have several options. For instance, you can drag a Speaking Rate slider to speed up or slow down the speech. You can also determine the kind of typing feedback you get: characters, words, characters and words, or no feedback. Additional switches let you turn on sound effects, change the pitch, and choose the default speech dialect. For example, you can choose an English dialect common to Australia, the United Kingdom, Ireland, or South Africa, along with, of course, the United States. You have additional speech choices from within these countries.

You have to know a new set of finger gestures when VoiceOver is on, which may seem difficult, especially when you first start using VoiceOver. This requirement makes a lot of sense because you want to be able to hear descriptions on the screen before you activate buttons. Different VoiceOver gestures use different numbers of fingers, and Apple recommends that you experiment with different techniques to see what works best for you. A VoiceOver Practice button is provided for this purpose.

We list just a few of the many available gestures here:

>> **Tap:** Select the item.

>> **Rotate two fingers:** This gesture has multiple outcomes that depend on how you set the rotor control gesture. To select your options, head to Settings ➪ General ➪ Accessibility ➪ VoiceOver ➪ Rotor. The rotor control gesture is similar to turning a dial: You rotate two fingertips on the screen. The purpose is to switch to a different set of commands or features. Suppose you're reading text in an email. By alternately spinning the rotor, you can switch between hearing the body of a message read aloud word by word or character by character. After you set the parameters, flick up or down to hear stuff read back. When you type an email, the flicking up and down gestures serve a different purpose: The gestures move the cursor left or right within the text. Here are some of main ones:

>> **Two-finger tap:** Stop speaking.

>> **Two-finger swipe up:** Read everything from the top of the screen.

>> **Two-finger swipe down:** Read everything from your current position on the screen.

>> **Three-finger swipe up or down:** Scroll a page.

>> **Double-tap:** Activate a selected icon or button to launch an app, turn a switch from on to off, and more.

Zoom

The Zoom feature offers a screen magnifier for those who are visually challenged. To zoom, double-tap the screen with *three* fingers. Drag three fingers to move around the screen. To increase magnification, use three fingers to tap and drag up. Tap with three fingers and drag down to decrease magnification. You can tap a Zoom Controller switch for quick access to zoom controls.

The Zoom feature does have a downside: When magnified, the characters on the screen aren't as crisp (although the Retina display is still pretty sharp), and you can't display as much in a single view. You can also choose to zoom full screen or zoom only a window. And you can drag a slider to choose your maximum zoom level, up to 15x.

Larger Text

You can make text larger in the Mail, Contacts, Calendars, Messages, and Notes apps. Drag the slider from left to right or from the small *A* toward the larger *A*. You can turn on a Larger Accessibility Sizes switch to enlarge the text even more in certain supported apps. (You may recall the Text Size option we mention earlier when describing the Display & Brightness setting.)

Bold Text

Bold Text is another setting you first met in Display & Brightness. If you don't think the text on your iPad is bold or bright enough, turn on the Bold Text switch. As we noted, doing so (or turning it off again) requires that you restart your iPad.

Button Shapes

Turn the Button Shapes setting on, and the left-pointing arrow at the top-left corner of the Settings pane (next to General) disappears and the word *General* appears inside a pencil-shaped button.

Increase Contrast

The Increase Contrast setting is another effort to bolster legibility. You can reduce the transparency of the screen to improve the contrast on some backgrounds. You can darken colors. And you can reduce the intensity of bright colors. Play around with these options to see whether they make a difference.

Display Accommodations

Under this setting, you can invert the colors on the iPad to provide a higher contrast for people with poor eyesight. The screen resembles a film negative. (You remember film, right?) You can also use color filters to help compensate for people who are colorblind. You can choose grayscale to reduce color altogether and go gray, or choose other color filters. Or select a Reduce White Point option to reduce the intensity of bright colors.

Hearing Aids

The iPad can communicate with hearing aids through Bluetooth. And Apple has designed a Bluetooth technology for use with custom iPad hearing aids.

Subtitles and Captioning

Aimed at people who are deaf or hard of hearing, the Subtitles and Captioning setting lets you turn on a Closed Captions + SDH switch to summon closed-captioning or subtitles. You can also choose and preview the style for the subtitles and create your own subtitle style.

Audio Descriptions

Toggling the Audio Descriptions switch enables the iPad to automatically play audio descriptions when available.

Mono Audio

If you suffer hearing loss in one ear, the iPad's Mono Audio setting can combine the right and left audio channels so that both channels can be heard in either earbud of any headset you plug in. A slider control can adjust how much audio is combined and to which ear it is directed.

REMEMBER

The iPad, unlike its cousin the iPhone, doesn't come with earbuds or headphones. You have to supply your own.

Speak Selection

When the Speak Selection setting is on, the iPad speaks any text you select. You also find a slider control to adjust the speaking rate. And you can highlight words as they are spoken. You find this option under Speech, along with a Speak Screen button that when enabled lets you swipe down with two fingers from the top of the screen to hear the screen's content.

Reduce Motion

We think the parallax effect of icons and alerts is cool, but your neighbor may not agree. By turning on the Reduce Motion switch, you can reduce the parallax effect and be fairly confident that your wallpaper will remain still.

On/Off Labels

Throughout this book, you read that when certain switches are on, green appears. If you turn on the On/Off Labels switch, you'll still see green, but you'll also see a nerdy 1 when the setting or switch is turned on or a little 0 when the switch is off.

Guided Access

Parents of autistic kids know how challenging it can be to keep their child focused on a given task. The Guided Access setting can limit iPad usage to a single app and also restrict touch input on certain areas of the screen. You can set a passcode to use when Guided Access is enabled and use Touch ID (on compatible models) to end it.

Switch Control

Several controls are represented under the Switch Control setting. The general idea is that you can use a single switch or multiple switches to select text, tap, drag, type, and perform other functions. However, turning on Switch Control changes the gestures and techniques you use to control your tablet and are presumably already familiar with. For example, the iPad can scan by or highlight items on the screen until you select one. Or you can take advantage of scanning crosshairs to select a location on the screen. You can also manually move from item to item by using multiple switches, with each switch set to handle a specific action. We recommend poking around this setting to examine these and other options.

AssistiveTouch

Turn on the AssistiveTouch setting if you need to use an adaptive accessory, such as a joystick, because of difficulties touching the screen. When this setting is on, a movable dot appears; tap the dot to access certain features, such as (but not limited to) notifications or Home. You can also create custom gestures through AssistiveTouch.

Touch Accommodations

Touch Accommodations lets you customize the touch sensitivity of your iPad. For example, you can change the amount of time you must touch the screen before your touch is recognized. You can also change how long your iPad treats multiple touches as a single touch. And you can enable a Tap Assistance option to allow any single finger gesture to perform a tap before a timeout period, which you can customize, expires.

Home-Click Speed

Tap the Home Button setting to choose a home-click speed. You can slow down the speed required to double or triple-click the Home button. On an iPad with

Touch ID, you can enable a Rest Finger to Open button that lets you open the iPad with Touch ID without pressing the Home button.

Accessibility Shortcut

Double-clicking the Home button launches multitasking. But you can set up the iPad so that triple-clicking the button turns on certain accessibility features. By doing so, you can turn on or off Guided Access, VoiceOver, Invert Colors, Color Filters, Reduce White Point, Zoom, Switch Control, and AssistiveTouch.

Storage

The About setting (covered earlier) gives you a lot of information about your device. But after you back out of About and return to the main General settings, you can find out how your iPad is using its storage. You can see what type of files take up how much space, and even see which apps are hogging the most storage and delete those you're no longer using.

Background App Refresh

Some apps continue to run in the background even when you're not actively engaged with them. If you flip the Background App Refresh switch so that green is showing, you can allow such apps to update content when an active Wi-Fi or cellular connection is available. The potential downside to leaving this switch turned on is a hit on battery life.

As it turns out, your iPad is pretty smart about when to refresh apps. iOS detects patterns based on how you use your iPad. It learns when your tablet is typically inactive — at night perhaps when you're in slumberland. And in some cases, apps are refreshed when you enter a particular location.

You can also turn on or off Background App Refresh for any individual app listed under this setting. Flip the switch to make the determination for each given app.

Restrictions

Parents and bosses may love the Restrictions tools, but kids and employees usually think otherwise. You can clamp down, er, provide proper parental guidance to your children or managerial guidance to your staff by preventing them (at least some of the time) from using the Safari browser, Camera, Siri & Dictation, FaceTime, Air-Drop, iTunes Store, Apple Music Connect, iBooks Store, Podcasts, News, or Game Center. Or you might not let them install new apps or make purchases inside the apps you do allow — or (conversely) let them delete apps. When restrictions are in place, icons for off-limit functions can no longer be seen. Tap Enable Restrictions, set or enter your passcode — you have to enter it twice if you're setting up the passcode — and tap the switch next to each item in the Allow or Allowed Content lists that you plan to restrict. Their corresponding settings should be off.

You can also restrict the use of explicit language when you dictate text. An asterisk (*) replaces a naughty word.

Parents have more controls to work with. For instance, you can allow Junior to watch a movie on the iPad but prevent him from watching a flick that carries an R, NC-17, or some other rating. You can also restrict access to certain TV shows, explicit songs and podcasts, and apps based on age-appropriate ratings. In Game Center, you can decide whether your kid can play a multiplayer game, add friends, or record what's on the screen. Apple lets you choose whether to let the kids read books with explicit sexual content. You can also restrict access to websites that have adult content.

If guilt gets the better of you, you can turn off restrictions. Open the Restrictions setting by again typing your passcode. Then switch the setting on for each item you are freeing up. Tap Disable Restrictions. You have to enter your passcode one more time before your kids and office underlings return you to their good graces.

Under Restrictions settings, you'll find privacy controls as well. For example, you can impose restrictions on the use of Location Services, as well as Contacts, Calendars, Reminders, Photos, Bluetooth sharing, and more. (For these and additional privacy controls, visit the dedicated Privacy setting.)

And in this area, you can allow or restrict changes made to your accounts, cellular use, background app refreshes, even volume limits.

There's a lot here, and even if you're liberal about policing your kids' activities, we recommend you poke around and consider all your options.

Use Side Switch

Users with iPads that have a side switch can choose whether it locks screen rotation or acts as a mute button.

REMEMBER

You won't see this setting on the iPad Pro since it doesn't have the side switch.

Date & Time

In our neck of the woods, the time is reported as 11:32 p.m. (or whatever time it happens to be). But in some circles, it's reported as 23:32. If you prefer the latter format on the iPad's status bar, tap the 24-Hour Time setting (under Settings ⇨ General ⇨ Date & Time) so that it's on (green).

This setting is just one that you can adjust under Date & Time. You can also have the iPad set the time in your time zone. Here's how:

1. **Tap Date & Time.**

You see fields for setting the time zone and the date and time.

2. **Tap the Time Zone field and make sure Set Automatically is turned off.**

The current time zone and virtual keyboard are shown.

3. **Tap X to remove the city currently shown in the Time Zone field, and tap the letters of the city or country whose time zone you want to enter until the one you have in mind appears. Then tap the name of that city or country.**

The Time Zone field is automatically filled in for that city.

4. **Tap the Set Date & Time field so that the time is shown; then roll the carousel controls until the proper time displays.**

5. **Roll the carousel controls to choose the proper month, day, and year until the correct date appears.**

6. **Tap General to return to the main Date & Time settings screen.**

You can also dispense with these settings and just have the iPad set the time automatically, based on its knowledge of where you happen to be. Just make sure to turn on the Set Automatically option.

Keyboard

Under Keyboard settings, you have the following options:

>> **Auto-Capitalization:** Automatically capitalize the first letter of the first word you type after ending the preceding sentence with a period, a question mark, or an exclamation point. Auto-capitalization is on by default.

>> **Auto-Correction:** The iPad takes a stab at what it thinks you meant to type.

>> **Check Spelling:** The keyboard checks spelling while you type.

>> **Enable Caps Lock:** All letters are uppercased LIKE THIS if you double-tap the shift key. (The shift key is the one with the arrow pointing up.) Tap shift again to exit caps lock.

>> **Shortcuts:** The iPad's virtual keyboard will display a shortcut bar with controls to copy and paste the text you've selected text, or to make that text bold, italic,

or underline. Don't confuse this Shortcuts setting with the "." Shortcut setting described later.

>> **Predictive:** When enabled, the iPad keyboard will suggest certain words that you might want to type next. Tap a suggested word to accept it. You can also flip the Predictive switch on or off right from the keyboard itself.

>> **"." Shortcut:** A period is inserted followed by a space when you double-tap the space bar. This setting is turned on by default; if you've never tried it, give it a shot.

TIP

You'll see another type of shortcut option, called Text Replacement, in which the keyboard presents a full phrase when you type a few letters. For example, typing the letters *omw* yields *On my way!* Tap the + under the Text Replacement setting to add a new phrase and the optional shortcut for that phrase. Saving a few letters is economical, don't you think?

You can choose to use an international keyboard (as we discuss in Chapter 2), which you enable from Keyboard settings. You can also enable the Split Keyboard option if you'd like to take advantage of this feature.

Apple gives you the power to substitute the default keyboard on your iPad for a custom alternative. Among the choices you might consider are Swype, SwiftKey, and Fleksy. For more on adding a third-party keyboard, consult Chapter 2.

Language & Region

In the Language & Region section, you can set the language in which the iPad displays text, plus the date and time format for the region in question. You can choose a Gregorian, Japanese, or Buddhist calendar, too.

VPN

After you tap VPN on the General settings screen, you see a control for VPN.

TECHNICAL
STUFF

A *virtual private network,* or *VPN,* is a way for you to securely access your company's network behind the firewall — using an encrypted Internet connection that acts as a secure tunnel for data. Some people use VPNs to encrypt their traffic or evade regional restrictions on content.

You can configure a VPN on the iPad by following these steps:

1. **Tap Settings ⇨ General ⇨ VPN ⇨ Add VPN Configuration.**

2. **Tap one of the protocol options.**

The iPad software supports the protocols *IKEv2* (Internet Key Exchange), *L2TP* (Layer 2 Tunneling Protocol), and *IPSec,* which apparently provides the kind of security that satisfies network administrators.

3. **Using configuration settings provided by your company, fill in the appropriate server information, account, password, and other information.**

4. **Choose whether to turn on RSA SecurID authentication, if the option presents itself.**

   Better yet, lend your iPad to the techies where you work and let them fill in the blanks on your behalf.

After you configure your iPad for VPN usage, you can turn that capability on or off by tapping (yep) the VPN switch in Settings.

Reset

As little kids playing sports, we ended an argument by agreeing to a do-over. Well, the Reset settings on the iPad are one big do-over. Now that you're (presumably) grown up, think long and hard about the consequences before implementing do-over settings. Regardless, you may encounter good reasons for starting over; some of these are addressed in Chapter 16.

Here are your reset options:

>> **Reset All Settings:** Resets all settings, but no data or media is deleted.

>> **Erase All Content and Settings:** Resets all settings *and* wipes out all your data.

>> **Reset Network Settings:** Deletes the current network settings and restores them to their factory defaults.

>> **Subscriber Services:** Reprovisions (or refreshes) your account and resets your authentication code. It will not show up on all models.

>> **Reset Keyboard Dictionary:** Removes added words from the dictionary. Remember that the iPad keyboard is intelligent. One reason why it's so smart is that it learns from you. So when you reject words that the iPad keyboard suggests, it figures that the words you specifically banged out ought to be added to the keyboard dictionary.

>> **Reset Home Screen Layout:** Reverts all icons to the way they were at the factory.

>> **Reset Location & Privacy:** Restores factory defaults.

Touch ID & Passcode

If you want to prevent others from using your iPad, you can set a passcode by tapping Touch ID & Passcode (or just Passcode on models without Touch ID) and then tapping Turn Passcode On. By default, you use the virtual keypad to enter and confirm a four-digit passcode. If you'd prefer a longer, stronger passcode, tap Change Passcode, and type your current passcode. Then tap Passcode Options, followed by Custom Alphanumeric Code, Custom Numeric Code, or 6-Digit Numeric Code. Now enter and confirm your new passcode, which can be almost any combination of the letters, numbers, and symbols available on the standard virtual keyboard. You'll also be presented with the option to use your new passcode as your iCloud security code, which is used to protect the passwords you've stored in iCloud Keychain.

You can also determine whether a passcode is required immediately, after 1 minute, after 5 minutes, 15 minutes, 1 hour, or 4 hours. Shorter times are more secure, of course. On the topic of security, the iPad can be set to automatically erase your data if someone makes ten failed passcode attempts.

You can also change the passcode or turn it off later (unless your employer dictates otherwise), but you need to know the present passcode to apply any changes. If you forget the passcode, you have to restore the iPad software, as we describe in Chapter 16.

From the Touch ID & Passcode setting, you can determine whether to allow access to the today view, the notifications view, or Siri, or Home control when the iPad is locked.

If you have an iPad Air 2, iPad mini 3, or any iPad Pro, we strongly recommend that you at least try Touch ID, the clever fingerprint authentication scheme that not only lets you bypass the lock screen by pressing your thumb or another finger against the Home button, but also lets you purchase stuff in iTunes, the App Store, and the iBooks Store. You can also take advantage of the Apple Pay mobile payments system, as mentioned earlier in the chapter, but (as of this writing) only for certain online transactions — not physical retail stores as is possible with compatible iPhone models.

You can store up to five fingerprints (yours and people you trust with whom you share the iPad). Tap Add a Fingerprint and go through the training session that you likely encountered back when you set up your iPad (consult Chapter 2 for details). If the iPad doesn't recognize your finger, you see Try Again at the top of the screen. You get three wrong tries before you're forced to use a traditional passcode instead, at least for this session.

As an added security measure, a regular passcode is required the first time you try to get past a lock screen after restarting the tablet.

If you want to delete an authorized fingerprint, tap the listing for the finger in question, and then tap Delete Fingerprint. Excuse our French, but you've just given the finger to the finger.

Promoting Harmony through Family Sharing

Earlier under Restrictions, we show you how to impose an iron fist when it comes to permitting iPad usage at home. Now we're going to try to make everybody in the clan happy again. Visit iCloud settings and consider setting up Family Sharing with up to six members of your family. Adults and kids can partake, but one grown-up must take charge as the family organizer. We figure it might as well be you, the person reading this book. You'll be the person presenting your iCloud Apple ID username and password, and the one on the hook for paying for iTunes, iBooks, and App Store purchases. As the family organizer, you can turn on Ask to Buy so that you can approve (or deny) purchases or download requests from other members of your clan.

When Family Sharing has been implemented, you can all share a calendar, photos, reminders, and your respective locations. Family Sharing may also help find a missing device through the important Find My iPad feature, which we describe at the end of this chapter.

WARNING

Should you leave Family Sharing, your account is removed from the group and you can no longer share content with everybody else. You won't be able to use DRM-protected music, movies, TV shows, books, or apps that another member purchased. And you won't be able to access the family calendar, reminders, or photos.

Family Sharing works with iOS 8 (and later) devices and OS X Yosemite and later on a Mac, and Find My Friends 3.0, Find My iPhone 3.1, and iCloud for Windows 4.0.

Settings for Social Media

Much as we all use our iPads to consume content, we also use it to exchange our own content — ideas, pictures and the like — with close intimates, colleagues, and yes, in some instances, people with whom we are trying to wield influence. The next set of settings is all about managing some of the most popular social networks and the people in our Contacts.

Twitter

In Twitter settings, you can add a new Twitter account and update your contacts so that Twitter uses their email addresses and phone numbers to automatically add their Twitter handles and photos. You also can choose yay or nay on whether you can use various apps with Twitter.

Facebook

Most of us know Facebook as a great service to help us stay in touch with relatives, associates, and old pals, rekindle relationships, and make new friends. But some people collect Facebook friends like baseball cards. If it seems like you're acquainted with all 2 billion-and-counting members of the mammoth social network, we know what you mean.

Fortunately, Apple kindly organizes your Facebook relationships on the iPad. If you turn on the Calendar and Contacts switches under Facebook settings on the iPad, your Facebook friends automatically populate your contacts list, complete with profile pictures as well as email addresses and phone numbers (if they made them public on Facebook). Birthdays and calendar appointments appropriately turn up in the Calendar app.

Think of these Facebook entries as live synced contact entries. If a person changes his or her phone number and email address on Facebook, that change will be reflected on your iPad, provided you have Wi-Fi or cellular coverage or the next time you do have coverage. And if your friends de-friend you — how cruel is that? — their contact info will disappear.

If the iPad can correctly match a Facebook friend entry with an existing contact entry, it will try to unify that contact under a single view. The Update All Contacts option under Facebook settings on the iPad serves a slightly different purpose. It tries to add Facebook profile information to contacts who are on Facebook but are not among your Facebook friends.

Flickr, Vimeo, Sina Weibo, Tencent Weibo

Yes, Flickr (online photo sharing), Vimeo (online video sharing), and Sina Weibo and Tencent Weibo (Chinese social networks if you've enabled a Chinese keyboard) get dedicated Settings areas from which you can enter your sign-in credentials to such services.

Sorting and displaying contacts

Do you think of us as Ed, Bob, and Bryan or Baig, LeVitus, and Chaffin? The answer to that question will probably determine whether you choose to sort your contacts list alphabetically by last name or first name.

In Settings, tap Contacts; scroll down to the Contacts section; and peek at Sort Order. Then tap Last, First or First, Last. You can determine whether you want to display a first name or last name first by tapping Display Order and then choosing First, Last or Last, First. You can also go with a short name to fit more names on the screen. You can choose a first name and last initial, first initial and last name, first name only, or last name only. If you prefer nicknames, you can choose those instead, when available.

You'll also see a Contacts Found in Apps switch that when disabled will remove unconfirmed contact suggestions. You won't see such autocomplete suggestions in Mail, the incoming call screens, or the Contacts app.

Find My iPad

We hope you never have to use the Find My iPad feature — though we have to say that it's darn cool. If you inadvertently leave your iPad in a taxi or restaurant, Find My iPad may just help you retrieve it. You need a free iCloud account and your iPad must be connected to a network of some kind.

Well, that's *almost* all you need. Tap Settings ➪ Apple ID ➪ iCloud and make sure Find My iPad is switched on.

Now, suppose you lost your tablet — and we can only assume that you're beside yourself. Follow these steps to see whether Find My iPad can help you:

1. **Log on to your iCloud account at** www.icloud.com **from any browser on your computer.**

2. **Click the Find iPhone icon.**

    Yes, even though the feature is Find My iPad on the iPad, it shows up as Find My iPhone on the iCloud site. Don't worry; it'll still locate your iPad — and, for that matter, a lost iPhone or iPod touch, and even a Mac computer, too.

Assuming that your tablet is turned on and in the coverage area, its general whereabouts turn up on a map in standard or satellite view, or a hybrid of the two. In our tests, Find My iPad found our iPads quickly.

Even seeing your iPad on a map may not help you much, especially if the device is lost somewhere in midtown Manhattan. Take heart.

3. **At the iCloud site, click the Lost Mode button.**

4. **Type a phone number at which you can be reached, as well as a plea to the Good Samaritan who (you hope) picked up your iPad.**

   Apple has already prepared a simple message indicating that the iPad is lost, but you can change or remove the message and substitute your own plea for the return of your tablet.

   The message appears on the lost iPad's screen.

TIP

To get someone's attention, you can also sound an alarm that plays for two minutes, even if the volume is off. Tap Play Sound to make it happen. Hey, that alarm may come in handy if the iPad turns up under a couch in your house. Stranger things have happened.

We also recommend turning on the Send Last Location setting in Find My iPad because it automatically sends the tablet's location to Apple when the device's battery is critically low. That way, you still have a puncher's chance of getting back a lost iPad even when the battery is knocked out.

TIP

Find My iPhone (which finds any iOS device) is also available as a free app. Another free app called Find My Friends will locate your friends on a map. Just hope that when you find a particular pal, he or she is not the one who snatched your missing iPad.

After all this labor, if the iPad is seemingly gone for good, click Erase iPad at the iCloud site to delete your personal data from afar and return the iPad to its factory settings. (A somewhat less drastic measure is to remotely lock your iPad by using a passcode.)

Meanwhile, the person who found (or possibly stole) your iPad cannot reactivate the device to use as his or her own, or to peddle, unless he or she successfully types in *your* Apple ID.

Even if you choose to erase the device remotely, it can still display a custom message with the information needed for someone to return it to you. If, indeed, you ever get your iPad back, you can always restore the information from an iTunes backup on your Mac or PC or iCloud.

We authors love a happy ending.

Chapter **16**

When Good iPads Go Bad

I n our experience, all Apple iOS devices — namely the iPad, iPhone, and iPod touch — are reliable. But every so often, a good iPad might just go bad. We don't see it as a common occurrence, but it does happen occasionally. So, in this chapter, we look at the types of bad things that can happen, along with suggestions for fixing them.

What kind of bad things are we talking about? Well, we're referring to problems involving

» Frozen or dead iPads

» Wireless networks

» Synchronization with computers (both Mac and PC) or iTunes

After all the troubleshooting, we tell you how to get even more help if nothing we suggest does the trick. Finally, if your iPad is so badly hosed that it needs to go back to the mother ship for repairs, we offer ways to survive the experience with a minimum of stress or fuss, including how to restore your stuff from an iTunes or iCloud backup.

Resuscitating an iPad with Issues

Our first category of troubleshooting techniques applies to an iPad that's frozen or otherwise acting up. The recommended procedure when this happens is to perform the seven *R*s in sequence.

1. Recharge

2. Restart

3. Reset your iPad

4. Remove your content

5. Reset settings and content

6. Restore

7. Recovery mode

But before you even start those procedures, Apple recommends you take these steps:

1. **Verify that you have the current version of iTunes installed on your Mac or PC.**

   You can download the latest and greatest version here: www.apple.com/itunes/download.

2. **Verify that you're connecting your iPad to your computer using a USB port.**

   TIP

   If you encounter difficulties here, we implore you to read the paragraph in the next section that begins with this:

   - *"Don't* plug the iPad's dock connector or Lightning–to–USB cable into a USB port on your keyboard, monitor, or unpowered USB hub."

3. **Make sure that your iPad software is up to date.**

   To check using iTunes on your Mac or PC,

   a. *Connect the iPad to the computer and launch iTunes, if it doesn't launch automatically.*

   If you connect more than one iDevice to this computer simultaneously, the button will say the number of devices (for example, *5 Devices*) rather than *iPad*. Click the button to display a drop-down list and select the device you want.

   b. *Click the Summary tab and then click the Check for Update button.*

To check with your iPad:

a. On the Home screen, tap Settings.

b. In the Settings list on the left side of the screen, tap General.

c. On the right side of the screen, tap Software Update.

If your iPad requires an update, you receive instructions for doing so. Otherwise, please continue.

If your iPad is still acting up — if it freezes, doesn't wake up from sleep, doesn't do something it used to do, or in any other way acts improperly — don't panic. The following sections describe the things you should try, in the order that we (and Apple) recommend.

If the first technique doesn't do the trick, go on to the second. If the second one doesn't work, try the third. And so on.

Recharge

If your iPad acts up in any way, shape, or form, the first thing you should try is to give its battery a full recharge before you proceed.

REMEMBER

Don't plug the iPad's dock connector or Lightning–to–USB cable into a USB port on your keyboard, monitor, or an unpowered USB hub. You *must* plug the cable into one of the USB ports on your computer itself because the USB ports on your computer supply more power than the other ports. Although other USB ports *may* do the trick, you're better off using a built-in one on your computer.

If your computer is more than a few years old, even your built-in USB ports may not supply enough juice to recharge your iPad. It'll sync just fine; it just won't recharge. If you see *Not Charging* next to the battery icon at the top of the screen, use the included USB power adapter to recharge your iPad from an AC outlet rather than from a computer.

TIP

Most *powered* USB hubs, the kind you plug into an AC outlet, will charge your iPad just fine. But *passive* or *unpowered* hubs — ones that don't plug into the wall for power — won't cut it when it comes to charging your iPad.

TIP

If you're in a hurry, charge your iPad for a minimum of 20 minutes. We think a full charge is a better idea, but a charge of 20 minutes is better than no charge at all. And for faster charging in any circumstances, turn off your iPad completely while it charges or at least put it in airplane mode. It's fine to use your iPad while it charges, but it will charge faster if you turn it off or put it in airplane mode.

Restart

If you recharge your iPad and it still misbehaves, the next thing to try is restarting. Start by restarting a recalcitrant app: Double-click the Home button, then swipe up on the misbehaving app in App Switcher.

You know how restarting a computer often fixes problems? Well, restarting your iPad sometimes works wonders, too, so that's what we'll try next.

Here's how to restart your iPad:

1. **Hold down the sleep/wake button.**
2. **When the slider appears, slide it to turn off the iPad and then wait a few seconds.**
3. **Press the sleep/wake button again until the Apple logo appears on the screen.**
4. **If your iPad is still frozen, misbehaves, or doesn't start, hold down the Home button for six to ten seconds to force any frozen applications to quit.**
5. **Repeat Steps 1–4 again.**

TIP

If your Home or sleep/wake button is acting up and you can't power down the usual way, try enabling Assistive Touch in Settings ➪ General ➪ Accessibility. A gray circle will appear on your screen; tap it and several options including on-screen versions of the Home and sleep/wake buttons appear. It may or may not help.

If these steps don't get your iPad back up and running, move on to the third *R:* resetting your iPad.

Reset your iPad

To reset your iPad, merely hold down the sleep/wake button and then hold down the Home button, continuing to keep both buttons down for at least ten seconds. When you see the Apple logo, release both buttons.

Resetting your iPad is like forcing your computer to restart after a crash. Your data shouldn't be affected by a reset — and in many cases, the reset cures whatever was ailing your iPad. So don't be shy about giving this technique a try. In many cases, your iPad goes back to normal after you reset it this way.

TIP

Sometimes you have to hold down the sleep/wake button *before* you hold down the Home button. If you press both at exactly the same time, you create a *screen shot* — a picture of whatever is on your screen at the time — rather than reset your iPad.

Unfortunately, sometimes resetting *doesn't* do the trick. When that's the case, you have to take stronger measures.

TIP

At this point, it's a good idea to back up your iPad's contents. On your iPad, go to Settings ⇨ iCloud ⇨ Backup and tap the Back Up Now button. Or connect your iPad to your computer and look in the Backup section of the Summary pane in iTunes, which also identifies when the last backup occurred.

Remove content

Nothing you've tried so far should have taken more than a few minutes (or 20 if you tried the 20-minute recharge). We hate to tell you, but that's about to change because the next thing you should try is removing some or all of your data to see whether it's causing your troubles.

To do so, you need to sync your iPad and then reconfigure it so that some or all of your files are *not* synchronized (which removes them from the iPad). The problem could be contacts, calendar data, songs, photos, videos, or podcasts. You can apply one of two strategies to this troubleshooting task:

>> **If you suspect a particular data type** — for example, you suspect your photos because your iPad freezes whenever you tap the Photos icon on the Home screen — try removing that data first.

>> **If you have no suspicions,** deselect every item and then sync. When you're finished, your iPad should have no data on it. If that method fixes your iPad, try restoring your data, one type at a time. If the problem returns, you have to keep experimenting to determine which particular data type or file is causing the problem.

If you're still having problems, the next step is to reset your iPad's settings and content.

Reset settings and content

Resetting involves two steps: The first one, resetting your iPad settings, resets every iPad *setting* to its default — the way the iPad was when you took it out of the box. Resetting the iPad's settings doesn't erase any of your data or media, so you can try this step without trepidation. The only downside is that you may have to go back and change some settings afterward. To reset your settings, tap the Settings icon on the Home screen and then tap General ⇨ Reset ⇨ Reset All Settings.

Be careful *not* to tap Erase All Content and Settings, at least not yet. Erasing all content takes more time to recover from (because your next sync takes a long time), so try Reset All Settings first.

If you're having network or connectivity issues, try Reset Network Settings. Now, if resetting all settings or network settings didn't cure your iPad, you have to try Erase All Content and Settings. Read the next warning paragraph first. Then tap Settings ➪ General ➪ Reset ➪ Erase All Content and Settings.

The Erase All Content strategy deletes everything from your iPad — all your data, media, and settings. Because all these items are stored on your computer or the cloud — at least in theory — you should be able to put things back the way they were by restoring your latest backup and then syncing. But you may lose any photos or screen shots you've taken, as well as any contacts, calendar events, reminders, playlists, and anything else you've created or modified on the iPad since it last synced.

After using Erase All Content and Settings, check to see whether your iPad works properly. If that didn't cure what ailed your iPad, the next-to-the-last *R*, restoring your iPad using iTunes, may help.

Restore

Before you give up on your poor, sick iPad, you can try to restore it. To restore, connect your iPad to your computer as though you were about to sync. But when the iPad icon appears in iTunes, click the Summary tab and then click the Restore button. This action erases all your data and media and resets all your settings.

If your computer isn't available, you can also trigger this step from your iPad by tapping Settings ➪ General ➪ Reset ➪ Erase All Content and Settings.

If Find My iPad (Settings ➪ iCloud ➪ Find My iPad) is enabled, you'll see a message to disable it before you restore your iPad.

Because all your data and media still exist on your computer (except for photos or screen shots you've taken, as well as email, contacts, calendar events, playlists, and anything else you've created or modified on the iPad since your last sync, as noted previously), you shouldn't lose anything by restoring except possibly email, photos, or text messages sent or received since your last backup. Your next sync will take longer than usual, and you may have to reset settings you've changed since you got your iPad. But other than those inconveniences, restoring shouldn't cause you any additional trouble.

Performing a restore deletes everything on your iPad — all your data, media, and settings. You *should* be able to put things back the way they were with your next sync; if that doesn't happen, for whatever reason, you can't say we didn't warn you. That said, you may still be able to restore from an iTunes or iCloud backup as described in this chapter's thrilling conclusion, a scintillating section we call, "Dude, Where's My Stuff?"

Recovery mode

So, if you've tried all the other steps or you couldn't try some or all of them because your iPad is so messed up, you can try one last thing: Recovery mode. Here's how it works:

1. **Disconnect the Lightning-to-USB cable from your iPad, but leave the other end of the cable connected to the USB port on your computer.**

2. **Turn off the iPad by holding down the sleep/wake button for a few seconds until the red slider appears onscreen, and then slide the slider.**

   Wait for the iPad to turn off.

3. **Hold down the Home button while you reconnect the Lightning-to-USB cable to your iPad.**

   When you reconnect the Lightning-to-USB cable, your iPad should power on.

    If you see a battery icon like the one shown in the margin, you need to let your iPad charge for at least 10 to 15 minutes. When the battery picture goes away or turns green instead of red, go back to Step 2 and try again.

4. **Continue holding down the Home button until you see the Connect to iTunes screen, and then release the button.**

   If you don't see the Connect to iTunes screen on your iPad, try Steps 1–4 again.

   If iTunes didn't open automatically already, launch it now. You should see a Recovery mode alert on your computer screen telling you that your iPad is in Recovery mode and that you must restore it before it can be used with iTunes.

5. **Use iTunes to restore the device, as we describe in the preceding section.**

Okay. So that's the gamut of things you can do when your iPad acts up. If you tried all of this and none of it worked, skim through the rest of this chapter to see whether anything else we recommend looks like it might help. If not, your iPad probably needs to go into the shop for repairs.

Never fear, gentle reader. Be sure to read the "If Nothing We Suggest Helps" section, later in this chapter. Your iPad may be quite sick, but we help ease the pain by sharing some tips on how to minimize the discomfort.

Problems with Networks

If you're having problems with Wi-Fi or your wireless carrier's data network (Wi-Fi + 3G or 4G models only), this section may help. The techniques here are short and sweet — except for the last one, restore. Restore, which we describe in a previous section, is inconvenient and time-consuming, and entails erasing all your data and media and then restoring it.

First, here are some simple steps that may help:

>> **Make sure that you have sufficient Wi-Fi or 3G or 4G signal strength, as shown in Figure 16-1.**

FIGURE 16-1:
Wi-Fi (top) and 3G or 4G (bottom) signal strength from best (left) to worst (right).

>> **Try moving around.** Changing your location by as little as a few feet can sometimes mean the difference between great wireless reception and no wireless reception. If you're inside, try moving around even a step or two in one direction. If you're outside, try moving 10 or 20 paces in any direction. Keep an eye on the cell signal or Wi-Fi icon as you move around, and stop when you see more bars than you saw before.

>> **Restart your iPad.** If you've forgotten how, refer to the "Restart" section, earlier in this chapter. As we mention, restarting your iPad is often all it takes to fix whatever is wrong.

If you have a Wi-Fi + 3G or 4G iPad, try the following:

>> **Make sure that you haven't left your iPad in airplane mode, as we describe in Chapter 15.** In airplane mode, all network-dependent features are disabled, so you can't send or receive messages or use any of the apps that require a Wi-Fi or data-network connection (that is, Mail, Safari, Maps, and the iTunes and App Store apps).

>> **Toggle airplane mode on and off.** Turn on airplane mode by swiping upward from the bottom of the screen to bring up Control Center and then tapping the airplane icon. Wait 15 or 20 seconds and then tap the airplane icon again to turn airplane mode off.

Toggling airplane mode on and off like this resets both the Wi-Fi and wireless data-network connections. If your network connection was the problem, toggling airplane mode on and off may correct it.

Apple offers two good articles that may help you with Wi-Fi issues. The first offers some general troubleshooting tips and hints; the second discusses potential sources of interference for wireless devices and networks. You can find them here:

```
http://support.apple.com/kb/TS3237
```

and here:

```
http://support.apple.com/kb/HT1365
```

If none of these suggestions fix your network issues, try resetting your network settings by tapping Settings ⇨ General ⇨ Reset ⇨ Reset Network Settings.

Finally, if nothing else has fixed your issue, you can try restoring your iPad, as we describe previously in the "Restore" section.

WARNING

Performing a restore deletes everything on your iPad — all your data, media, and settings. You should be able to put things back the way they were with your next sync. If that doesn't happen, well, consider yourself forewarned.

Sync, Computer, or iTunes Issues

The last category of troubleshooting techniques in this chapter applies to issues that involve synchronization and computer–iPad relations. If you're having problems syncing or your computer doesn't recognize your iPad when you connect it, here are some things to try.

We suggest that you try these procedures in the order they're presented here:

1. **Recharge your iPad.**

   If you didn't try it previously, try it now. Go to the "Resuscitating an iPad with Issues" section, earlier in this chapter, and read what we say about recharging your iPad. Every word there also applies here.

2. **Try a different USB port or a different cable if you have one available.**

   It doesn't happen often, but occasionally USB ports and cables go bad. When they do, they invariably cause sync and connection problems. Always make sure that a bad USB port or cable isn't to blame.

   If you don't remember what we said about using USB ports on your computer rather than the ones on your keyboard, monitor, or hub, we suggest that you reread the "Recharge" section, earlier in this chapter.

3. **Restart your iPad and try to sync again.**

   We describe restarting in full and loving detail in the "Restart" section, earlier in this chapter. You might also want to restart your computer at this point, just in case.

4. **Reinstall iTunes.**

TIP

Even if you have an iTunes installer handy, you probably should visit the Apple website and download the latest-and-greatest version, just in case. You can find the latest version of iTunes at `www.apple.com/itunes/download`.

More Help on the Apple Website

If you try everything we suggest earlier in this chapter and still have problems, don't give up just yet. This section describes a few more places you may find help. We recommend that you check them out before you throw in the towel and smash your iPad into tiny little pieces (or ship it back to Apple for repairs, as we describe in the next section).

First, Apple offers an excellent set of support resources on its website at `www.apple.com/support/ipad/setup`. You can browse support issues by category, search for a problem by keyword, read or download technical manuals, and scan the discussion forums.

Speaking of the discussion forums, you can go directly to them at `http://discussions.apple.com`. They're chock-full of useful questions and answers from other iPad users. If you can't find an answer to a support question elsewhere, you can often find it in these forums. You can browse by category or search by keyword. Either way, you find thousands of discussions about almost every aspect of using your iPad.

Now for the best part: If you can't find a solution by browsing or searching, you can post your question in the appropriate Apple discussion forum. Check back in a few days (or even in a few hours), and some helpful iPad user may well have replied with the solution. If you've never tried this fabulous tool, you're missing out on one of the greatest support resources available anywhere.

Last, but certainly not least, you might want to try a carefully worded Google search. You might just find the solution.

If Nothing We Suggest Helps

If you tried every trick in the book (this one) and still have a malfunctioning iPad, consider shipping it off to the iPad hospital (better known as Apple, Inc.). The repair is free if your iPad is still under its one-year limited warranty.

TIP

You can extend your warranty for as long as two years from the original purchase date, if you want. To do so, you need to buy the AppleCare Protection Plan for your iPad. You don't have to do it when you buy your iPad, but you must buy it before your one-year limited warranty expires. The retail price is $79, but we've seen it for less, so it might pay to shop around.

Here are a few things you need to know before you take your iPad in to be repaired:

>> *Your iPad may be erased during its repair,* so you should sync your iPad with iTunes or iCloud and make a backup before you take it in, if you can. If you can't and you entered data on the iPad since your last sync, such as a contact or an appointment, the data may not be there when you restore your iPad upon its return.

>> Remove any accessories, such as a case or screen protector.

TIP

Although you may be able to get your iPad serviced by Best Buy or another authorized Apple reseller, we recommend that you take or ship it to your nearest Apple Store, for two reasons:

>> **No one knows your iPad like Apple.** One of the Geniuses at the Apple Store may be able to fix whatever is wrong without sending your iPad away for repairs.

>> **The Apple Store will, in some cases, swap out your wonky iPad for a brand-new one on the spot.** You can't win if you don't play, which is why we always visit our local Apple Store when something goes wrong (with our iPads, iPhones, iPods, and even our laptops and iMacs).

If you've done everything we've suggested, we're relatively certain that you're now holding an iPad that works flawlessly. Again.

That said, some or all of your stuff may not be on it. If that's the case, the following section offers a two-trick solution that usually works.

Dude, Where's My Stuff?

If you performed a restore or had your iPad replaced or repaired, you have one more task to accomplish. Your iPad may work flawlessly at this point, but some or all of your stuff — your music, movies, contacts, iMessages, or whatever — is missing. You're not sunk, at least not yet. You still have a couple of tricks up your sleeve.

>> **Trick 1: Sync your iPad with iTunes and then sync it again.** That's right — sync and sync again. Why? Because sometimes stuff doesn't get synced properly on the first try. Just do it.

>> **Trick 2: Restore from backup.** Click the Summary tab in iTunes and then click Restore Backup. If Find My iPad (Settings ⇨ iCloud ⇨ Find My iPad) is enabled, you'll first see a message to disable it before you restore your iPad. Then the Restore from Backup dialog appears and offers you a choice of backups, as shown in Figure 16-2. Select the one you want, click the Restore button, and let the iPad work some magic.

TIP

If you have more than one backup for a device, as Bob has for his iPads in Figure 16-2, try the most recent (undated) one first. If it doesn't work or you're still missing files, try restoring from any other backups before you throw in the towel.

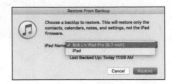

FIGURE 16-2:
Select the appropriate backup and click the Restore button.

These backups include photos in the camera roll, text messages, notes, contact favorites, sound settings, and more, but not media you've synced, such as music, videos, or photos. If media is missing, try performing Trick 1 again.

If you aren't holding an iPad that works flawlessly and has most (if not all) of your stuff, it's time to make an appointment with a Genius at your local Apple Store, call the support hotline (800-275-2273), or visit the support web page at www.apple.com/support/ipad.

Chapter **17**

Accessorize Your iPad

A nyone who has purchased a new car in recent years is aware that it's not always a picnic trying to escape the showroom without the salesperson trying to get you to part with a few extra bucks. You can only imagine what the markup is on roof racks and navigation systems.

We don't suppose you'll get a hard sell when you snap up a new iPad at an Apple Store (or elsewhere). But Apple and several other companies are all too happy to outfit whichever iPad model you choose with extra doodads, from wireless keyboards and stands to battery chargers and carrying cases. So just as your car might benefit from dealer (or third-party) options, so too might your iPad benefit from a variety of spare parts.

Accessories from Apple

Our roster of worthwhile accessories begin with the options that carry the Apple logo:

» **Apple Smart Cover:** No iPad has ever shipped with a case in the box, but you can find cases aplenty just the same. Apple's iPad case is more cover than case, which is probably why it's called a *Smart Cover* instead of a *Smart Case*. Made specifically for iPads, it's ultra-thin and attaches magnetically. Flip the cover open (even just a little), and your iPad wakes instantly; flip it shut, and your iPad goes right to sleep. The case is available in numerous bright colors in polyurethane ($39–$49) or leather ($69).

>> **Apple Magic keyboard:** The various virtual keyboards that pop up just as you need them on the iPad are fine for shorter typing tasks, whether it's composing emails or tapping a few notes. For longer assignments, however, we writers are more comfortable pounding away on a real-deal physical keyboard.

The $99 Apple Magic keyboard is a way to use a decent-enough aluminum physical keyboard without tethering it to the iPad. It operates from up to 30 feet away from the iPad via Bluetooth, the wireless technology we discuss in Chapter 15. The keyboard has a built-in lithium-ion battery, which you can charge by plugging it into the supplied Lightning–to–USB port on a computer or (via an adapter) to your iPad. Apple claims battery life of a month or more.

That said, many compatible Bluetooth keyboards and keyboard covers and cases can be used with any iPad, plus smarter cases for Pro models, such as . . .

>> **Apple Smart Keyboard (for iPad Pro):** Apple built special keyboard-and-cover combinations for its iPad Pro models, the aptly named iPad Pro Smart Keyboard. The prices are $169 for the 12.9-inch iPad Pro, $159 for the 10.5 inch, and $149 for the 9.7 inch. All three are 4mm thick, which is quite thin.

The keyboard connects to the iPad Pro via the smart connector on the edge of the Smart Keyboard and on the side of iPad Pro. Making that connection is a tad tricky at first. And beyond typing, you get the added benefit of using the Smart Keyboard as your Smart Cover.

>> **Camera connector:** iPads don't include a USB port or an SD memory card slot, which happen to be the most popular methods for getting pictures (and videos) from a digital camera onto a computer. So, you'll need either Apple's Lightning–to–USB–camera connector or its Lightning–to–SD–card connector ($29 each).

>> **Travel adapter:** If you're traveling abroad, consider the Apple World Travel Adapter Kit. The $29 kit includes the proper prongs and adapters for numerous countries around the globe, and it lets you juice up not only your iPad but also iPhones, iPod touches, and Macs.

Listening and Talking

You've surely noticed that your iPad didn't include earphones or a headset. That's probably a blessing because the earphones and headsets Apple has included with iPods and iPhones since time immemorial aren't that good.

Wired headphones, earphones, and headsets

Search Amazon for *headphones, earphones,* or *headsets,* and you'll find thousands of each available at prices ranging from $10 to more than $1,000. Or if you prefer to shop in a bricks-and-mortar store, Target, Best Buy, and the Apple Store all have decent selections, with prices starting at less than $20.

TIP

Much as we love the shopping experience at Apple Stores, you won't find any bargains there because Apple-branded products are rarely discounted, including the company's own Beats brand of headphones.

With so many brands and models of earphones, headphones, and headsets available from so many manufacturers at so many price points, we can't possibly test even a fraction of the ones available today, and this is all subjective anyway. That said, we've probably tested more of them than most people, and we have our favorites.

Bob is partial to his SR60i from Grado, which is legendary for offering astonishingly accurate audio at an affordable price (around $80). Find out more at www.gradolabs.com. Ed likes sweet-sounding, albeit pricey (about $300) Bose QuietComfort series acoustic noise-canceling headphones.

For earphones and earphone-style headsets, Bob still likes the Klipsch Image S4 headphones and S4i in-ear headset with mic and three-button remote. At around $79 and $99, respectively, they sound better than many similarly priced and more expensive offerings.

Bluetooth stereo headphones, earphones, and headsets

We don't spend much time using Bluetooth (wireless) stereo headphones and headsets, but we thought we'd at least plant the seed. The idea is that with Bluetooth stereo headphones, earphones, and headsets, you can listen to music wirelessly up to 33 feet away from your iPad. If this sounds good to you, we suggest that you look for reviews of such products on the web before you decide which one to buy. A search of Amazon for *stereo Bluetooth headset* brought up thousands of items, with prices starting as low as $11.99.

Bob has been happy with his BlueAnt Pump HD Stereo Sportsbuds, a Bluetooth stereo headset he occasionally uses with his iPhone and iPad. Although discontinued (and replaced by a new, more expensive model he hasn't tested), the original model is still available at Amazon for under $30.

Finally, we love our Apple AirPods ($159), which work with almost all iPhones and iPads and are more comfortable and sound better than their similar-looking wired counterparts (the ones in the box with iPhones but not iPads). About the only drawback is their price: $159.

If price is no object, consider wireless versions of the Bose QuietComfort noise-canceling headphones (about $350) or other high-end headphones.

Listening with Speakers

You can connect just about any speakers to your iPad, but if you want decent sound, we suggest you look only at *powered* speakers, not *passive* (unpowered) ones. Powered speakers contain their own amplification circuitry and can deliver much better (and louder) sound than unpowered speakers. Prices range from well under $100 to hundreds (or even thousands) of dollars. Most speaker systems designed for use with your computer, iPod, or iPhone work well as long as they have an auxiliary input or a dock connector that can accommodate your iPad.

Desktop speakers

Logitech (www.logitech.com) makes a range of desktop speaker systems priced from less than $25 to more than $300. But that $300 system is overkill for listening to music or video on your iPad, which doesn't support surround sound anyway. If you're looking for something inexpensive, you can't go wrong with a Logitech-powered speaker system.

Bob is a big fan of Audioengine (www.audioengineusa.com) desktop speakers. They deliver superior audio at prices that are reasonable for speakers that sound this good. Audioengine 5 is the premium product priced at $349 per pair; Audioengine 2 is its smaller but still excellent sibling priced at $199 per pair. They're available only direct from the manufacturer, but the company is so confident that you'll love them that it offers a free audition for the speaker systems.

Bluetooth speakers

Like Bluetooth headsets, Bluetooth speakers let you listen to music up to 33 feet away from your iPad. They're great for listening by the pool or hot tub or anywhere else you might not want to take your iPad.

Ed likes the Bose SoundLink wireless mobile speaker, which fetches around $300.

Bob has the Ultimate Ears Boom wireless speaker/speakerphone ($199.99), of which he says, is the best-sounding $200 Bluetooth speaker he ever tested. Ultimate Ears recently introduced Mega Boom ($299.99), which is (all together now) a bigger version of the Boom with bigger sound and Bob's current best-sounding pick at that price point.

AirPlay speakers

The newest type of speakers you might choose for your iPad support Apple's proprietary AirPlay protocol, which takes advantage of your existing Wi-Fi network to stream audio and video from your iPad (or other compatible iDevice) to a single AirPlay-enabled speaker or audio/video receiver. The biggest differences between AirPlay and Bluetooth speakers are

>> Bluetooth can stream music only in a compressed form; AirPlay can stream music (and video) uncompressed. So, a speaker with AirPlay should sound better than a similar speaker with Bluetooth.

>> Bluetooth's range is roughly 30 feet; AirPlay's range is up to 300 feet. You can't extend Bluetooth's range; Wi-Fi range can easily be extended with inexpensive routers such as Apple's AirPort Express ($99).

>> iTunes (on your computer) can use AirPlay to stream audio or video to multiple speakers or audio/video receivers, with individual volume controls for each device; Bluetooth streams to only one device at a time.

Wrapping Your iPad in Third-Party Cases

Much as we like the Apple iPad case, other vendors offer some excellent, different options:

>> Abas, www.abas.net

>> Targus, www.targus.com.

>> Griffin Technology, www.griffintechnology.com

>> iLuv, www.i-luv.com

>> Zero Chroma Vario, at www.zerochroma.com

>> Twelve South BookBook, www.twelvesouth.com

>> LifeProof nüüd, www.lifeproof.com

Standing Up Your iPad

The Griffin Tablet Stand ($14.99) is so unusual that we just had to include it (see Figure 17-1). It's a dual-purpose desktop stand made of heavy-duty aluminum. You can open it to hold your iPad in either portrait or landscape mode for video watching, displaying pictures (a great way to exploit picture frame mode, as we describe in Chapter 9), or even reading. In upright mode, it's also the perfect companion for the Apple wireless keyboard (or any other Bluetooth keyboard). Or close the legs and lay it down, and it puts your iPad at the perfect angle for typing on the on-screen keyboard.

The iKlip Studio Stand (www.ikmultimedia.com; $29.99), shown in Figure 17-2, may not look as cool as Griffin's, but it's lightweight and folds flat. And it has rubber feet that don't slide around when you tap the screen. Bob says: "I love my iKlip Studio Stand. Wherever my iPad goes, my iKlip Studio Stand goes with it."

Courtesy of Griffin Technology

Courtesy of IK Multimedia

FIGURE 17-1:
The Griffin Tablet Stand is a unique, dual-purpose tabletop stand for your iPad.

FIGURE 17-2:
iKlip Stand is adjustable, portable, and easy to set up and use.

6

The Part of Tens

Explore our ten favorite free apps in the App Store. You'll find clever apps that serve as a superb way to enjoy digital comics, settle disputes over any movie, ever, and even help you identify the name of an unfamiliar song.

Peruse our ten favorite not-for-free apps for the iPad, including one very addictive game and apps that let you create and mail picture postcards, make your own movies with Hollywood-style special effects, and control your Mac or PC remotely from your iPad.

Chapter **18**

Ten Appetizing and Free Apps

K iller app is familiar jargon to anyone who has spent any time around computers. The term refers to an application so sweet or so useful that just about everybody wants or must have it.

You could make the argument that the most compelling killer app on the iPad is the very App Store we expound on in Chapter 11. This online emporium has an abundance of splendid programs — dare we say killer apps in their own right? — many of which are free. These cover everything from food (hey, you gotta eat) to showbiz. Okay, so some rotten apples (aren't we clever) are in the bunch, too. But we're here to accentuate the positive.

With that in mind, in this chapter, we offer ten of our favorite free iPad apps. In Chapter 19, we tell you about our favorite iPad apps that aren't free but are worth every penny.

We show you ours, and we encourage you to show us yours. If you discover your own killer iPad apps, by all means, let us know — our email addresses are at the end of the Introduction to this book — so that we can check them out.

TripCase

We travel more than most people and are somewhat set in our ways. Before a trip, we use our computers to print boarding passes, hotel and rental car details, and any other info we might need while in transit. The printouts are strictly analog, so they don't notify us (or anyone else) of gate changes or flight delays or cancellations. And, of course, they can't remind us to check in. Still, the system works reliably unless we lose our printed documents.

It may be old school, but it's the best we could do until recently. What we wished and hoped for was a single intelligent repository for travel-related information, one that was smart enough to alert us of gate changes, weather delays, flight cancellations, and the like, and one that was easy to configure, convenient to use, and free.

What we found is TripCase, which is all that and more. It's a free app (and website) that organizes details of each trip in one place, with reminders and flight alerts delivered directly to your iPad.

TripCase has a lot to like, but one thing we like best is that it's drop-dead simple to add your travel events — without copying and pasting or even typing. We merely forward our confirmation emails — for flights, hotels, rental cars, and other travel-related services — to trips@tripcase.com. TripCase parses the details, creates an itinerary, and sends us an email to confirm that our trip is ready to view in TripCase. We've forwarded confirmations from at least a half dozen travel providers, and TripCase has never failed to interpret them correctly. (And you can always enter details the old-fashioned way — by copying and pasting or typing.)

After TripCase has your info, you can view it in the TripCase app or in any web browser. The app is well-organized, with a timeline view of the itinerary (as shown in Figure 18-1), and details are but a tap away (as shown in Figure 18-2). TripCase also includes an action view with flight alerts, reminders, and other messages. Any way you look at it, TripCase does most of the work for you.

TripCase can even help you locate an alternate flight based on your original reservation should your flight be cancelled or delayed. And it reminds you to check in and print boarding passes 24 hours before each flight. Sweet!

TripCase's motto is "stress-free travel." Although it may not make travel stress free — or increase the legroom in and around a cramped airline seat — it definitely makes travel less stressful.

FIGURE 18-1:
The timeline view shows you everything you need in the order you're likely to need it.

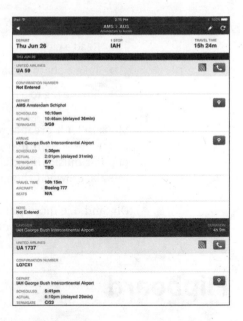

FIGURE 18-2:
Tap any item in the timeline to see its details.

Shazam

Ever heard a song on the radio or television, in a store, or at a club and wondered what it was called or who was singing it? With the Shazam app, you may never wonder again. Just launch Shazam and point your iPad's microphone at the source of the music. In a few seconds, the song title and artist's name magically appear on your iPad screen, as shown in Figure 18-3.

In Shazam parlance, that song has been *tagged*. Now, if tagging were all Shazam could do, that would surely be enough. But wait, there's more. After Shazam tags a song, you can

>> Buy the song at the iTunes Store

>> Watch related videos on YouTube

FIGURE 18-3:
Shazam can often identify obscure songs like this one by Dr. Mac and his All GarageBand Band.

- » Tweet the song on Twitter if you set up Twitter in Settings
- » Read a biography, a discography, or lyrics
- » Take a photo and attach it to the tagged item in Shazam
- » Email a tag to a friend

Shazam isn't great at identifying classical music, jazz, show tunes, or opera, nor is it adept at identifying obscure indie bands. But if you use it primarily to identify popular music, it rocks (pun intended). It has worked for us in noisy airport terminals, crowded shopping malls, and even once at a wedding ceremony.

Oh, and one more thing: You can have Siri (with Shazam's assistance) identify a song for you even if you don't have the Shazam app installed.

Flipboard

If imitation is (as the cliché goes) a form of flattery, Apple reaped high praise on Flipboard when it unleased the News app as part of iOS 9 (revamped with iOS 10). Apple's News seems to share much in common with Flipboard, the latter being a socially oriented personal magazine app that we're confident news and information junkies will like a lot.

To get started with Flipboard, tap the topics you're interested in: business, technology, sports, arts & culture, wine tasting, music, cute animals, and a lot more — over 30,000 topics, in fact.

Flipboard then delivers articles based on your selections, all presented in a handsome, intuitive interface. Swipe left and right to move from page to page. Tap on the articles you want to read. Fine-tune the articles that Flipboard delivers by tapping a thumbs-up (more like this) or a thumbs-down (less like this) icon.

By choosing "weird" as one of his topics, Ed was able to read articles he was unlikely to stumble upon otherwise, including a story out of the Daily Mail in the UK that revealed "The weirdest things dentists have found in patients' mouths."

Trust us, you'll find articles in Flipboard that are a lot more appetizing than that one. As a bonus, you can link Flipboard to various social media accounts.

Movies by Flixster

We like movies, so we both use the Flixster app a lot. Feed it your zip code and then browse local theaters by movie, showtimes, rating, or distance from your current location. Or browse to find a movie you like and then tap to find theaters, showtimes, and other info, as shown in Figure 18-4. Another nice feature is the capability to buy tickets to most movies from your iPad with just a few additional taps.

FIGURE 18-4:
Find out showtimes, watch the trailer, or get more info on the director or cast with a single tap.

We appreciate that we can read reviews, play movie trailers, and email movie listings to others with a single tap. We also enjoy the movie trailers for soon-to-be-released films and DVDs. Other free movie showtime apps are out there, but we like Flixster the most.

IMDb Movies & TV

While we're on the subject of the silver screen, we couldn't resist opening IMDb, shorthand for Internet Movie Database (owned by Amazon). And what a database it is, especially for the avid filmgoer. This vast and delightful repository of all things cinema is the place to go for complete cast/crew listings, actor/filmmaker bios, plot summaries, movie trailers, critics' reviews, user ratings, parental guidance, famous quotations, and all kinds of trivia.

You can always search for movies, TV shows, actors, and so on by typing a name in the search field at the top of the screen. You can also browse various menu choices to find current movies by showtimes, what's coming soon, or what's popular. You can browse TV recaps, too, or find people born on the day you happen to be looking and poking around the app. It's also fun to check out Trending Celebrities on IMDb. The recent roster included Jaimie Alexander, Tom Hardy, Alexandra Daddario, Priyanka Chopra, Emilia Clarke, Johnny Depp, Leonardo DiCaprio, Marion Cotillard, Natalie Dormer, Michael Fassbender, Rooney Mara, among many others.

One piece of advice to movie buffs: Avoid IMDb if you have a lot of work to do. You'll have a hard time closing the curtain on this marvelous app.

Netflix

Flixster, IMDb, and now Netflix. You've no doubt detected a real trend by now, and that trend is indeed our affection for movies and TV shows. If you love TV and movies, too, you're sure to be a fan of the Netflix app. Over time, Netflix, the company that built its reputation by sending DVDs to subscribers through the mail, started streaming movies and TV shows over the Internet to computers, TVs, and other consumer electronics gear. You can now add the iPad to that list.

From the iPad, you have more or less instant access to thousands of movies on demand. And although these titles aren't exactly current blockbusters, we know you'll find plenty of films worth seeing. You can search by *genre* (classics, comedy, drama, and so on) and *subgenre* (courtroom dramas, political dramas, romantic dramas, and so on).

What's more, Netflix produces its own popular shows, including *House of Cards*, featuring Kevin Spacey, which Ed binged on, *Orange Is The New Black*, and the huge hit *Stranger Things*.

Although the app is free, you have to pay Netflix streaming subscription fees that start at $7.99 a month. You also need an Internet connection, preferably through Wi-Fi, although Netflix works on 3G and 4G models as well.

WARNING

Remember what we tell you about streaming movies over 3G or 4G and be mindful of your data plan.

Comixology

The Comixology app is a fantastic way to read comic books on a touchscreen. Its online store features thousands of comics and comic series from dozens of publishers, including Arcana, Archie, Marvel, Devil's Due, Digital Webbing, Red 5, DC Comics, and Zenescope, as well as hundreds of free comics.

Furthermore, many titles are classics, like issue #1 of *The Amazing Spider-Man*. Released in 1963 for $0.12, a copy in excellent condition goes for at least $25,000 today! We're enjoying this out-of-print classic in pristine condition on our iPads, as shown in Figure 18-5, for a mere $16.99 (or free with a $5.99 unlimited monthly subscription).

Other comics are priced from $0.99 per issue, though many issues of many series are available for free as a teaser.

Finally, this app provides a great way to organize the comics you own on your iPad so that you can find the one you want quickly and easily.

New releases are available every Wednesday, so visit the web store often to check out the latest and greatest offerings. Both the store and your personal comic collection are well organized and easy to use. And reading comics in Comixology is a pleasure you won't want to miss if you're a fan of comics or graphic novels.

Amazon bought this app (and its eponymous maker, Comixology) in 2013, and it's not as good as it used to be. The current version still requires you to visit the Comixology website to buy comics, which you then download to the Comixology app. Before Amazon, the Comixology app had its own built-in comic bookstore, which made buying a comic more convenient and straightforward. We hope Amazon will reconsider and bring back the in-app store someday. However, even with the convoluted buying process, we still don't know of anything that offers a better reading experience for comics and graphic novels.

FIGURE 18-5:
Comixology is the best way to read comics on your iPad.

Epicurious Recipes & Shopping List

We love to eat. But we're writers, not gourmet chefs, so we'll take all the help we can get when it comes to preparing a great meal. And we get a lot of that culinary assistance from Epicurious, which easily lives up to its billing as the "Cook's Companion." This tasty recipe app comes courtesy of Condé Nast Digital.

With more than 33,000 recipes to choose from, we're confident you'll find a yummy one in no time. From the Home screen, you can browse categories, often timed to the season. Around the time we were writing this book, recipe collection categories included Halloween Treats, Vegetarian Thanksgiving, Lunches Kids Love, and Chocolate Desserts. To which we say, "Yum." Some recipes carry reviews.

If you tap Search instead, you can fine-tune your search for a recipe by food or drink, by main ingredient (for example, banana, chicken, pasta), by cuisine type, and by dietary consideration (low-carb, vegan, kosher, and so on), among other parameters.

When you discover a recipe you like, you can add it to a collection of favorites, email it to a friend, pass along the ingredients to your shopping list, summon nutritional information, or share it on Facebook and Twitter.

If you want to sync favorite recipes on your iPhone and iPad through a personal recipe box on Epicurious.com, you can now do so for free.

Bon appétit.

Evernote

Before we even talk about the Evernote iPad app, let's take a quick look at the problem Evernote resolves for us: storing our little bits of digital information — text, pictures, screen shots, scanned images, receipts, bills, email messages, web pages, and other info we might want to recall someday — and synchronizing all the data among all our devices and the cloud.

Evernote (www.evernote.com) is all that and more, with excellent free apps for iOS, Mac OS X, Android, and Windows, plus a killer web interface that works in most browsers.

You can create notes of any length on your iPad by typing, dictating, or photographing. You can add unlimited tags to a note, and create unlimited notebooks to organize your rapidly growing collection of notes.

TIP

You can even annotate images and PDFs in Evernote notes, using another free app from Evernote called Skitch, which we also recommend without hesitation.

Getting words and images into Evernote couldn't be much easier, but the info will be useless if you can't find it when you need it. Evernote won't let you down, with myriad options for finding and working with your stored data. In addition to the aforementioned tags and notebooks, Evernote offers searching and filtering (Tags and Notebooks) to help you find the note you need, as shown in Figure 18-6.

Two other nice touches are worth noting:

>> Notes are automatically tagged with your current location (as long as you create them on your iPad or other location-enabled device), so you can filter by Places.

>> You can attach reminders to notes and receive notifications on the date and time you chose. Best of all, you'll be notified on your iPad as well as on your other iDevices, Macs, PCs, and on the Evernote website!

Our two favorite features are that Evernote syncs notes with all your devices and the cloud automatically and that everything we've mentioned so far — creating, organizing, and syncing notes — is free.

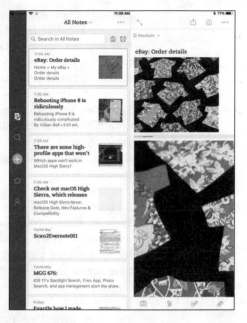

FIGURE 18-6:
Evernote's main screen only hints at how easy it is to create and find notes.

Bob likes Evernote so much that he recently upgraded to the premium plan ($7.99/ month or $70/year), primarily to increase his monthly upload limit to 10GB and to get the capability to search for text in PDFs. A Plus plan, for $34.99 per year with a 1GB upload limit, is also available.

Pandora Radio

We've long been fans of Pandora on other computers and mobile devices, so we're practically delirious that this custom Internet radio service is available *gratis* on the iPad. And you can play Pandora music in the background while doing other stuff.

Pandora works on the iPad in much the same way that it does on a Mac or PC. In the box at the upper left, tap + Create Station and type the name of a favorite art-ist, song title, or composer via the iPad keyboard, and Pandora creates an instant personalized radio station with selections that exemplify the style you chose. Pan-dora will also suggest some stations you might like based on the stations you've already established, and you can browse genre stations.

Along the left panel of Figure 18-7, you see some of the eclectic stations Bob created. Tapping Shuffle at the top of the list plays musical selections across all your stations.

Suppose that you type *Beatles.* Pandora's instant Beatles station includes performances from John, Paul, George, and Ringo, as well as tunes from other acts.

And say that you type a song title, such as *Have I Told You Lately.* Pandora constructs a station with similar music after you tell it whether to base tunes on the Van Morrison, Rod Stewart, or another rendition.

You can help fine-tune the music Pandora plays by tapping the thumbs-up or thumbs-down icon at the bottom of the screen associated with the music you've been listening to during the current session.

FIGURE 18-7:
Have we told you lately how much we like Pandora?

Pandora also takes advantage of the generous screen real estate of the iPad to deliver artist profiles, lyrics, and more. (Refer to Figure 18-7.) You may see ads, too, unless you opt for Pandora Plus ($4.99 a month) or Pandora Premium ($9.99 a month), premium upgrades that eliminate them. Both plans add other benefits as well, such as permitting you to more often skip music you don't like, on-demand listening, and more.

TIP

If you tap the share icon below an album cover of the currently playing song, you can write a message about the song, and then share it on Facebook or Twitter or email it. Other options in Pandora let you bookmark the song or artist that's playing or head to iTunes to purchase the song or other material from the artist directly on the iPad (if available). You can instantly create stations from artists or tracks or also indicate when you're tired of a track.

REMEMBER

Before we leave the realm of the free apps, we'd like to remind you of an 11th freebie — a free app so wonderful that we devoted almost an entire chapter (Chapter 10) about it. The app is iBooks.

Chapter **19**

Ten Apps Worth Paying For

I f you read Chapter 18, you know that lots of great free apps are available for your iPad. But as the cliché goes, some things are worth paying for. Still, none of the ten for-pay apps we've chosen as some of our favorites are likely to break the bank. As you're about to discover, some apps in this list are practical, and some are downright silly. The common theme? We think you'll like carrying these apps around on your iPad.

Bill Atkinson PhotoCard

Who is Bill Atkinson? He had a hand (or both hands) in the first Macintosh computer, as well as the MacPaint and HyperCard Mac applications. Today he's a world-renowned nature photographer, which brings us to his app. Bill Atkinson PhotoCard is a free app that lets you create gorgeous high-resolution postcards and send them via either email or the US Postal Service.

But the reason we love it is that you can have printed postcards sent via USPS for $1.50 to $2.00 per postcard, depending on how many print-and-mail credits you purchase. The 8.25-x-5.5-inch postcards are, in a word, stunning. Printed on heavy glossy stock on a state-of-the-art HP Indigo Digital Press and then laminated for protection, they're as beautiful as any postcard you've ever seen.

You can use one of the 200 included Bill Atkinson nature photos, as shown in Figure 19-1, or you can use any picture in your Photos library. You can add stickers and stamps, as shown in Figure 19-1, and you can even add voice notes to emailed cards.

TIP

If you're still uncertain, download the app (it's free) and try it. Send an email postcard or two to yourself. After you've seen how gorgeous these

FIGURE 19-1:
Your postcard can feature one of Bill Atkinson's gorgeous nature photos.

cards can be and how easy the app is to use, we think you'll spring for some print-and-mail credits and take your iPad on your next vacation as Bob always does.

Words with Friends — Best Game

This brings us to perhaps the only time in this entire book that two of your authors had a disagreement. Bob and Ed love word games and puzzles, but Bob loves Words with Friends — Best Game, whereas Ed prefers the real thing: namely, SCRABBLE.

Words with Friends — Best Game is the most social game Bob has found — and a ton of fun, too. Because it's turn-based, you can make a move and then quit the app and do other stuff. When your friend makes his next move, you can choose to be notified that it's your turn by sound, on-screen alert, a number on the Words with Friends icon on your Home screen, or any combination.

TIP

Although this app sold for $2.99 previously, when we checked the price for this edition we noticed that it was now free. There's no guarantee it'll remain free, so if you like word games, it's worthwhile to see if you can still grab a copy for $0.

Bob says: "Even if you can't, it's easily worth three bucks. After you have a copy, feel free to challenge me if you like; my username is boblevitus (although I often have the maximum 20 games going, so keep trying if I don't accept your challenge right away)."

ArtStudio — Draw and Paint

Do you fancy yourself an artist? We know our artistic talent is limited, but if we were talented, ArtStudio — Draw and Paint is the program we'd use to paint our masterpieces. Even if you have limited artistic talent, you can see that this app has everything you need to create awesome artwork.

We were embarrassed to show you our creations, so instead we whipped up Figure 19-2, which shows just the options for just one of ArtStudio's tools (there are dozens and dozens more).

Here are just some of ArtStudio's features:

FIGURE 19-2:
ArtStudio for iPad's Wet Paint Brush Settings and brush options.

» Offers 25 brushes, including pencils, a smudge tool, bucket fill, and an airbrush. Brushes are resizable and simulate brush pressure.

» Allows up to five layers with options, such as delete, reorder, duplicate, merge, and transparency.

» Provides filters, such as blur, sharpen, detect edges, and sepia.

Don't believe us? AppSmile.com (www.appsmile.com) rated it 5 out of 5, saying, "This is what Photoshop Mobile wishes it had been." SlapApp.com (www.slapapp.com) also rated it 5 out of 5 and said, "I've dabbled in quite a few painting and drawing apps and this one has 'em all beat by a long shot." And by all means, check out what talented artists can do with ArtStudio at www.flickr.com/groups/artstudioimages.

At $4.99, it's a heck of a deal for a thoughtfully designed and full-featured drawing and painting app. If you're not ready to invest $4.99, check out ArtStudio — Draw and Paint LITE, a free version that offers a taste of the real deal but with smaller canvases, limited layer and export support, and fewer custom brushes.

Pinball Crystal Caliburn II

Good pinball games require supremely realistic physics, and Pinball Crystal Caliburn II ($3.99) nails it. The way the ball moves around the table and interacts with bumpers and flippers is so realistic that you'll think you're at an arcade. The app is so realistic, in fact, that you can shake the table to influence the ball's movement.

Another hallmark of a great pinball game is great sound effects, and this game doesn't disappoint. The sounds the ball makes when it bounces off a bumper, is hit with a flipper, or passes through a rollover are spot-on and authentic.

If you like pinball, we think you'll love Pinball Crystal Caliburn II on your iPad. LittleWing (the developer) recently released an iOS version of its original pinball hit, Tristan, which also sports realistic physics and sounds and is also a lot of fun.

Art Authority for iPad

We've already admitted to being artistically challenged, but that applies only to making art. We appreciate good art as much as the next person. That's why we're so enthusiastic about Art Authority, even at $9.99.

Art Authority is like an art museum you hold in your hand; it contains more than 100,000 paintings and sculptures by more than 1,500 of the world's greatest artists. The works are organized into period-specific rooms, such as Early (up to the 1400s), Baroque, Romanticism, Modern, and American. In each room, the artworks are subdivided by movement. For example, as Figure 19-3 shows, the Modern room

FIGURE 19-3:
Exploring virtual art galleries with the iPad.

has works of Surrealism, Cubism, Fauvism, Dadaism, sculpture, and several more.

You'll find period overviews, movement overviews, timelines, and slideshows, plus a searchable index of all 1,500+ artists and separate indices for each room.

TIP

Developer Open Door Networks includes an Art Near Me feature, which lets you search for art in your vicinity. And the app has artwork and rooms optimized for the Retina display. And the Art Real Size feature adds the perspective of understanding how big or small a work really is. Video has also been added for hundreds of major works. If you love art, check it out.

And let us point out a kid-friendly K-12 version with still close to 100,000 paintings and sculptures. It costs $7.99; "inappropriate" nudity for the youngsters has been eliminated.

Solar Walk

We like to gaze at the heavens, but we often have no clue what we're looking at. Solar Walk, a handsome animated $4.99 guide to the night sky from Vito Technology, will delight astronomy students and anyone fascinated by outer space, even if purists scoff that Pluto, no longer considered a planet, is included in the model of the solar system. (The official name of the app is Solar Walk — Planets System, Orbits, Moons & Size. Whew.)

From the start, you're taken on a virtual tour through the galaxy. You can search planets — Figure 19-4 shows Saturn — satellites, stars, and more. You can even travel through time and space with a time machine feature. Animated movies cover topics such as Earth's cycles, solar eclipse, and the moon's phases.

FIGURE 19-4:
Learning about beautiful Saturn in Solar Walk.

What's more, the app can exploit 3D, provided you supply your own *anaglyph*-style cyan-red 3D glasses. And if you hook the iPad up to a 3D TV using an HDMI adapter, you can get a true sense of the depth and sheer size of the solar system in 3D, while controlling what you see on the screen through the iPad.

Without 3D, you can use AirPlay to mirror what's on the iPad screen on the bigger TV screen, provided you have an Apple TV.

One thing we find frustrating: Solar Walk is heavy on in-app purchases. For example, you'll have to pay 99¢ to watch a 3D animation showing a repair of the Hubble telescope, though you can get a high-resolution bundle with numerous extras for $2.99.

Action Movie FX

With Action Movie FX, it's a breeze to add big-budget Hollywood-style special effects to video you shoot with your iPad. Action Movie FX comes from producer J. J. Abrams's Bad Robot Productions, best known for TV shows such as *Alias* and *Fringe* and feature films including *Star Trek* and *Super 8.* We expected the app to be pretty good, and it is — it may well be the most fun app we've ever used to make videos with an iPad.

The free version features eight big-budget movie effects, such as missile attack, avalanche, and meteor from outer space, as well as phaser fight and photon torpedoes from Abrams's epic theatrical release *Star Trek into Darkness.* In other words, Action Movie FX lets you add Hollywood-style special effects to your videos so you can "destroy" people, places, pets, and other stuff in a variety of fun and interesting ways.

Making a video with Action Movie FX couldn't be easier. Just launch the app, select the scene you want to use, tap Start, and shoot a minimum of five seconds of video. It's better if the footage is of someone or something that will remain still, unlike Bob's dog Zeke, the slightly blurry miniature vizsla in Figure 19-5.

FIGURE 19-5:
An alien bursting out of Bob's dog.

When you've finished filming, you can adjust the timing as well as resize and reposition the special effects. When you're satisfied with your creation, your masterpiece appears after a bit of processing; you can then share it, save it to your Camera Roll album, adjust its timing again, or shoot another video.

FIGURE 19-6:
A jet taking out several vehicles on a quiet street.

The free effects are great, but we found ourselves wanting more and have purchased most of the ten currently available FX packs, for $0.99 each. They're mostly great, but our absolute favorites are the Jet (shown in Figure 19-6) and Alien Burst (refer to Figure 19-5).

The videos are HD, and look great in a text message or an email displayed on any device. The videos look fabulous on your iPad, but also look surprisingly good on a bigger display such as the one on a Mac, a PC, or an HDTV.

Finally, you just can't beat the price — your first eight effects are free. But we're betting that you'll like it enough to pop for one or more $0.99 FX packs. Either way, we're pretty sure you'll have as much fun as we have adding special FX to your videos.

Facetune 2 for iPad

You don't really think those drop-dead gorgeous models are really that drop-dead gorgeous, now do you? They had "work done." And the portraits that show these men and women in their best light were doctored, touched-up, and made to look perfect.

The free Facetune app (with in-app purchases) can make you look perfect, too — okay, we'll amend that to say it promises to make you look better. (As we know, you have to work with what you've got.)

After uploading a photo or taking pictures in the app with the camera on your iPad, you can tap the Facetune controls shown in Figure 19-7. Facetune smooths wrinkles, whitens teeth, heals zits, changes the contours of your face, gives you a full head of hair if you're lacking, and even defocuses the image to minimize imperfections in your face.

When you reach perfection, you can save the finished product to your Camera Roll album, share it by email, or post it on Facebook, Twitter, Tumblr, Messenger, or Flickr.

FIGURE 19-7:
Facetune can make Ed look better.

Dark Sky Weather

You can find many fine weather apps in the App Store. We rely on Dark Sky a lot because of the app's uncanny capability to inform us not only whether it will rain or snow at our current location but also when it will rain or snow pretty much down to the minute and within one hour of the time that you begged the question. Figure 19-8 shows what the main Dark Sky screen looks like.

If you've ever been caught in a downpour without a raincoat or an umbrella — and who hasn't?— you'll wish you had sprung for this $3.99 app.

You get some basic weather info too, including a detailed daily forecast, a seven-day forecast, and details on

FIGURE 19-8:
There's some precipitation in this particular Dark Sky forecast.

wind, humidity, and pressure. Dark Sky will also let you know when the sun will rise and when it will set. Through some cool simulations, you can map the path of upcoming precipitation or even go back a few days. But for us, the real draw is the down-to-the-minute prediction feature, which in our experience has been right more often than wrong.

It's not necessary to keep the app open to get word of an impending storm; Dark Sky can dispatch a notification shortly before rain or snow is supposed to start. Dark Sky is powered by a homegrown and aptly named weather service called Forecast.

Parallels Access

If you're like most of the iPad community, you mostly use your iPad for consumption: watching movies, listening to music, playing games, and browsing the web. You engage less often in productive activities on the iPad, mostly because it lacks a physical keyboard. (We're assuming here that you did not spring for an accessory keyboard for the iPad Pro or other iPads.) As a result, you still schlep a laptop with you on the road even though you also carry the iPad.

Parallels, a company best known for letting you run virtualized versions of Microsoft Windows on Macintosh computers, may eliminate the need to carry the extra machine. Its Parallels Access iPad app ties into a subscription service that lets you tap into your home or office PC remotely, whether it's a Windows PC or a Mac.

What sets Parallels Access apart from other apps that provide remote access to computers is that you can get to use *all* the programs that reside on your PC or Mac, including the proprietary software that your company may employ. Moreover, you can interact with those applications on the tablet as if each were designed for the iPad, and even use a browser running Adobe Flash on the iPad.

You start any PC or Mac desktop application on the iPad from a familiar looking launcher screen with icons for the apps you use most often. Such a screen is shown in Figure 19-9. You can add or remove icons to this launcher screen.

Parallels, as the company puts it, "applifies" PC/Mac programs so that the software is modified on the tablet to display iPad-style buttons for actions such as copy, paste, and select. And touch gestures on the iPad substitute for mouse moves on your computer. For example, tapping is like clicking with a mouse; two-finger tapping is equivalent to a right-click. Hold your finger against the display in an Excel spreadsheet, say, and an iPad magnifying glass appears.

You can use your voice to dictate text remotely onto the home or office computer. And you can listen to music on the iPad that resides on your faraway computer, too — no, the folks back home or in the office will not hear what you're hearing; the app is set up so as not to disturb them.

Parallels Access can't completely make up for the lack of a physical keyboard on the iPad. But the on-screen Mac or Windows keyboards that appear in the app display any dedicated special keys unique to Mac or Windows keyboards.

FIGURE 19-9:
Parallels Access lets you run programs on a Mac or PC from the iPad.

The Parallels Access app is free to download, as is the agent program you must install on each Mac or PC that you choose to access. A single-user Parallels Access subscription is $19.99 per year for an unlimited number of devices (iPads and iPhones running iOS 8 or higher, Android tablets and phones running Android 4 or higher, Kindle Fire running Fire OS 3.0 or later, and any device with an HTML5 web browser) and up to five computers (PCs running Windows 7, 8, 8.1, or 10, and Macs running Mavericks or later).

Index

Symbols and Numerics

About the Authors

Bob LeVitus, often referred to as "Dr. Mac," has written or cowritten more than 80 popular computer books, including *iPhone For Dummies, iPad For Dummies,* and *macOS High Sierra For Dummies,* all for John Wiley & Sons, Inc. His books have sold millions of copies worldwide. In addition to books, Bob has penned the popular "Dr. Mac" column in the *Houston Chronicle* for more than 20 years and has written for pretty much every magazine that has ever used the word *Mac* in its title.

Edward C. Baig writes the Personal Technology column in *USA TODAY* and makes regular video appearances on the web and TV. Ed is also the author of *Macs For Dummies* and cowriter (with Bob LeVitus) of *iPhone For Dummies.* Before joining *USA TODAY* as a columnist and reporter in 1999, Ed was on the editorial staff at *Business Week, U.S. News & World Report,* and *Fortune* magazine.

Bryan Chaffin is the cofounder and editor-in-chief of *The Mac Observer,* as well as the cohost of The Apple Context Machine podcast and Pop.0 video podcast. In addition to writing for several print magazines, he has contributed to or coauthored five *Dummies* titles, including *Incredible iPad Apps for Dummies.* Bryan is shopping his first novel, *Accidental Intelligence.*

Dedications

I will never tire of dedicating books to the best wife ever. Lisa LeVitus has taught me pretty much everything I know about almost everything I know (other than technology). She's been dedicated to me for more than 30 years, so dedicating every book I write to her is the least I can do. Finally, as usual, I dedicate this book also to my grown-up kids, Allison and Jacob, who love their iPhones and iPads almost as much as I love them (my kids, not my gadgets).

— Bob LeVitus

I dedicate this book to my beautiful and amazingly supportive wife, Janie, and to my incredible kids: daughter Sydney, son Samuel, and canine Sadie. The book is also written in the memory of my "doggie son," Eddie, Jr., and my mom, Lucille, and dad, Sam. I love you all.

— Ed Baig

I dedicate this book to the women in my life, listed alphabetically because I'm not stupid: Heather, JJ, Laura, Nancy, and Vicki. Thank you, ladies, for making everything a lot better.

— Bryan Chaffin

Authors' Acknowledgments

Special thanks to everyone at Apple who helped us turn this book around so quickly: Steve Dowling, Greg (Joz) Joswiak, John Richey, Keri Walker, Trudy Muller, Tom Neumayr, Janette Barrios, Christine Monaghan, Andy Bowman, and everyone else. We couldn't have done it without you. We apologize if we missed anybody.

Big-time thanks to the gang at Wiley: Steve "Still Pretty Mellow All Things Considered" Hayes, Susan "just one more little thing. . ." Pink, and technical editor Ryan Williams, who has no humorous nickname yet but did a rocking job. We also want to thank our invaluable proofreader, Debbye "Hawkeye" Butler, who again did a tremendous job. Finally, thanks to everyone at Wiley we don't know by name or humorous nickname. If you helped with this project in any way, you have our everlasting thanks.

Bob adds: Extra special thanks to my super-agent of nearly 30 years, Carole "Swifty" Jelen. And to Bryan Chaffin, for exceptional editorial contributions under extreme time pressures. Nicely done, Bryan!

Ed adds: Thanks to my agent, Matt Wagner, for again turning me into a *For Dummies* author. I'd also like to thank my *USA TODAY* friends and colleagues for your enormous support. Most of all, thanks to my loving family for understanding my nightly (and weekend) disappearances as we raced to get this project completed on time. They all keep me sane.

And finally, thanks to you, gentle reader, for buying our book.

Publisher's Acknowledgments

Executive Editor: Steve Hayes

Project Editor: Susan Pink

Copy Editor: Susan Pink

Technical Editor: Ryan Williams

Proofreader: Debbye Butler

Production Editor: Siddique Shaik

Cover Image: @ kacha somti/Shutterstock